# JACOB'S WOUND

# JACOB'S WOUND

## WOUND

*A Search for the Spirit of Wildness*

## TREVOR HERRIOT

FULCRUM

GOLDEN, COLORADO

Library of Congress Cataloging-in-Publication Data

Herriot, Trevor.
  Jacob's wound : a search for the spirit of wildness / Trevor Herriot.
    p. cm.
  Includes bibliographical references (p.      ).
  ISBN 978-1-55591-616-9 (pbk.)
   1. Nature--Religious aspects--Christianity. 2. Qu'Appelle River Valley (Sask. and Man.)--Description and travel. I. Title.
  BR115.N3H47 2009
  231.7--dc22
                        2008048706


Printed on recycled paper in the United States of America by Malloy Inc.
0  9  8  7  6  5  4  3  2  1


Cover Art:
Mashel Teitelbaum (1921–1985)
*God's Acre*, 1945, oil on masonite, 76.5 x 58.5 cm
McMichael Canadian Art Collection,
Gift of the Teitelbaum Family 1987.47.1


Fulcrum Publishing
4690 Table Mountain Drive, Suite 100
Golden, Colorado 80403
800-992-2908 • 303-277-1623
www.fulcrumbooks.com

*In memory of wild places lost to ignorance, greed, and fear*

*And Jacob said, "Please accept the gift I offer, for in fact I have come into your presence as into the presence of God, since you have received me kindly. So accept the gift I have brought for you, since God has been generous to me and I have all I need." And he urged him, and Esau accepted.*

— Genesis 33:10–11

# CONTENTS

*Acknowledgments*                    *xiii*

## INTRODUCTION
*Birds of Pentecost*          *3*

## PART ONE
### Ascending Hakkarmel
*Shelter 1*              *15*
*El Marahka I*           *20*
*Shelter 2*              *24*
*El Marahka II*          *28*
*Shelter 3*              *31*
*El Marahka III*         *33*
*Shelter 4*              *49*
*El Marahka IV*          *52*
*Shelter 5*              *59*
*El Marahka V*           *62*
*Shelter 6*              *66*
*El Marahka VI*          *77*
*Shelter 7*              *88*
*El Marahka VII*         *93*
*Shelter 8*              *102*
*El Marahka VIII*        *107*
*Shelter 9*              *114*

| | |
|---|---|
| *El Marahka IX* | *117* |
| *Shelter 10* | *120* |
| *El Marahka X* | *124* |
| *Shelter 11* | *142* |

## PART TWO
### From Mount Carmel

| | |
|---|---|
| *Wild Grace* | *147* |
| *Pilgrims* | *155* |
| *At the Riverside* | *163* |
| *Fresh Wounds* | *168* |
| *Songs* | *175* |
| *Scapular I* | *185* |
| *Scapular II* | *190* |
| *Leaven I* | *219* |
| *Leaven II* | *227* |
| *Leaven III* | *235* |
| *A New Small-Rented Lease* | *245* |
| *Into the Presence of God* | |
|     *1. Descend* | *289* |
|     *2. Rise* | *307* |
|     *3. Converge* | *319* |
| *An Evening Prayer* | *350* |

## POSTSCRIPT

| | |
|---|---|
| *Wind Birds* | *361* |
| | |
| *Notes* | *365* |
| *Bibliography* | *369* |

# ACKNOWLEDGMENTS

Help came in ways surprising and varied as I worked on this book. Many of those I would like to acknowledge also make appearances in the narrative: Paul Goossen of the Canadian Wildlife Service; Mike and Lorran Wild; Grace Stevenson; Don McKay; Ron Rolheiser; Rob Wright; Father James Gray; my children, Kate, Jon, Sage, and Maia; Noreen Strueby; Duane Guina; Brewster Kneen; Nolan Bodnarchuk; Peter Farden; Noel Star Blanket; Robert Stacey; Archbishop Peter Mallon; and Harold and Audrey Zettl.

There are those who helped shape my thinking in the conversations we have had together: Noel Star Blanket, Heather Hodgson, Rob Wright, Laura and Gene Forrester, and John Dipple. Of particular significance were my conversations and correspondence with Father James Gray. I thought of him often as I reworked drafts or struggled for ways to listen to my material.

I am particularly grateful to those who read some or all of the manuscript, offering suggestions. These include Ross Laird, Myrna Kostash, Sean Virgo, David Perrin, Michelle Sanche, and Heather Hodgson. I would like to single out Gary Ross, who was enthusiastic about the project early on, and Ron Rolheiser, who not only allowed me to borrow so many of his thoughts and phrasings but commented on the manuscript in detail during its latter stages.

Jackie Kaiser, my agent, has faithfully guided me through several transitions during the conception, writing, and editing. Dinah Forbes, my editor at McClelland & Stewart, was gentle with a manuscript that must have seemed rather unruly at first glance. I appreciated her cheerful questions and suggestions, helping me to create a more navigable and appealing book. Thanks also to the copy editor, Heather Sangster, for finding my mistakes and polishing sentences, and to Jean Okemasis and Arok Wolvengrey for assistance with spelling Cree words.

With apologies to anyone who I may have forgotten to name, these are the people who have provided important corrections, comments, and advice, improving the book immeasurably. None is responsible for the errors and weaknesses that remain.

Groups I wish to acknowledge include the Benedictine brothers of St. Peter's Abbey in Muenster, the Saskatchewan Writers/Artists Colonies, and the Saskatchewan Writers Guild. I am especially grateful for writing grants I received from the City of Regina, the Saskatchewan Arts Board, and the Canada Council. Each allowed me to devote myself fully to research and writing for several months at a time.

I am also indebted to my employer, SaskTel, and my managers there for supporting my writing and allowing me time off to work on the manuscript for three summers running.

I have no hope of repaying my debts to my in-laws, Jack and Louise Sutherland, whose unbounded generosity and support has made every difference. Without them to help Karen look after the children when I have to be away and without Jack taking up many of the chores and home repairs that would normally fall to me, I would not be able to write.

My parents, Norm and Jeanne Herriot, remain a steadfast influence. The older I become the more I understand that their decency, hard work, and faithfulness to one another and to the family have been the primary blessings of my life.

Finally, there is my wife, Karen. With ever-increasing grace and forbearance, she creates the world in which I can write and yet remain a husband and a father of four children. Any thanks I say here will sound paltry, for she deserves more than I will be able to give her in a lifetime.

# BIRDS

# OF

# PENTECOST

A long the pebbled margins of certain prairie lakes, a small plover the color of sand makes its living. It struts and whirrs where waves have been, stopping momentarily to pick at the bits of life that inhabit a shoreline. If you walk too close, it will, like most shorebirds, run away. If you persist, it will fly up, offering a single clear note as complaint before it circles back behind you or heads farther down the shore. For this soft and plaintive cry we call it the piping plover. It is a sound that belongs to the beach or to the wind that moves above its stones. Shorebirds, in voice and manner, are birds of the moving air. *Wind birds,* Peter Matthiessen named them—spirits of the long migration that ride on swept-back wings and bear in their breasts the utterance of wildness. To listen to a piping plover is to hear the wind eddying through a small body, resonating in an intricate tube in its throat, and returning again as a lyric that fits within larger harmonies.

The notes of the piping plover, like other phrases within the Holocene music of this continent, are heard less frequently now than they were even twenty years ago. Officials have noticed the change and are concerned. Worry of this kind generally leads to counting and so these days we census piping plovers and much else that is running away from us. We gather numbers because in legislatures, boardrooms, and courts a story does not cut any ice. Until the results are in, everything else is merely anecdotal.

It was Pentecost Sunday when I left home to help count piping plovers at Lake Diefenbaker. Weeks later, our records were added to totals for the lake, the province, the nation, and the continent, contributing to figures that biologists and wildlife officials will use to estimate populations and revise recovery plans for the species. It was the anecdotal evidence, though, that remained with me long after the count: some memories, a couple of sketches made on the beach, and a few pages of notes scribbled down when the day was over. None of it will save plovers or their habitat. The drawings I pinned above my desk. The notes and memories took over the book

I thought I was writing, replacing it with an interlude of narrative and argument pondered between two separate encounters with a wild bird on the morning after Pentecost.

A week of weeks after Easter, Pentecost carries its own load of narrative. It marks a time when a people divided were brought together in wind and fire by their share in a larger story. We, and here I mean people of Christian ancestry, are the offspring of that story, and regardless of what we may think of it now, we bear in our flesh its familiar trajectory from Ash Wednesday to Easter Sunday. For my part, though, I keep on the lookout for even the smallest signs of Pentecost, a convergence of the irreconcilable, translated one to the other, tongued with fire by the bewildering winds of heaven.

We began the plover survey, the four of us, walking into a hard gale out of the east along the expanse of sand that shows up here and there on the shores of Lake Diefenbaker whenever the water is low. This man-made lake, a section of the South Saskatchewan River dammed for hydroelectric-power generation, has become the world's most important body of water for nesting piping plovers. They come in the hundreds here in years when the water is low and the beaches wide. Hundreds, too, have had their nests washed away in June when the Rocky Mountain meltwater arrives and the dam gates, closed to maximize power generation, raise the water level several feet virtually overnight.

As every year passes, the reservoir waters eat away at more of the alluvium that once underlay the grassy hilltops of the old river valley, creating these vast sand and gravel flats. For much of the morning we were walking through acres of what used to be shoreline vegetation, mostly mare's tail, now caked in sand and some distance from the water's edge. Heading into the wind, our line of four watchers abreast covered 250-yard swaths of habitat as we passed along the beach, the wind swirling the sand around our ankles in strange, mesmerizing strands like snow drifting over a highway. I covered the zone nearest the inlet of a small creek where marbled godwits, sanderlings, semipalmated sandpipers, and willets were foraging. A raven stooped over the carcass of a large pike on the shore.

We walked only sixty or seventy yards apart, but the sound of wind and blowing sand made it impossible to hear so we resorted to hand signals. Now and then I'd see the others stop, wave one another over, and kneel beneath the wind to look ahead at something, make some notes, and amble on again like pilgrims on a prayer walk. Paul—our leader and the one with the radio, the Global Positioning System gear, and spotting scope—had to record the exact location of each new nest we found. Everyone else seemed to be finding nests. It was not until later in the morning, when we'd turned our backs to the wind and were headed west on a sweep nearer the reservoir, that I found my first one, a female a few paces ahead of me squatting on the sand.

I discovered her in a pause between gusts when the airborne grit settled long enough for me to see. The haze dropped like a veil and there she was: the orange on her bill, a couple dabs of darker brown against the white and bleached-sand tones of her face and back. She seemed barely perturbed by the sandstorm, an image of faith amidst inexorable forces. Then the wind rose again and all I could see was a beige band of air streaming away from me beneath the sky's distant blue. A pile of sand gathered against my legs and lower back as I crouched, staring into the brown wall hiding the plover.

Pentecost or not, the wind couldn't blow hard enough to give me the wild tongue of a prairie shorebird. I had no way to speak apologies for all that we have destroyed beneath this reservoir—the ancient gathering place, a sacred buffalo rock, the historic home and hunting grounds of the Sandy Hills Cree, and the headwaters of a sleepy river that first drew my ancestors to the New World and that has since become the gutter of our heedless tenure within its heartland.

I looked to my left and saw my cohorts strung out at intervals, hunkered down as I was, backs to the sandstorm like Bedouin herdsmen. In my ears there was the wind's howl and the loud patter of sand particles striking my jacket. Before calling Paul over, I got out a notepad and scribbled a sketch of her facing into the gale, body pressed down into the beach, feathers rippling with the air's wild vibration. I resisted a momentary urge to leave her undiscovered, unstaked by the coordinates of our best intentions, and stood to give Paul the signal for "nest."

There was a good chance, Paul had said when we started out in the morning, that we'd see the first fledglings of the year later at another stretch of beach where he'd been keeping an eye on a well-advanced nest. But I just wanted to hold on to this one, as she was now, pregnant with possibilities and metaphor: a mother, small and alone, brooding over the troubled world in a howling wind.

I had spent the previous night in my one-man tent, camping away from roads in the aspen-bush sand dunes on the other side of the reservoir. I lit a small fire and listened to the questioning cries of a hundred Franklin's gulls in the upper stories of air, where they scooped chironomids from ecstatic pillars that looked like smoke spiraling up into the darkening sky. Its light filtered through a dust-choked horizon, the new moon rose blood red. Not long after nightfall, the wind came up, filled the fly of my tent to billowing, pulled its stakes out of the sand, and kept me restless, half awake, and dreaming desolate dreams of our ungodly passage in this land.

The prairie I saw that night had no lark song, no badgers, no antelope or buffalo. Only grass museums where captive-bred burrowing owls and other creatures were managed and interpreted in displays sponsored by Monsanto and Hoechst. The lifeways I'd known as a small child visiting uncles and aunts in the valley were as distant as the buffalo-hunting cultures they replaced; the land strewn with the casualties of cash-crop economics, modern agriculture, and other occasions of sin: gardens gone to weeds, horse barns empty and atilt, homesteads burned in a fool's windrow fire, the milk separator waiting to be salvaged by antiques collectors, the home quarter gathered up in grain operations that span whole townships.

A while ago, well before I was born, something stopped the music that played behind more hopeful dreams. We have been mourning ever since, in our stories, our politics, and our nostalgia, for all that we lost in removing the native grass and its people from the prairie: fertility, traditions, community, biodiversity, landscapes, medicine wheels, burial grounds, opportunities, and innocence.

The days of grieving are ending now. Old ways and first dreams are in the tomb. There are fresh ones birthing in the light of day, born of mixed parentage, the colonized and the colonizers, the remains of the native adapting to the persistent and alien, creating a new prairie world beneath our feet.

On this morning, blasted by Pentecostal winds, I walked on the shores of a lake made by our hubris above the headwaters of the only river that has a claim upon my blood. Counting birds endangered by our sins, I searched as well for the blessings of our past, for ways to release the old life from our grasp, that we might turn and lean into the new spirit stirring life from the sand.

But first there had to be a week of weeks, each sun rising on a little less regret, a little more blessing. It began as life often begins—with a death.

At the far end of the river without any beginning, by the mouth of a creek once called the Little Cutarm, and before that *kīskipitonēwi-sīpīsis*, I saw someone rise and walk into the water in the slow gait of the old ones. It was *mihkināhk*, on whose back the first people say this land rests. He slipped into the creek leaving sharp tracks printed deep into the gray alluvium—a wild script promising fresh stories to replace the ones that were passing away.

I'd spent the day with a beloved aunt in Saint Anthony's, a hospital in a town twelve miles back along the creek, where she was breathing the soft blows of death. Something unkind but not unbidden pressed down on the place where she kept the stories I have always thought of as my narrative ligaments to the valley. The subsistence life embraced by those stories disappeared decades ago; now the stories themselves would follow.

The redbrick hospital, named for an old desert mystic, offered a serenity I have felt in monasteries. The hours passed quietly between us in her room, she holding fast to a remnant of life, me looking for a graceful way to let the last storyteller of the clan go. While she squeezed my hand, I read psalms, muttered inadequate prayers, and offered sips of water. With each breath, a moan escaped from her mouth. Sometimes she would try to form words, but there was little I could understand. She said my name, she asked for water, and once she asked me to sing. "Sing," I said, "what should I sing?" Slowly, her lips pursed from an "ah" to an "m," then came a harder, guttural sound, barely there, ending with a soft sibilance. I thought she disliked that hymn, but I sang it anyway, forgetting more words than I remembered: "When we've been there ten thousand years, bright shining as the sun...how precious did that grace appear, the hour I first believed."

All afternoon, people drifted in and out of the room like ghosts. Smiling and patting before moving on, they were somehow less alive than the one they had come to see for the last time. When I arrived, there was an angel named Cecille at her side who told me she had gone for a bicycle ride to the edge of town after rising at six that morning. She had her binoculars with her as always but couldn't recognize a duck that was all black except for some white on its head and it dove into the slough just like that. Some visitors came after the funeral let out next door at Saint Anthony's Church. It was old Mrs. Sapara they said, the name on the grocery store when I was a boy living on the other side of town. Later, an old man with the palliative bearing of a chaplain stopped in for a few seconds. Thirty-five years ago he was the druggist behind the high counter whenever we came to get penicillin or cough syrup. According to Cecille, he retired decades ago but couldn't stop making his daily rounds at Saint Anthony's.

Everyone had gone, even Cecille, and I was all alone with my aunt when she asked me to sing. The light of late afternoon slanted in through half-drawn blinds and across her bed. After I ran out of lyrics, I leaned over to kiss her and she held me fiercely to her cheek with the arm that still worked. We stayed like that a long time, my tears falling against her skin until I broke her embrace and pulled away. I said good-bye and she said my name many times, was still saying it when I left.

Toward twilight I drove down to the valley, looking for easy consolation—something I can always find on the tributary's last run to the river. I set out from the homestead site where my grand-parents had left their mark upon the grass: a cellar, some weeds, chimney bricks, a bedspring. Past the current landowner's hay bales, across the valley road I found the creek again and trudged along its muddy margins. Late spring, the flow was still strong from the last of the snowmelt. Some drifts remained high in the oak-shaded clefts of each ravine. No more than a canoe length from bank to bank, the creek fell in riffles and small rapids stepping down to the river through the maples and willows ahead of me.

Nearing the confluence, I heard the harsh rattle of a kingfisher, and then a splash and the thin, piping call of a wood duck. I stopped to look for the birds, turned and saw a tangle of metal at the base of a small tree on the ashen, silt-coated grass where the flooding river had moved only days before. It was a battered and rusty fish trap grown over by weeds and saplings. Homemade, it had corroded iron hoops and galvanized chicken wire on the outside with an inverted cone of wire pointing inward from either end. *Grandpa*—forty years of poach-ing from this river, using tricks he learned as a boy on the Thurso River in Caithness. It's been another forty since he stopped. I stared down at the traps and felt time curve in the maple branches overhead. I was a full lifetime away from the days he first drew life from these waters, but that lifetime—that of his eldest daughter breathing into the silence of her hospital room—now seemed behind and distant, less present than the poacher and his proprietary dreams.

I wanted to stand with the maple trees, girdled by the turn of seasons, to wear years like scars and face the present through the accretions of summers and winters gone. When I went back to the mouth of the creek, someone was waiting for me there. Not recognizing him at first, I saw only a circle in the gray, glistening mud—a round portal, the lid upon countless flood times. I stepped closer and then he stirred. His great beaked head rose out of the muck, then the claws beneath his carapace emerged and he walked down to the water's edge and slipped unafraid into the flow of things.

*Mihkināhk.* Recognition stirred embers I'd let grow cold, turned me back upon my tracks. People here have named him the Ancient One who bears the land and its stories on his back. A large male snapping turtle like this one can live forty years or more. The only creatures in this valley that live longer walk on two legs. Venerable, solitary, and loyal to one stretch of water, the snapping turtle lives like a hermit holed up in a creekside anchorage, watching the rise and fall of river life. This one may well have seen my grandfather, been seen by him. I stayed there on the mud trying to read the ciphers of the old turtle until another splash drew my attention to the creek mouth where the kingfisher was emerging, minnow in its bill, water shedding from its blue mantle in mercury-colored droplets.

The face of God is commonplace on such days. Driving east from home that morning, I had stopped at the edge of the city to pick up a hitchhiker, a middle-aged Indian woman carrying a jacket and a daypack. She was headed to a town in Manitoba to see her daughter.

"Got a message from her last night—just said, 'I need you, Mom.'"

We talked about teenagers, about losing people we love, about addictions. She had moved to the city from rural Manitoba recently to help another daughter in trouble. A single mom, the girl had become addicted to codeine and the children were selling beadwork to pay for their mom's vice.

"She wouldn't straighten out, wouldn't listen, eh. So one night I come and the kids were still awake at two in the morning with school the next day. So I called Social Services and they come and took the kids for a bit. Oooh, she was mad at me. But she's straightened around now and you should see those kids. They're involved in everything—sports, things at the school. I'm proud of her now."

For an hour or more we talked in this way, with the highway rolling on past towns named Indian Head, Sintaluta, Wolseley, and for the time being it was possible to imagine a way across the divide between her race and mine, a rift formed long before residential schools and broken treaties. At Whitewood I had to turn off the highway, so we parted ways at a roadside gas station.

"How long does it usually take you to get home?" I asked.

"I'll be there by supper."

When the day was over, I drove past a burning stubble field and turned back onto the highway at Whitewood to join the westbound traffic heading for Regina. *She'll be with her daughter by now.*

I opened a window and caught a draft of the hospital-gown smells of Saint Anthony's again. The last storyteller was dying, but something would remain. A spirit that flies up out of rivers, drifts in tree branches, and walks out of mud, resurrected in ways I may not recognize. It is always this way when we give up on dreams, and escape to sorrow and consolation. But it all comes again in faces and words unfamiliar at first, then searing remembrance into the heart, turning us back to Galilee.

The car radio played the last few bars from an old Don McLean song about lost innocence, and in the dusked and grieving prairie fields little men tended fires bright with colors borrowed from the inside of the sun.

PART ONE

# Ascending Hakkarmel

# SHELTER 1

---•---

*There ain't nothing more to write about, and I am rotten glad of*
*it, because if I'd a knowed what a trouble it was to make a book I*
*wouldn't a tackled it, and—ain't a-going to no more. But I reckon*
*I got to light out for the Territory ahead of the rest, because Aunt*
*Sally she's going to adopt me and sivilize me, and I can't stand*
*it. I been there before.*

—Mark Twain, *The Adventures of Huckleberry Finn*

Amen, Huck. Mark Twain, my all-time favorite atheist, had a
healthy distaste for religion, but in writing that great novel,
and in choosing to conclude it with those words, he was, unconsciously, drawing from the mythic waters that run beneath all religious striving. At the other end of the story, Huck is getting fidgety
and lonesome, feeling walled in by the "sivilizing" schemes of Miss
Watson, the old maid of the moment. She brings on the spelling
books, the table manners, and, worst of all, the religion, until he
longs for his liberty. It finally comes when he gets to the river, but
first he has to escape his origins as the son of the town drunk.

This distancing from family and the orthodoxy of the day in an
adventure in the wilderness follows the ancient pattern set down by
the prophets, teachers, and saints who have marked each advance of
our religious evolution. Abraham, Moses, Elijah, Buddha, Jesus of

15

Nazareth, Saint Benedict, Muhammad, Saint Francis of Assisi—all found their way by losing it, by turning their backs on civilization and lighting out for the Territory.

It's the same impulse that sends us out of doors when the world of Miss Watson is too much with us. Something in the heart recognizes that, just as religious truth springs forth beneath the Bodhi tree, in the desert, on the mountaintop, or at the riverside, our own salvation, our hope for personal transformation and understanding, requires a certain willingness to lose our way in uncharted terrain. The straight lines surveyed by others are of little use here. We've been there before, and it generally leads to more civilization, less of the Territory.

The stories I have written down in these pages come from a period of being lost in the boundary land where religion, Christianity in particular, has from time to time made contact with wildness. Writing in this vagrant way—led by instinct, pattern recognition, and other spirits—suited the terrain and subject. It was a bit like the long walks with my father hunting for grouse years ago, which I still regard as my first way into wildness. On an October afternoon we'd set off along the edges of something, a stand of poplar, a ravine, a railway easement. We'd walk for hours, quiet and alert for the flushing birds, yet surprised nonetheless at the sudden *thwirr* of wings just ahead.

The margins of myth, nature, and history that drew me onward, as indistinct as they were at times, marking boundaries between the civilized and the wild, the orthodox and the pagan, allowed plenty of room for speculation. There was little to constrain me from imagining the intricacies of Creation and its particular unfolding here and now on these plains—not the biologist's standards of scientific rigor nor the theologian's fear of heresy.

Once or twice the impulse to make the most of this latitude caught me with my guard down. There was the afternoon, late in the summer, when I found myself naked and alone in a large tipi staring up at the smoke hole trying to understand what I'd seen there at midnight, what it is about a little less shelter that can shift a lens in the spirit.

The tipi did not belong to me, though for that summer it rested on our meadow just north of the cabin. For the land I will, with reservations, admit ownership, though Karen and I and the children call it just that—"the Land"—in part because of those reservations. "Our land" sounds presumptuous, and terms such as "acreage" have come to imply a level of subjugation and comfort that we aspire to eschew. For a while we considered inventing a name for the place, but everything that came to mind sounded pretentious, bearing either the bathos of a ruined estate or the vulgarity of a condominium project. When we began to hear our youngest children tell their friends "we're going to the Land," we knew it had been named well and good.

We purchased the property, seventy acres of Qu'Appelle Valley hillside, meadow, and coulee, ten years ago. The first two years we came here to camp in summer and began searching for abandoned and moveable farmhouses in the vicinity. My father and I spent a good piece of the second summer getting to know one another better as we built a foundation for a small, one-and-a-half-story house a friend had located just north of the valley.

The day we surveyed the building site and drove in the stakes, a male mountain bluebird landed atop the transit. It remained with us, visiting the work site almost daily as we contoured the excavation, hauled sand, hammered together forms, and poured concrete. When the house finally lurched down our road and groaned its way onto the new moorings, the bluebird perched on the west gable for a moment. That year I put up a dozen bluebird houses on the property.

꙳

Not unlike bluebirds, we spend time in houses to create a zone of comfort, to raise a barrier between ourselves and the biting, prickling, digging, cooling, heating, blowing world outside. Nature, for its part, no sooner encounters one of our barriers than it sets about finding ways to get through it. Even as I write this in my cabin bedroom, three flies are using me as a salt lick and landing pad. We have had skunks dig into the cellar, raccoons tear into the attic, crickets serenade us from beneath our beds, and moths dive-bomb us from above. What's more, we have good reason to believe that our cabin's presence on this meadow has granted the local deer mouse population an evolutionary leg up in their ascent toward the zenith of rodentia, whatever that turns out to be. Though we have had no luck in getting the old pond at the base of our hillside to retain its share of spring runoff, I spend a weekend every April siphoning another pond that would make perfectly adequate frog and duck habitat were it located anywhere other than my cellar. I will leave you to imagine our gardening efforts.

This, I know, sounds like complaint, but it is this life within a broader margin of intercourse between ourselves and nature that keeps us coming out here whenever we can. Here there is always something hidden in the grass just ahead, waiting to leap into the air and stir our blood memory of a time before injury and exile.

As someone who has been contemptuous of white people who put on Indian ways, I was reluctant at first to use the tipi, a little embarrassed and uneasy about the whole thing. Soon after it was up, though, the kids wanted to try sleeping in it. That first night, I awoke to a loud shriek I could not place as owl, coyote, house cat, or bear. Curious, I slipped outside into the moonlit meadow for a look, silence all around, nothing moving but the northern lights rippling across the sky in great scarves of orange and red.

That was when I remembered the recent sightings of cougars up the valley. Back in my sleeping bag, I stared up at the wheeling heavens through the smoke hole, and for a moment somewhere between waking and sleep I was in a womb looking out upon hills ablaze with holy fire.

# EL MARAHKA I

———————————•———————————

I saw a play once in which a grieving woman dreams nightly of her dead lover. In the end, after coming to terms with his life and her regrets, she has one last dialogue with him in her dreams. "But I'm afraid I will forget," she cries, holding on to him. "Don't forget," he answers, "just let go."

It was a cliché, something you'd hear from a therapist on afternoon television perhaps, but, voiced by actors onstage, it suggested a deeper remembrance, a wider disengagement. Watching the two lovers in a last embrace of their spirits, I thought again about how this culture—North America in general and my own prairie culture in particular—clings to distorted memories, nursing a burden of nostalgia and regret even as we blunder forward in ways disrespectful of all that might yet offer blessings and wisdom from the past. The Untouched Wilderness, the Heroic Pioneer, and the Vanquished Savage all persist in our contemporary encounters with the wild, the rural, and the aboriginal. Their resilience is a tribute to roots deep in Old World soil.

In idle moments I find myself wondering about those roots and that soil, asking unanswerable questions, imagining pathways back to a time when and a place where we were ourselves native in wildness. Archaeology, in unearthing physical evidence, marks the coordinates well enough but leaves us to guess at the exact forces that prompted each adaptation in our emergence as spiritual creatures. Myth and metaphor take up the slack. A long walk out of

Eden is one way we have carried it in the imagination, but I have come to think of it as an ascent on the Mountain of the Lord—one that we embarked upon when the sacred myths of hunters gave way to the sacred texts of shepherds and farmers.

Exile, it has been suggested, happens in that signal shift from tongue to script. That sounds right to me. Writing posits a measure of distance between self and world. Even so, it is the familiar arm's reach of our reality, and while words on a page will never rescue us from Babylon, they make for a serviceable home away from home. Songs of longing and redemption, stories of loss, abandonment, consolation, and reconciliation still speak to us from some of the oldest writing we have thought holy. That may still be the best we can hope for when we resort to text: to relocate ourselves in hymns that console, stories that reconcile.

In trying to write my own way toward a more graceful encounter with the wild, the rural, and the aboriginal, I realized early on that I would need a running start. I would have to begin by retracing our wanderings away from wildness and back again. With no exact entry into the mind and heart of the hunter, I took refuge in the old texts, the Bible in particular, as a rough archive of the human spirit at certain critical horizons in our evolution as the primates who got religion. Don't worry. As I rummage through those verses, I do not look for their value or meaning in their small residue of documentary fact, nor in their imputed Providence. For my purposes, and for the narrative at hand, the great truths in myth, poetry, and prophecy—those that have accompanied us for good or ill to this present moment—are more than enough.

After comparing his lover's breasts to the twins of a gazelle, the bridegroom in Song of Songs praises her profile with a reference to the heights of Carmel. In the Hebrew scriptures, the

Mountain of the Lord is known as Hakkarmel, roughly "the garden land," an actual place in Palestine long renowned for its beauty. Christians call it Mount Carmel, and local Palestinians know it today as either Kurmul or Jebel Mar Elias, the Mountain of Saint Elias. Some say Elias, the prophet Elijah, lived somewhere on the mountaintop, which rises from six hundred feet above the Mediterranean in a ridge running ten miles southeast to where the altars of El Marahka stand against the seventeen-hundred-foot-high summit.

El Marahka, "the burning" or "the sacrifice," was there long before Elijah, and long before El Marahka there were other burnings on the mountain. For sixty thousand years, human beings have been, accidentally or intentionally, setting Mount Carmel's pine forests alight. So say the forest ecologists who study the Aleppo pine forests of Carmel National Park and Nature Reserve. Abraham Haim and Gidi Ne'eman of the University of Haifa have found that the flora and fauna of the mountain's east Mediterranean pine forests require a half century to recover fully from a fire. With burns of varying ages and sizes, the fire history of the forest landscapes creates a succession and diversity of vegetation communities, which in turn are reflected in local animal distribution and density.

Likewise, the fire history of humankind in this region is bound up with a succession and diversity of religions. Jewish, Christian, Druze, and Baha'i believers have come to this place to lift their prayers to the one God. And before them, pagan hunters and herdsmen came here to make their lives sacred in the eyes of a multiplicity of spirits and gods. All, appealing to one or many gods, climbed to the southeast point of Hakkarmel to burn sacrifices on altars. Now and then, when the grass was dry, the fire would have jumped the pyre and burned a path uphill to the pines. At El Marahka, in the shadow of the pine forests, the Druzes of neighboring villages still come to perform a yearly sacrifice, participating in the ritual that gave life to our religions, that mimicked and abetted the rhythms of fiery transformation present in nature.

The difference seems to be that in nature an underlying unity persists within diversity, whereas in our religions we choose to ignore and even do violence to the bonds that could hold our spiritual yearnings together in a rich and healthy community of differentness. If the Creator cannot be happy with one kind of beetle, why would one religion be enough?

The common ground is here at El Marahka, where tumbled stones remember the times of shared sacrifice. Elijah is claimed as a prophet by Jewish, Christian, and Islamic believers, and in the eighteenth century, local leaders from all three faiths would join together to celebrate a feast in his name. How extraordinary those celebrations must have been. What was said? What was not said? Did anyone think of inviting the pagans?

# SHELTER 2

---

*To light a fire is the instinctive and resistant act of man when,
at the winter ingress, the curfew is sounded throughout Nature.
It indicates a spontaneous, Promethean rebelliousness against the
fiat that this recurrent season shall bring foul times, cold darkness,
misery and death. Black chaos comes, and the fettered gods of earth
say, Let there be light.*

—Thomas Hardy, *Return of the Native*

The first time we talked about the possibility of raising a tipi at
the Land it was early November, one last night at the cabin
before the snow would block our road. Friends drove out to stay the
weekend with us on the valley rim: Mike and Lorran with their two
little ones, Megan with her two. We sat around the woodstove that
evening and Lorran told ancient Chinese tales by the light of our
gas lamp. There was one about a brocade that became a castle and
another about a garlic farmer whose crop was stolen while he slept.
We listened, Megan nursed her youngest boy to sleep, and later the
adults went out to look at the stars. The constellations of late fall
appeared at our bidding: Pleiades, Taurus, Cygnus, Ursa Minor,
Draco, all in turn. We mapped the skies from brim to brim, as duck
wings whistled overhead in dark passage—a sound with a chill in it.
On the horizon, just beneath the half moon, the milt of the winter's
first clouds appeared. As we went back inside to the fire, Mike said
he'd like to raise a tipi on the meadow the next summer.

Heading for the outhouse at dawn the next day, I caught a few snowflakes on my shoulders. Two jays screamed; an owl cried softly across the coulee. By that evening, people in Weyburn were using snowmobiles to rescue travelers trapped in cars half buried in snow.

The snows came deep in the following days and weeks, and with them the bittersweet sensation that we had joined in the passing of one season into another and measured the heat and light of our spirits against the coming darkness. That winter, reading the bonfire scene in the opening chapters of Hardy's *Return of the Native*, I flipped back through our desk calendar to check the date of that last night at the Land. It was the fifth of November, Guy Fawkes Day, or Bonfire Night as it is still known and celebrated in England. In the novel, Hardy's peasant "heath-folk" of mid-nineteenth-century Wessex are telling ghost stories and exchanging gossip around a towering bonfire they have built to mark the fifth of November. Their fire was on top of the Rainbarrow, an ancient ceremonial and burial mound on Hardy's fictional Egdon Heath where first Druids and later Saxons gathered to light fires "at the ingress of winter." The novel's bonfire-makers, mostly furze- and heath-cutters and their sons, look out over the dark face of the heath and see thirty other fires on near and distant hilltops, blazing "like wounds in a black hide," each representing a specific locality to the Rainbarrow men though they could see nothing of the landscape to aid their recognition.

The bonfire scene establishes early on the novel's thematic tension between heath (heathen) values on the one hand and civilized Christian values on the other. The pagan wildness of the land itself has its congener in the folk wisdom, superstitions, and lifeways of the peasants who dwell within the narrow margin that Egdon Heath allows for humanity. Most of the novel's main characters, though, are educated, pensioned landowners who do not crease their hands with dirt, but merely dwell on the edges of the heath where they can best avow the Christian code of conduct that sustains propriety and keeps the wild and pagan out of doors and out of mind. The narrative's ultimate tragedy and romantic pathos is a playing out of the tension that occurs when the heath asserts its dominion over the lives of those who had thought themselves, by the exercise of their will and desire for a more civilized life, beyond the powers of nature.

The pagan and the Christian infuse one another on every page of the book. The heath-folk may seldom go to church, but they, too, have their notions of Christian rectitude. Likewise, although Eustacia Vye, the primary female character, hates the heath and longs for city life, she is said to have "Pagan eyes, full of nocturnal mysteries."[1] One of the book's minor characters, introduced at the opening bonfire scene, is "a faltering man with reedy hair [and] no shoulders" who embodies the very flaw that leads to the undoing of the main characters. His name is Christian and he is, significantly, the youngest son of an ancient furze-cutter, a mischievous old codger whom Hardy casts in the pagan, heath-en mold. The old man, named Cantle (he *is*, literally, a fragment of the old ways of the heath and heathen), is the first to sing ("with a voice of a bee up a flue"[2]) and dance a jig around the fire.

As the other revelers talk of a man no woman will consent to marry, young Christian stands off to one side, away from the light of the bonfire, teeth chattering, limbs quaking with fear and worry. The others push him toward the fire and begin questioning him. In his "thin, jibbering voice," Christian lets it be known that he is such a man never to be married, for he was born at the new moon. The heath-folk give him their pity for they know that a man-child born under a moonless sky will never be a man fit to marry. "No moon, no man," they say, and Christian, in a statement that reminds us of the blending of religious tradition that once kept rural peasantry nearer the earth, replies, "I'd sooner go without drink at Lammas-tide than be a man of no moon."[3] Talk turns to ghosts that visit single men and then the people, two by two, begin to dance around the fire—all, that is, but Christian, who "stood aloof, uneasily rocking himself as he murmured, 'They ought not to do it—how the vlankers do fly! 'Tis tempting the Wicked one, 'tis.'"

# EL MARAHKA II

———————————————•———————————————

N ow the hallways are cold as catacombs, though the baptismal font still drains through stone laid upon stone to commit the holy water down from high altars to the soil beneath the church's foundations. And still people stand well above that moistened earth and read of kings, of the day Elijah made the sacrifice that burned the heights of Carmel into our history.

We read of kings who lived three thousand years ago, of Ahab's misbegotten reign, of Israel's surrender to his philistine wife, Jezebel. She, handmaiden of Baal, brought with her 450 priests and prophets of her pagan god and set about slaughtering the prophets of Yahweh, god of Abraham, Isaac, and Jacob. She found all save the one whom Yahweh favored above the others. Elijah, sheltered in Yahweh's protection, watched from the wilds as his people hobbled along to the music of two gods. Then, out of the desert Elijah came suddenly before Ahab with a message of Yahweh's displeasure. "There will be a drought," he said, "and even the dew will be withheld. It will not end except upon my order."

Then Yahweh spirited his prophet away to the desert again at the side of the Wadi Cherith, east of Jordan. While the Israelites suffered in a barren land, Elijah drank from the stream and ate food brought by Yahweh's ravens, bread in the morning and meat for his supper.

Two years passed. A wilder Elijah, the mud of Cherith's shores caked in his hair, came again to the King of Israel. To end the

drought and settle this matter of conflicting gods, he invited Ahab
to hold a contest of sacrifices atop Mount Carmel. "Bring the
people of Israel and the 450 priests of Baal who sup at Jezebel's
table," he said. Ahab was desperate for rain in his land and so he
had the people fast in preparation and gather at the appointed time
around the old altars of Carmel. There Elijah, the lone priest of
Yahweh, appeared before them and invited the prophets of Baal to
slaughter a bull and place it on an altar pyre ready to be lit. He told
them they were not to light the fire themselves but had to call on
their god to light it for them. The Baalites dismembered the bull,
built a makeshift altar, heaved the carcass on, and set to praying and
prancing around the pyre. They carried on, moaning and limping,
long into the day, with Elijah taunting them. "Call louder," he said.
"Perhaps your god is just asleep or busy." Dusk approached but not
a spark came to the altar of Baal.

With the priests of Baal exhausted, Elijah set to work. Silently, he
repaired the old altar of Yahweh, which had fallen to ruin. Twelve
stones he placed on the ground, one for each of the twelve tribes
of Jacob. Around these he dug a deep trench. Next, he gathered
wood for the fire, the pine and oak of Hakkarmel, into a massive
pyre. This done, Elijah took another bull and disemboweled it in
a deft movement of his knife running from pelvis to sternum. He
laid the sacrifice on the pyre and asked others to drench the altar,
the wood, and the bull with twelve large jarfuls of water until the
trench itself was overflowing.

With the stage set, Elijah waited. The eyes of Israel were on
his altar, and the time for the customary evening sacrifice was
approaching. At the moment sanctioned by Yahweh and kept in
the traditions of his forefathers, Elijah stepped forward and called
on his God to win back the hearts of the people. The altar pyre
burst into a great holocaust, illuminating the crest of Carmel. The
bull fell to ashes and the flames licked the trench of water dry. The
Israelites repented then and there, turning back to Yahweh as Elijah

seized the prophets of Baal and slaughtered them down at the dry riverbed of Cisson.

Elijah then told Ahab to end his fast, saying, "I can hear the sound of rain." Climbing again to the heights of Carmel, the prophet bowed down to the earth, putting his face between his knees. After his prayer, he commanded his servant to go up to the summit and look out to the sea. Six times the servant went up and six times he came back to report a cloudless sky. On the seventh trip, he returned to report a cloud, small as a man's hand, rising from the sea. At this, Elijah sent the servant down to warn Ahab to harness his chariot and get away from the mountain and back to the courts of Jezreel before the rains filled the Wadi Cisson and blocked his path. Soon the rain came in torrents and Cisson turned into a ferocious river that washed the slain priests of Baal out to sea. Ahab crossed the riverbed just in time and made for Jezreel. Elijah, protected by the hand of Yahweh, tucked up his cloak and, like the wild herald he was, ran before Ahab to the outskirts of town.

# SHELTER 3

—————————————————•—————————————————

L ike everyone else, I get out of town to be in a place where a good chunk of nature remains available to my senses. When our souls want restoring, we do not go sit in the middle of parking lots. We go where life is a little less scripted, a little less conscripted.

An older couple stopped by for a visit one afternoon while we were out at the Land. Retired people, well-off, well educated. We sat in front of the cabin gazing out over the valley and Lake Katepwa in the middle distance. On cue, the woman said, "My, what a place you have here! I can just feel the stress melting away."

You hear such talk, the same clinical terms, from people for whom a gravel road is an adventure. The wind fresh from poplars and meadows eddies through their blood and yet they are at a loss to name the thing that moves them. One step beyond constructed and landscaped surfaces and we are in terra incognita. We are dying within our shelter. People used to die of exposure. Nothing gets a piece of us anymore if we can help it. Wind, rain, ice, and sun, the creatures that bite or hook into us, wait for us on the other side of doors and walls and caskets.

Once, children inoculated themselves with mud and microbes. Remember? People pulled foals from mares. Woke to crowing birds. Who stumbles now in storm from porch to barn door? The long hours lying in grass are gone. Time with lambs and calves, bird nests and dragonflies made us. Time apart from them is unmaking us.

I dreamed last night of horses escaping from crude corrals that I had made. Arriving after a long absence to find the hay and water drawn down, I opened the gate an inch and they burst out upon the unfenced fields and I was lost as to how to get them back. How *do* I get the horses back? My daughter's dreams, the nightmares of a housebound three-year-old in midwinter, are of foxes. The fiery-red brush sweeps across her unconscious, and she is scared of its wild touch. Now she runs in terror if she finds herself alone in a room. Yet every morning she insists on wearing the same skirt, the shiny bronze one her mother sewed out of faux snakeskin.

Predawn dispatches from the cerebellum urge a lowering of barriers, a return to the senses: abandon shelter, find communion in exposure. See this luffing sail, hear this canine howl, taste this bread, smell this violet, touch this stone. Blessed are the unwanted abrasions, invasions, and privations; the grace of all that, in eluding and pursuing our flesh, draws us nearer sacrament.

# EL MARAHKA III

———————————————————•———————————————————

*We can never be too Pagan when we are truly Christian, and the old myths are eternal truths held fast in the Church's net.*

—Michael Fairless, *The Roadmender*

The story of Elijah's sacrifice and violence at Mount Carmel (1 Kings 18–20) is but one moment in our civilization's passage toward monotheism. A hundred generations have come and gone with various claimants to the rightful worship of the one true God, but still we can identify with the Israelites who were drawn by the energy they found in pagan worship, while hanging on to their faith in Yahweh. Like us, they hedged their bets, kept one foot in each camp, and waited for new developments.

Illuminated by the warm afterglow of the Enlightenment, we think we are beyond the reach of gods, certainly pagan ones. After all, the churches are growing empty and we have given our souls over to moral relativism, psychotherapy, and the marketplace, haven't we? Or are we waiting, like the Israelites, for someone to take us up a mountain? A pilgrimage, some pyrotechnics from I Am Who Am, and we might easily return to the faith of our fathers. The religious press keeps watch for doves on the horizon: "83.7 percent of North Americans profess belief in God." Or "One in four Internet searches is for religious or spiritual material."

Now that we are Enlightened we can measure everything: belief, hope, prayer—it can all be tallied. Trouble is, a recent poll

shows that 8.2 out of 10 mystics believe enlightenment has actually been set back by the Enlightenment. William Blake comes to
mind here. Born into the teeth of the Enlightenment, Blake threw
himself headlong into bewilderment. While others bowed to the
new reign of reason, Blake turned away from the naked vanity
on parade and engraved songs in praise of the imagination. We
may fuel our science and industry with Cartesian and Newtonian
combustibles, but our souls still run on the same fires of bewilderment and imagination that seared William Blake's poems into our
literature.

Innocence was Blake's pearl of great price. In two poems that
together form a single parable, "Little Girl Lost" and "Little Girl
Found," innocence is regained by the family's immersion in wildness. The child, lost in the "desart," falls asleep and then is delivered
tenderly by wild beasts to a cave where she remains in the keeping
of lions, leopards, and tigers. Her parents, having lost their own
innocence and their child, walk the wilds in fear and sorrow searching for her. After seven days, a lion finds them and "their fears allay
/ When he licks their hands / And silent by them stands." The
lion, who wears a crown, leads the parents back to the cave. In the
closing lines they look upon their "sleeping child / Among tygers
wild. / To this day they dwell / In a lonely dell; / Nor fear the
wolvish howl / Nor the lion's growl."

After searching the woods for seven days and regaining their
lost innocence at the touch of a wild but gentle beast that wears
a crown, a man and a woman abandon their fears and embrace
the wilderness. There is something Christian bedding down with
something pagan here, but when a religious poet gives us visions
of renewal in nature we call it mysticism. Christian or pagan, Blake
drew on a wild energy that has been around since well before
Abraham stayed his hand.

*Nor fear the wolvish howl.* I did not know the late Canadian poet
Anne Szumigalski but those who did say she drew inspiration from

Blake and would often recite his poems. A film about her life and work shows her at home, sitting in her living room and talking about gardening, her love of wild things, her habit of dancing whenever the spirit moved her. At one point in the interview she says, "I have two religions—my left hand is pagan and my right hand is Christian…or is it the other way round?"

Jesus of Nazareth, Francis of Assisi, John of the Cross, Teresa of Avila, Hildegard of Bingen, Julian of Norwich, Meister Eckhart, and Teilhard de Chardin. The further we get from our last dance at El Marahka and other hilltops, the more we are interested in people who found other ways to sacred fires. Bookstores are doing a brisk trade these days in new editions of writing by and about these mystics, shelving them next to how-to guides for the aspiring Druid or Wiccan.

*Deserere*: to unjoin. Away to the desert, the wilderness, the *midbar*, the *arabah*, we go. Not sandy dune land, but the barren places left over to wilder culture, to grazing animals and their nomadic herders. The desert is the place where you go to be unjoined, detached from things. A landscape made of what *remains*. A hermit remains in the desert, becomes a remnant of his former self, and learns how to dwell in the mansions of creation. The remnant plains of Judea had their wild beasts, their herdsmen, their mystics; the glacial outwash and till plains of the northern prairie had theirs. What drives a saint or a Black Elk out into the desolate places anyway?

Saint John of the Cross, whose *Ascent of Mount Carmel* is founded upon a detachment from creaturely existence with its base desires and appetites, had his grotto where he could pray in solitude. He would often leave the monastery near Segovia and go alone to a place hollowed out in the rock and overlooking the river. Later, at Baeza, he purchased some property in the mountains as a retreat for himself and the others in his order. Thinking of his place apart, he wrote verses proclaiming, "My Beloved is the mountains / and lonely wooded valleys, / strange islands, / and resounding rivers."

Who is that fierce little pagan within, the one who pecks away with his pointed stick at a chink in the monastery wall, who keeps driving us out into the thorny plains, away from the clapboard enclosures of civilized life? We think we know where he came from, what he left behind. The acacia savanna of the Great Rift, the habitat that forced him upright on two legs to see above the encircling grass. Some time later, he wandered north across the Levant, began herding sheep, learned to write, and heard the voice of Yahweh. It wasn't long, nor without bloodshed, before he had made stones into walls and earth into bread. Inside the walls, his every longing save the spiritual one is gratified, yet table manners are little consolation when something—a vagrant restlessness, an inclination of the remnant within walls for the wholeness without—stirs his memory of the veld.

"The Spirit," Matthew said, drove Christ out into the wilderness for forty days. Mark added, "He was with wild beasts." Comfort, power, meaning, identity were behind him somewhere in a box in town. Before him spread the wide curving plains of Judea, scrubby native pasture, rock rose, and thorny broom.

Empty belly, hot days, cold nights: Jesus fasts and prays. Satan, the fallen spirit, arrives bearing the standard temptations and empty promises. First off, Jesus confronts the temptation to give into appetites mindlessly.

"If you're the Son of God," says the Evil One, "command these stones to become loaves of bread." It's that same primary sin, the first apple-grabbing transgression that always leads away from Eden.

*You are the great one, so forget about the rules and take what you want. It's easy. Go ahead, you deserve it.*

Christ's answer restores the correct order of things with the ancient guideline for rightful living in relation to creation: "Man shall not live by bread alone, but by every word that proceeds from the mouth of God." God's first words? "Let there be light." A lot of utterances followed after that one and near as we can tell the words show no sign of abating. Precious little light reaches the murky, abyssal plains of the Atlantic Ocean's Angola Basin, but last year taxonomists identified twenty-two new species of crustacea living there at a depth of three miles.

Even the toughest mystic would be hard-pressed to make a go of it on the unlit plains of the Angola Basin, but there's no denying it has desert value in spades. "Through the dark cold and the empty desolation, / The wave cry, the wind cry, the vast waters / Of the petrel and the porpoise." Lines from T. S. Eliot, in the closing of "East Coker," the second quartet. A desire to embrace all that proceeds from the mouth of God drives you out of the monastery and "Into another intensity / For a further union, a deeper communion…"

I asked a theologian once what wilderness means in the New Testament and he said, "Wilderness asks the purification question."

When the longing is fierce enough to overwhelm the human desire for comfort, safety, and community—the tool-grabbing urge that turned the earth into walls and bread in the first place—the bravest souls go out to the desert. There are demons living there they must wrestle, vexatious spirits that over time turn out not to be desert dwellers after all, but stowaways smuggled in their fears and desires.

The Desert Fathers carried their share of demons with them

out into the barren places of Egypt. During the third century AD, young men and women who were to become the first Christian monks and nuns began leaving the cities and towns of their birth and going into the desert to find out for themselves what it is to be "a people apart." Their religion had come of age, as they had, within the walls of the Roman polis. The decades of persecution had passed—Nero and the other emperors with a penchant for watching Christians die painful deaths were long gone. The church was mainstream now and rising toward its first taste of privilege. Cut off from their Jewish roots, "the People of the Way" (Acts 9:2), as the early Christians called themselves, came increasingly under the influence of contemporary Hellenistic philosophy with its preference for spirit over matter. An ideal of extreme asceticism and renunciation of all material desire had settled into the faith as a requirement for salvation.

In the Egyptian countryside, however, the old gods and idols were alive and well. Christians believed they had chased the demons out of the city and into the desert where they worked their evil among the goatherds and tribal nomads, pagans all. *Paganus*, "of the country," became the rubric for circumscribing all the old religious customs lingering in the wilderness of Christendom.

Having reached adulthood and their Christian identity upon the entitlements of family and urban society, the generation of aspiring ascetics grew restless, disenchanted with the social order, as young people will. The desert was awash in demons and called to them as a place where they could test themselves in the wilderness as Jesus had in his early days. Before long there were hundreds of men and women living in loose collections all over the desert. Only a few generations had passed since Christ vacated the tomb and already we were heading off to conquer pagan spirits in the wild. Nevertheless, the desert mystics anchored the faith in wilderness and over time bore the good fruit of Christian mysticism and the entire Western monastic tradition.

The purification question comes up smartly when you have abandoned the script of your name, comfort, and civil society in favor of an exile that will by stages prove the self to be no more than a wave cresting in an ocean, the paradox of a differentiation within unity. The Desert Fathers (and mothers—there were many women too) lived as hermits in caves and rough huts, subsisting on bread and water, the goodwill of others, and the grace of God. Many became ascetic athletes, rivaling one another in their extremes of self-abnegation. A good hermit, it was said, should eat and sleep as little as possible and his tunic must be ragged enough that if left on the road no one would be tempted to take it. Battling evil spirits was part of daily life. But the demons they wrestled had followed them from the city like the weed seeds that clung to the soles of their sandals. Loneliness, fear, attachment to the comforts and pleasures of life—these were the spiritual enemies that came into their huts. And the weapons they took up—self-denial, acts of service, walking, praying, meditating—eventually made their way into the religious life of most Christian monastic orders.

Imagine these first nuns and monks striking forth to purify the wilderness, not knowing that it would purify them, expecting to conquer the evil outside the city in a realm they feared but did not understand. They walked out of the profane and twittering world, away from distraction, the apathy and stale exhalations of society, and into the axis mundi of land unspoken, unbroken, seamless and enveloping. Sitting in the ashes of their exile, they came to know the smell of their fear and ignorance, the taste of their helplessness in the hands of God. The waiting in hunger and abstention, the sleeping against the cold, uncaring earth, the breathing, praying, and shouting against the dark absences of others—it was a descent that served them not as mortification but as the hand that clears away the leaves that choke the surface of the desert spring. And grace came in spite of their weakness because grace comes freely in the desert. If the holy spirit descended upon any of the Desert

Fathers it was because wildness is the dwelling place not of demons but of God's very breath within the ragged and tendriled lives bursting into the light of this place or that, the spiritual presence within locality, bearing its scent and mood and shade.

And the pilgrims, too, came from the city. The first spiritual tourists, they sought the counsel of the wisest of the fathers. Returned home and told of men and women whose faces shone like lightning. Who reached skyward with the tips of their fingers aflame like lanterns. Who said, "Go, cast your weakness before God and you shall find rest." And, "To be a monk you must become like a consuming fire."

Desert words, purification words from mystics ignited by the wild spirit of creation. Fasting away from appetites and desires long enough to achieve a certain attenuation of the self, a mystic becomes a frail vessel permeable and open to the possibility of being-*with*. Interbeing, as the Buddhists say, a return to the Ground of Being, the water beneath the wave, the soil beneath the desert flower where the mystic locates compassion in the contiguous substrate of matter running like wildfire consuming and renewing in the combustion of creation all that lives, dies, and lives again.

Church historians link the rise of Western monasticism in Gaul and Italy to the early tradition of the desert hermits in Egypt. By the fourth century, European monks and nuns were beginning to live in community, basing their religious practice in large part on accounts of the lives of these "eastern" desert mystics. *Via Antonii*, a book about Saint Anthony, the most famous of the Desert Fathers, made the rounds, as well as the writings of John Cassian. Cassian, one of the first to write about Christian contemplative prayer, is said to have formed a bridge between Eastern and Western monasticism (and mysticism) by coming out of Egypt and helping to found two monasteries in Marseilles. The monks and nuns in these early monasteries followed the ascetic ideals of the Desert Fathers, but Cassian urged them to live in community and to cooperate with one another rather than compete as superhermits.

Around the year 500, another young Christian, perhaps twenty years of age and born into the Italian aristocracy, turned his back on school and career prospects and walked out of Rome. He wasn't sure what he was going to do or where he would end up, but he knew something was calling him out of the city and its embattled, trade-weary streets. His name, Benedict, calls to mind words that bless, and it was his words, and deeds, that over the next forty years of his life would bless Europe with the organizing model for religious community that has come to characterize Western monasticism.

After leaving Rome, he made his way to the Simbruini Mountains, through oak and beech woodlands and past the two springs that form the headwaters of the Aniene River. Forty miles from the city he arrived at the entrance to a steep-walled valley where a bridge across a small man-made lake joined the broken-down archways of a decaying villa on one side to a set of derelict Roman baths on the other. The site had once been a grand country estate for Nero, but the day Benedict walked by, the marble pillars, porticos, and casements were already overgrown, crumbling, and well on their way back into the rock cycle. Climbing a steep path up the side of the mountain ravine, Benedict came upon a cave that would be his home for the next three years. Five hundred feet below, the lake, a stretch of the Aniene withheld by a dam, reflected some light into the valley's gloom. Over time, the place came to be known as Subiaco, "by the water." Hanging on the mountainside not far above the cave was a small monastery where a handful of monks living like alpine marmots scrabbled out a meager existence. One of the monks befriended the young Benedict, gave him a habit to wear, and lowered food to him at regular intervals.

The histories of Benedict say little more of his time in the grotto and show him emerging suddenly three years later to build twelve small monasteries in the valley. Each monastery housed

twelve monks—young people who had apparently been drawn to
Subiaco by the stories of Benedict's sanctity and wise counsel. He
lived several years at Subiaco as abbot in charge of these monasteries, forming his first experience of communal living, and eventually
bearing fruit in the tenets of what we now call the *Rule of Saint
Benedict.*

Benedict's biographers believe that he wrote his rule after he
had left Subiaco and the Simbruini Mountains to build another
monastery atop Monte Cassino. But they say his first act (hagio-
graphers seem rather preoccupied with saints' "first acts" upon
arrival in a heathen territory) was to smash the local shrine dedicated to Apollo, a small chapel with an idol and an altar where the
locals were still offering the occasional sacrifice to the Roman god.
Benedict then built his new chapel on the very spot, thereby enact-
ing the second task of the venturing saint, which is usually followed
in the hagiography with a sentence or two remarking upon the
haste with which the local pagans, who were simple country folk
after all, abandoned their old ways and converted to Christianity.
It seems Yahweh's prophet on Hakkarmel persists on other moun-
taintops, haunting the stories of evangelizing saints.

Not surprisingly, Benedict's biographers never ask whether the
pagan values of the countryside might have influenced the saint,
his religious community, or his church. A man lives in a cave for
three years halfway up a mountain and overlooking a river valley,
emerges finally like Jonah from the belly of Leviathan, and then
begins establishing the religious communities that have from age
to age anchored Christian monasticism to the landscape and rural
culture. Yes, his work and evangelizing left its mark on the land
and on the local peasantry—indigenous traditions, sacred places,
and customs were destroyed and replaced by Christian ones. The
historic accounts are proud and clear on that point. But what of
the new monastic communities and the spiritual trajectory of the
church as a whole? Is it important that one of the most influential

popes of the age, Gregory I, was first an abbot of a Benedictine monastery and left his community to step in as Holy Father?

Benedict, regardless of what we think of his dealings with pagans, led a movement and wrote the guidelines that returned Christianity to its roots as a profoundly communitarian faith. At Subiaco and Monte Cassino, he worked, ate, and celebrated with simple people whose pagan ways made them, like the Samaritan woman at the well in John's gospel, the excluded ones who nevertheless inclined naturally to the Word as the willow reaches for water. To Benedict, a sophisticated son of Rome, their humility, sharing of resources, and openness to strangers might have seemed a native embodiment of Christ's injunctions. Scripture provided the authority, but I cannot help wonder if the illiterate heathens of Subiaco and Monte Cassino, in their sin and virtue, were not the unacknowledged example when Benedict finally sat down to write the communalist principles of his rule.

> Let all things be common to all,
> as it is written,
> and let no one say or assume that anything is his own.

And later,

> He who needs less should thank God and not be discontented;
> but he who needs more
> should be humbled by the thought of his infirmity
> rather than feeling important
> on account of the kindness shown him.
> Thus all the members will be at peace.

Regarding the communal rearing of children,

> But children up to 15 years of age

shall be carefully controlled and watched by all,
yet this too with all moderation and discretion.

On hospitality, a value that has remained central to all Benedictine communities,

Let all guests who arrive be received like Christ…
In the reception of the poor and of pilgrims
the greatest care and solicitude should be shown,
because it is especially in them that Christ is received.

Hospitality to strangers, meaningful work that benefits the entire community, collective effort in gardens, kitchens, nursery, and school, choral chanting of ancient prayers—these, the fundamentals of Benedictine monastic life, came at least in part from a pagan influence that Christians seldom acknowledge.

There is a pattern in all of this running off to the desert and back again; a rhythm I can't quite name or make coherent. Generations flow by in privilege and comfort, centuries perhaps of religious hegemony, the church high on its dogma, power, and esteem. Corruption and decay follow privilege, and soon the young and spiritually restless want to turn away, find purification in places outside the civil domain and its moribund orthodoxy. Inevitably, the adventurous ones head out to the wilderness, hole up in a cave, and embrace a life of hardship. By stages they learn that there is always wildness in one's hunger, but seldom any in its satisfaction. One or two may, like Benedict, become mystics, prophets, or saints. They talk of battling demons and converting pagans and wreak havoc with the original lifeways of the land of their exile. Time passes, languages and gods fade away, but in the end pagan values are once again tilled into the fresh soil that gives new spiritual energy for the next turn of the wheel.

And the turning will not slacken for any man's will. Each of us too small a part, but if it runs it runs on forces in the flesh as old and wild as fire and water.

*Wild.* I've been using that term carelessly, avoiding the urge to pin it down. We feel compelled to corral its meaning, but the word, like all that it attends, flees our grasp, and definition fails to satisfy. Of the many attempts by philosophers, naturalists, and ecologists I have found, the one I have settled on is not so much a definition as an observation. What's more, it comes from a poet and bird-watcher, and it fell into my hands while I was staying at a monastery.

Saint Michael's, a retreat center run by Franciscan brothers, rests on a slump plain in the Qu'Appelle Valley where Boggy Creek coulee contributes its share of water, white-tailed deer, native grass, and wood ticks to the great postglacial spillway. In late summer, writers gather at Saint Michael's for nine days to work on their manuscripts and learn from guest authors. It is called the Sage Hill Writing Experience, and the year I attended the mornings were too exquisite to waste on writing, but just right for retreat. My crucifixed and Bibled room, with its traces of all the other sinners who had leaned on the desk before me, turned me out of doors. I would head out after breakfast each day to walk along Boggy Creek's floodplain and sidehills, trying my best to move as one of Thoreau's Saunterers, looking for holy land, equally vagrant and at home everywhere.

Rosy purple spikes of blazing star dotted the hilltops along with some late milk vetchs and skeletonweed. I saw the hind parts of things that left off sauntering to get away from me: deer, a porcupine, ground squirrels, a garter snake. I had three glimpses on three different mornings of a Cooper's hawk. I'd come around the base of the same knoll, oblivious, not thinking of the hawk, and just as the crowns of some poplar trees would come into view, I'd remember, "Oh, the hawk" just in time to see it tail-ruddering back into the bush. And on the crest of another hill there was a single flower in bloom that I could not name. I squinted at its yellow florescence day after day, unable to even place it in a family, never mind genus or species. These things—one I could name but not see and one I could see but not name—are the remnants of wilderness that eluded me on those mornings outside the monastery.

The poet said, "By 'wilderness' I want to mean not just a set of endangered spaces but *the capacity of all things to elude the mind's appropriations*" [italics mine]. Don McKay was teaching the poetry course at Sage Hill while I learned alongside the nonfiction writers, all of us struggling to understand our own appropriations.

Toward the end of our time at Saint Michael's, Don handed me a copy of an essay he had published on poetry and the wild, entitled "Baler Twine: Thoughts on Ravens, Home, and Nature Poetry." I read the piece that night knowing it would be good. Don's poetry, like the best writing, lives outside the barricades where we keep safe all that we own and categorize. As for literary categories, I guess I'd have to call him a nature poet, though I picture him hanging out in bosky dells more to get a good look at a hermit thrush than to let the wind blow through his harp strings. Still, he is someone who writes of and with nature, evoking the truths of creation that we also meet in Lao-tzu or the psalms of David. McKay has an uncanny knack for seeing and attending to the remnant wilderness in things, in an old car, in a hand tool, or in a raven strung to the fence with baler twine. And he somehow manages to do it without letting his own literary grasp of our most distinctive tool, language, wring the wilderness from his poetry. In McKay's cosmos, things are observed with humility, playfulness, and a pagan eye.

Since meeting Don at Saint Michael's, I have spent two summer afternoons bird-watching with him and Tim Lilburn, another fine nature poet I seem to catch up with at monasteries. Each June the two of them run a poetry and nature workshop at Saint Peter's Abbey, a Benedictine community in Muenster. Twice they have asked me to join them for a day to help show their participants some of the local landscape and birdlife. I meet them on a gravel road just north of the Quill Lakes, where waterfowl and shorebirds breed amidst the saline remnants of a once vast glacial lake. We park the vehicles and in scattered groups walk the cordgrass meadows on an isthmus between two of the lakes—shallow inland seas running to all horizons and blanched in the sun, nearly as white as the alkali soil at our feet. Every now and then we gather to peer through the spotting scope at godwits, avocets, canvasbacks, or pelicans. More walking, then we crouch to name a plant or to find the marks on a wood tick that betray its sex. By the end of the afternoon, people are marveling at the names and habits of creatures and comparing insect bites and sunburns. After returning to the abbey, we talk more over a meal of food grown by the Benedictine brothers and prepared by local women who work in their kitchen. The first year I came, we headed out to the abbey woods after supper to see a family of long-eared owls Don had found days before. The parents flew off at our approach but the four fledglings stayed and swung precariously from poplar branches too thin to hold their weight. We stood there, the nature poets and I, staring at new owls in the dusk and silence. A moment of reverence passed between us unre-marked upon, then the poets returned to their rooms in the abbey and I drove home thinking of wildness and poetry.

Seems I can't walk anywhere these days without at least a passing thought for the wilderness pondered in McKay's "Baler Twine." Just last week I was returning home along downtown alleys and came across a pair of old running shoes dangling from a power line. They looked so odd there, twenty feet above the pavement, not quite in repose, expectant, as though waiting for the right moment to leap down and run away. Then I saw the birds. Two house sparrows were filling up one of the shoes with grass and little sticks. The cock sparrow perched just above his nest and sang his unlovely song, but it sounded to me like the voice of all that we do not own.

From "Baler Twine" again:

> That tools retain a vestige of wilderness is especially evident when we think of their existence in time and eventual graduation from utility: breakdown. To what *degree* do we own our houses, hammers, dogs? Beyond that line lies wilderness. We probably experience its presence most often in the negative, as dry rot in the basement, a splintered handle, or shit on the carpet. But there is also the sudden angle of perception, the phenomenal surprise which constitutes the sharpened moments of *haiku* and imagism. The coat hanger asks a question; the armchair is suddenly crouched: in such defamiliarizations, often arranged by art, we encounter the momentary circumvention of the mind's categories to glimpse something's autonomy—its rawness, its *duende*, its alien being.[1]

And it is all one song rising from the desert stones: *nor fear the wolvish howl, for man does not live by bread alone, but by every word that proceeds from the mouth of God, and by a further union, a deeper communion. Become like a consuming fire, let no one say or assume that anything is his own. Beyond that line lies wilderness.*

# SHELTER 4

W hen we get a heavy rain at the Land, water runs along the ruts worn into our access road, which slopes steeply from the hilltop down to the meadow where our cabin sits. Within minutes, the road—a smattering of gravel stuck into gumbo from glacial lake Indian Head—becomes slicker than the belly of a jack-fish, utterly impassable to all but four-wheel-drive trucks. A good storm comes down the valley and, if I don't drive our car up the hill, we are marooned on our meadow until the road gets a chance to dry. Other days we are at the mercy of the north wind as it gains speed along the full length of Lake Katepwa and rushes up the valley slopes to rattle the windows and make the rafters groan. Deck chairs, canoes, wheelbarrows, and anything else not tied down become airborne and land in the leeward coulee, hung up in the chokecherries like bad environmental-art installations. In the dry days of late summer we try to be careful with fire, but we've had two close calls nonetheless where Karen and I have had to beat the grass with rugs, while the older children run with buckets of water and the younger ones stand on the deck screaming in unre-lieved terror.

Mud, rain, windstorms, and prairie fire—these are not the pleasant hours at the Land. When a squall that might become a tornado peels back my eyelids and flashes lightning all around our little cabin, I will catch myself thinking of the comfort and safety of the city, but it is always tempered by the satisfaction that comes with the preparation for and encounter with weather. I feel it every time I look at the western sky before bedtime: thunderclouds and a rising wind—should I put the canoe in the lee of the cabin, get the car off the meadow while I can? And other times, when I've misjudged and the storms take us by surprise in the middle of the night and I rush outside in my underwear to drive the car up the road before it runs with mud. I walk back, shivering in the rain, the hilltop illuminated with each thunderbolt, and I pause to bow to the wild power of the storm. My feet set in mud, rain running down the small of my back, the woollen gray world suddenly ablaze in the blue fire of lightning—at such moments a longing overtakes me that I cannot entirely account for. It feels like desire, without anything in mind, and all I can say for certain is that it has some-thing to do with my body's heat against the cold, and the wet and the fury of the night.

If we stay in our shelters and rarely allow ourselves to feel the rough edges of our being, we diminish our participation in the exchanges, the metabolic dance that binds us to the rest of cre-ation. Metabolism is the physiology of desire, the great yearning for an interchange of energy, the fire within our appetites. One of the surest signs that we have become strangers in nature is that we have lost the ability to feed ourselves well even in the midst of apparent plenty. What happens to your spirit when you eat one in three meals at fast-food restaurants and the other two out of instant-meal packages? How can eating be a sacred practice, an entry into creation's wholeness and interdependency, when the lives that become part of us have been irradiated, genetically modi-fied, drugged, poisoned, and otherwise desecrated by the unholiest of human industries? Some cope by closing their eyes and stuffing down another burrito. Others, not surprisingly, become unduly focused on the way the body uses food. They starve themselves, or eat and then induce vomiting, or find themselves morbidly obsessed with the working of their bowel, or give themselves over to one nutritional program after another looking for something that will ensure health and longevity.

There once was a woman, a graceful and tender soul, afraid to place the world within herself, afraid as well to place herself within the world. Her footsteps led from greengrocer to kitchen to toilet and back again. In the fearful fastness of her palace stockade she gazed upon her viscera, bleached her clothes, ate uncontaminated greenery, and looked hopefully toward the day when she'd find only rabbit turds in her toilet bowl. She would have had a child, only that would require a messy mingling. She would have had a garden, only that would require even messier mingling and anyway she didn't like earthworms. She did like pictures of herself in nature, usually with fluffy clouds in a blue sky, but outside there were always ticks and spiders and mosquitoes, and no practical way to control the temperature.

Some folks said four days alone in the coulee with nothing but a jug of water might do her a world of good. Some said she might benefit from a week shearing sheep or hoeing potatoes. Eventually she disappeared—died or moved quietly away, no one really knows. She remained a topic of curiosity and discussion for some time afterward, because, with all her quirks, she had come perilously close to the truth—like the poet who uses too many words.

# EL MARAHKA IV

---

"Who is fit to climb God's mountain / and stand in his holy place?"[1] the shepherd-king asked. It is tempting to try to sneak back up along the old pathways. Some have tried it in their hearts, to return to that preliterate age of magic and myth, to the time before the written word usurped the shaman's power. Halfway to the top they decided that was far enough and set up camp. First thing they did was get a printing press and start publishing newsletters and books for the aspiring pagan. And that was where it ended: with one mystery appropriating another.

David's answer? "Whoever has integrity: / not chasing shadows, / not living lies." The neopagan shortcut is fraught with shadows because we let the genie out of the bottle three thousand years ago. Once a powerful tool, the alphabet, is harnessed to a powerful idea, monotheism, the resulting Word unleashed upon the world leaves us wounded and exiled. If we are unfit to make the climb, it is because we are hobbled by the same exile and desire that made the Israelites dance in obeisance to two gods. "How long," asked Elijah, "do you mean to hobble first on one leg then on the other?" The Israelites had no reply for that question and I wonder if we are any nearer an answer today.

A Christian by birth, culture, and upbringing, like many of my time, I have had my lapses and relapses away from and back toward the church, in my case Roman Catholicism. There is no shortage of justification for leaving the church—its culpability in the conquest of the New World and the oppression of its peoples, an entrenched fear of women, a record of attracting and hiding sexually deviant priests, pewfuls of self-serving and smug parishioners, corrupt and dogmatic hierarchy, lifeless liturgies, and so on. All fine and virtuous reasons to proudly join the ranks of former Catholics, but the last time I shook the dust of Catholicism from my feet, leading the way up onto the moral high road was my ego, freshly wounded in a personal encounter with ecclesial cowardice.

Karen and I were young enough to know everything then. That the premier's wife and another one of the most influential Catholics in the diocese—both major donors in the church's recent fundraising campaign—had been in for tea with the archbishop before he called us in. That we were right and they were wrong. That the missives we'd written in the social-justice newsletter, aimed at the province's Conservative government, had made their mark. That the archbishop had promised them the political attacks would stop. And that now, after our chastening and a final pudgy-fingered blessing—go and sin no more—we'd stride righteously away from his office, away from the church that had finally proven itself beneath our virtue.

We'd long ago lost our tolerance for all that was retrograde in Catholicism: all that was decaying, backward-looking, afraid of women and other sources of change and renewal. We'd lost our patience, our hope for transformation, and our place in the church, but we would find something else. We were happy to go and knew that somewhere outside the church we'd locate that exemplary community of spiritual seekers who are all secure enough in their faith to honor the wilderness in God, to celebrate the unruly and protect the innocent, and to ignite the fires that unite us in mercy, pity, peace, and love.

During those five years away from Catholicism, though, I learned that life rages on with all of its corruption, loss, and disappointment regardless of where one stands in relation to church walls. The nonpareil circle of worship never materialized. Friends and relatives got sick. Beloved ones died: one of sorrow, many of age and disease. Governments continued their obsession with free trade, national security, and limitless growth. Farms continued to look more and more like firms, and rural people moved away to find jobs in distant cities where they bumped up against aboriginal people fleeing overcrowded and impoverished reserves.

Birds disappeared. Each spring I counted migrant songbirds in the mornings and tried vainly to convince myself that the numbers were not declining. Maybe it was just another overflight, or a natural dip in a long, sine-wave trend. Next spring, it won't be quite so bad. Sure, tropical deforestation, fragmentation of our boreal woodlands, and pesticide use are reducing the forest bird populations, but maybe things aren't as hopeless as we think. The loss of local-breeding prairie species was even harder to wish away. It took just three years for the small pastures near the city to give up their last few burrowing owls, chestnut-collared longspurs, Sprague's pipits, and Baird's sparrows.

I think I got weary of things going away, of sudden absences, until I was blind to small renewals, life hatching forth surprisingly as it does—not perfectly or on the terms of yesterday, but in new and surprising ways. I go to church now for the same reasons I have taken to walking a woebegone strip of native grass that runs along the railway tracks where they leave the city.

Last time I went, I found a killdeer nest—four pointy-ended eggs, turned inward and nestled in a perfect little mandala. To get there, I walk west out of the city on a street that crosses the creek, turns to gravel, and leads past ball diamonds, a golf course, a nursery, and the Royal Canadian Mounted Police (RCMP) grounds before things quiet down. If I keep up a good pace it takes me fifteen minutes from my doorstep to reach the first meadowlark song. All along the walk I am a stone's throw from the main Canadian Pacific Railway (CPR) line, the one that laid steel upon the dreams of Eastern capital in the 1880s, the one that Chief Piapot failed to stop with his tipi roadblock, the one that, on a summer afternoon in 1882, bore a private train, with CPR founder Sir Cornelius Van Horne and a gaggle of local dignitaries aboard, to the creek crossing where they stopped long enough to drink a toast and name the town in honor of a dowager queen who would never see these plains. We live a block from the line, and at night when the freights go by slowly I wake to the rattle of doorknobs and the low rumble of fifteen thousand tons of God-knows-what-all rolling east or west. Our children count boxcars from their bedroom windows and there is a sign at the end of our street commemorating the two thousand relief-camp refugees who jumped off the train right there in June 1935 only to be bludgeoned, shot at, and chased out of town by the RCMP on Canada Day three weeks later.

The railway and its grassy easement are a blessing, a curse, and the reason I am drawn to this path out of the city. It makes for a mournful walk, a transect raw with the fresh wounds of our encampment here on the Qu'Appelle plains. I see fewer birds, fewer butterflies, fewer frogs every time I go, but I keep going. Between the gravel road and the railbed, there runs a strip of unmowed grass, weeds, and ditch puddles—a scrap of uncultivated land that ranges from seventy-five to two hundred feet wide. Much of it is littered with old tires, aluminum cans, and rotting lumber; almost all of it matted down with bromegrass, crested wheatgrass, thistles, absinthe, and other introduced species. It is an unkempt, shaggy place. Joggers and dog walkers stay away in droves.

Hidden in the weeds, and still within the western limits of the city, a vestige of native grass and forbs runs here and there in discontinuous patches along the railway easement. I can span the narrowest pieces with my outstretched arms. Other places it may be twenty or thirty feet wide. With cropland on one side and the railroad and city on the other, this remnant of the old buffalo prairie is several miles away from any other. Aggressive weeds from other continents are encroaching on each patch, mingling with native grasses, three-flowered avens, asters, cinquefoil, and sage. There is not much good to be said for these Eurasian weeds, though they green up quickly in spring, keep the soil in place, and provide richer habitat than a wheat field.

Whenever I am out walking the easement, questions arise about the mix and unfolding of life there. Each step intersects points in time and space where the prairie remnant is changing and becoming something different here and now beyond human will somewhere within the mysteries of divine will. I flush two game birds from the snowberry in front of me and it is a thrill until I realize they are gray partridge, another introduced species. But I *like* gray partridge. From the standpoint of ecology, nonnative is always bad and native is always good. Ideally there would be no mixing. In thrall to the lesser gods of science, I can't escape the coin-toss view of life as good or bad, true or untrue, native or alien. Walking the remnant, I catch myself cursing the untrue, the bad, and the alien, lamenting all that is gone, all that seems to be going: the prairie I knew as a boy, its birds, its self-reliant people and their stories, and its innocence, or at least my belief in its innocence. I stand in the midst of a landscape made by our transgressions and then something always surprises me. A circle of avens blooming on the ground as perfect in its green and red as an advent wreath. A mat of moss phlox silver and white covering a patch of ground the size of our front garden. Once, I watched a female Brewer's blackbird transform her drab brown cowl into her secret beauty—a veil of shimmering turquoise beadwork that hovers just above the surface of her back and wings to be seen only by her mate when the sun is just so.

Walking back into town on Sunday mornings I have heard the bells pealing from the towers of the cathedral. Holy Rosary is a mile and a half back along the avenue and when I look up at the city's skyline, the twin spires gleam above elms and rooftops. All of my children were baptized there with water that ran over their heads through the font basin and down to the cold clay beneath the nave of the church. Once, on a May afternoon, I spoke sacred vows to their mother as we stood together beneath its vaulted ceilings facing a church full of family and friends. And on Sunday mornings now I stand shoulder to shoulder there with people whose theology and politics I may not like. Even so, we face our sins together, begging communal forgiveness and embracing communal hope in the reconciliation of irreconcilables, in belief in the unbelievable, in the life gestating within all that seems to be dying.

I am not sure what it is that keeps me returning to a prairie remnant and to church, but it feels the same. I stand within and bear witness to weeds, garbage, railway, and a few scattered wild things, all in one place, pay homage to the lives that are passing there, as my own is, as all lives are, face our trespasses with courage, ask for forgiveness, and dwell in the light as dim as it is amid the darkness. Now and then, there is a paschal moment when the hidden beauty of a blackbird shines forth on a spring morning, reminding me of regenerative powers that wait beneath and within.

When I went back to the cathedral again a few years ago, I saw the unity in our ragtag diversity for the first time. The God who spun off 350,000 different beetles wouldn't be impressed by a homogenous battalion of worshippers anyway, no matter how virtuous or wise. So, here we are then, all in it together. Some looking for comfort amidst privilege and probity. Others hoping to shore up a flagging faith. Some seeking a private encounter with the Divine. Others seeking to merge with a body of believers. Some hoping to dissolve the pain of reality in the waters of heaven's promise. Others hoping to chasten themselves by facing the truth of our brokenness. Some nursing their piety with novenas while they cling to a mildewed dogma. Others holding fast to the prospects for religious renewal offered in new theology.

Despite all that divides us, we share in a struggle to believe the good news in a world where bad news is abundant and always easier to believe. Hammered by the believable lies that justify billion-dollar assaults in the Middle East, pesticides that support our "feed-the-world" mania, and technology that promises to help anyone have a baby and everyone live longer, we gather to the clanging of bells and try to see the truth in the body we form, in the Divinity who is a parent, a child, and a spirit all at once, in the standing up of the dead, and in the regaining of the lost.

Lost sheep, lost treasures, lost sons—this religion is so much about losing one's way or losing the richness of life, longing for it, and then regaining it amidst great feasting and celebration. If we've lost our way on the Mountain of the Lord, on our ascent from pagan hunter to post-Enlightenment Christian, how else to regain the path than to backtrack to the place where we veered away from God's own wildness? People can try to jump back along the journey to the rites of distant ancestors, but it makes more sense to start where the spoor is still fresh, where you can share sacraments in a living body of bodies who still believe in the possibility of transformation. What better place to reckon the sins of our civilization than here, in the church that once sang hosannas upon its reckless advance?

In solidarity with the spiritually unfit everywhere, I am making my way back to El Marahka to stand with the Israelites. There we will wait for Elijah to come along, disembowel the bull, toss it on the pyre, douse it with water, and call upon God's fire.

# SHELTER 5

T he following June we chose a site for the tipi. Mike had
arranged to buy the poles from a tipi-maker named Grace who
lives on the Pasqua Reserve a few miles upstream in the valley.

"You'll see the tipi poles standing in front—you can't miss it,"
said Grace. We piled our families into our vans and headed up
the valley road, through Standing Buffalo Reserve, across Sioux
Crossing, and up a long coulee onto the plains just south of Pasqua
Lake. The road to Grace's curved past a crescent-shaped slough in a
little draw on one side of her yard. We parked by the freshly stripped
tipi poles standing in a cone by the driveway and walked through
a circle of poplar and spruce trees enclosing the yard. Passing more
stacked tipi poles and a large woodpile by the garage, we were met
by Grace at her door.

A member of the Pasqua Saulteaux First Nation, Grace lives in
a small bungalow with her two-year-old son and her mother. She
has an open, easy way about her, a smile that lets you know when
she is teasing, and infinite patience with white folks who are over-
excited at the prospect of raising their own tipi. As we walked back
out to the fresh poles, one of the children found a young chipping
sparrow on the driveway. "Better put it back in a tree or the dogs'll
get it," said Grace.

Taking a measuring tape from her jeans pocket, Grace began
measuring poles, helping us select the right ones to use. The poles
were twenty-two- to -thirty-foot lengths of tamarack shipped

in from a First Nations healing lodge in Manitoba. Still the rich blond color of newly peeled wood, they would soon darken and season into durable supports for the tipi. Tamarack is tough, dense wood, much harder than the lodgepole pine often used for Plains tipis. Neither species, though, occurs in this part of the Northern Great Plains. Traditionally, the local poplar would have had to suffice, though some bands would have got straighter poles either in trade or by traveling to the tamarack bogs of the northern forests two hundred miles away. To the Nakota (Assiniboine), Cree, and Saulteaux people of Qu'Appelle, straight poles with the right kind of taper would have been great treasures.

Four to five inches thick at the butt end, the poles have to be stout enough through the first three-quarters of their length to support the canvas or skins. Then they taper quickly over the remaining five to eight feet to form the fine, elegant lines that knit the tipi into the realm of air and clouds. In this way the lodge forms a respectful bridge between earth and sky. "Some people shave the ends of their poles down to a fine point," said Grace as we began loading the poles on top of our two vehicles.

"The right poles are important. People get pretty darn protective of them when they get a good set. Each pole represents something, the old people say—you know, Obedience, Respect, Humility, different things." Grace offered what she knew cautiously, deferentially, and for the time being we managed to ignore the gulf between her world and mine, and the history that precedes such moments.

She told us how the poles are to be erected in a circle following the path of the sun. That was when we invited her to come for the tipi-raising gathering we had planned for later in the summer.

"Sure. I'll come, but I should warn you now about one thing." She gestured to our clutch of children running in and out of her gate chasing the dogs. "You've got to be careful sleeping in a tipi unless you want more little ones."

Mike and I looked at our wives and laughed, relieved that Grace wasn't telling us we needed an elder's blessing or a particular dispensation to ordain our adoption of the tipi. She went on to tell us more about the tipi, how the elders say it was given to the people as a sacred way of drawing life energy up from the earth, bringing that which longs to be born into the light of day. "A tipi is a better kid magnet than a swimming pool. It'll bring 'em in from a *long* way off...a month after I had my first sleep in a new tipi I made, I found out I was pregnant—so be careful!" We laughed again, said our good-byes, and returned to lives where such mystery is granted no quarter.

# EL MARAHKA V

It may have been restlessness that put us up on Mount Carmel in the first place. The Israelites' hobbling dance sprang from a spiritual unease that was relatively new back in the ninth century BCE. Four hundred years earlier, their ancestors were suffering under slavery in Egypt, waiting for Yahweh to live up to His end of the bargain and deliver them out of bondage. Early on in Exodus, there is a broken verse right at the point where Yahweh is hearing the cries of the Israelites and preparing to appoint Moses as their leader. Interesting that there would be a gap in the narrative here and that scholars have somehow resisted the temptation to fill it in through three thousand years of translation, transcription, and editorial gloss. The second chapter ends with this unfinished statement: "God looked down upon the sons of Israel and he knew…" Knew what? The editors of *The Jerusalem Bible* say, "The verse does not yield satisfactory sense; probably the end is missing." Other gaps in the Bible are filled in, but not this one and so we are left with an irresistible opportunity to speculate and reimagine this critical pause in our spiritual ascent.

It seems possible that the God of Abraham looked down upon his people and knew that they were ready for a change, ready to take a new step. The Israelites, Moses among them, had descended from tribal herdsmen living in the land between the River Jordan and the desert west and south of Palestine that is drained by the Wadi of Egypt. (Before that were the hunter-gatherers, the vanquished ones who in the caves of Hakkarmel left scant traces of their passage dating back 150,000 years.) A preliterate, oral culture, the early Israelites would have kept their social bonds intact with stories of ancestral heroes—heroes who came alive in their imaginations as their words and deeds were spoken ritually in the telling and retelling. Like all ancient peoples and indigenous cultures, they would have experienced the Divine within the revealed world available to their senses.

David Abram, an ecologist and philosopher, says that the early Hebrew people shared with the Navajo and the Lakota "a reverence for the air" as "the breath of God [that] permeates all of nature."[1] Then why choose the people of the Middle East? Why did they make the shift from pagan worship to strict monotheism so early?[2] Why not the Hindu, the Greeks, the Navajo, or the Aztecs?

The answer, I am beginning to believe, is in the advent of agriculture and the alphabet. If you want spiritual restlessness on a scale that will bring a major shift in religious evolution, take an oral culture of hunters and gatherers, bring them through a phase of pastoral nomadism, then place them in a colonizing and oppressive agricultural economy and introduce them to the new power of the written word.

Agriculture came first. Israeli archaeologists have found skeletons and decorative objects in burial sites on Hakkarmel that they call "Natufian," a Stone Age hunter-gatherer culture that lived in the region 12,000 years ago. By the time of Moses (1250 BCE is our best guess), virtually all hunter-gatherer cultures of the Middle East had been wiped out by pastoral and agrarian cultures. In the terms of the Hebrew scriptures, once the people had seen their nakedness and been cast out of the Garden, they faced a choice: either follow the ways of Abel and herd-grazing animals or follow the ways of Cain and till the soil for a living. The tillers, as we know, rose in numbers and prominence by stockpiling their grain against famine, while the tribal herdsmen of the region remained satisfied with their wandering subsistence life one step nearer the innocence of Eden.

The steps are significant here in marking levels of our appropriation of nature and the restlessness it brings. By domesticating wild goats or sheep, the early pastoral tribes were in effect conscripting a piece of nature to their own utility. The life of an individual ewe from birth until its slaughter becomes the tool of the herdsman. Nevertheless, the ewe retains a great deal of wildness. This is, again in Don McKay's terms, that portion of its existence that is not used or usable as tool: its gamboling on the hillside, its voice, its tail-wagging pleasures, its interdependencies with the grasses and forbs it grazes, its nourishment for the occasional predator. Likewise, the unfenced land used by the grazing animal and the shepherd is not "used up"; it retains the majority of its ecological integrity. Equally important, the shepherd need not own the land. He is free to move and follow the weather and the herd and in this way sustains something of his own wildness. Neither land, nor herd, nor shepherd is completely conscripted to the use of civilization.

The appropriation ratio changes dramatically, though, as soon as a civilization makes the shift to the cultivation of crops. Suddenly, ownership of land, particularly fertile floodplains, becomes important, worth fighting over. More of the life cycle and ecology of the land in use comes under human control. Perhaps most significant of all, cultivation and the accumulation of resources allows for surplus food to be stored and used or sold at a later date. Storage would seem harmless enough in itself, but it was the fuel that drove the world's first expansionist empires. In a pastoral culture, the primary source of food—animal flesh, cheese, and milk—limits the number of people that can be fed by any given flock. Everyone in the family or tribe is active in either rearing children or procuring food. Standing armies and an expanding population, on the other hand, require huge surpluses of food, which can only be provided by the cultivation of grain crops by a class of farmers and their slaves. Once a valley's fertility is exhausted, more land must be taken. Food and agriculture suddenly become tools of colonization, a phenomenon that implies a higher order of appropriation. Things aren't just used, they are used up—whole ecologies, landscapes, and human cultures. Hunter-gatherer and pastoral peoples disappear, massacred, enslaved, and assimilated by the land-hungry nations of grain producers. The margin for wilderness narrows sharply, and the gods begin to reflect the embattled and controlling natures of the civilizations that pay their tribute. And, for the first time in history, people experience mass exile, a separation from the land of their ancestors and their birth.

# SHELTER 6

Naturalist Carl Zimmer writes about a bush that defends itself from caterpillar infestations. When the caterpillars begin munching on the bush's leaves, the bush releases smelly molecules that draw parasitic wasps from a long distance away. The wasps arrive in battalions and deposit their eggs in the caterpillars. As the eggs begin to hatch, the wasp larva eat the caterpillars from the inside out, unintentionally saving the bush.

We live in an eat *and* be eaten world. Zimmer says that every living thing has at least one parasite in it or on it, and more than half of the biosphere's organisms are parasites themselves. Our own species has taken the parasitism strategy to an extreme, boosted by our technologies beyond the reach of natural selection. Yet, despite our illusions about hygiene, we remain hosts ourselves. All of us still roll out the red carpet for fellow travelers. Your digestive tract has a flora and fauna all its own, among which are many beneficial microbes. Viruses and bacteria thrive within ecological niches in your mouth, respiratory tract, and vascular system. Through the course of your life you have likely been a home, incubator, and food source for arthropods, fungi, entire yeast colonies, and all manner of microscopic beings, including the demodicids that right now are foraging in the follicles of your eyelashes. Your body is not *your* body; it is *every*bodies'. Like every large mammal, a human being is a mobile ecosystem, and though you may scrub your flesh inside and out and eat only the purest of the pure, there is no way to keep yourself to yourself.

This lively little truth scares us because it disabuses the modern mind of one of its most cherished fables—that we are autonomous individuals living in an orderly, predictable universe. We have refined our habitats and ourselves so much that we no longer seem able to recognize the raw, chaotic realities on the ragged edge of ecological interchange, in which every creature gives up bits of itself in the little lives and deaths of the great metabolic dance. Behind our firewalls, we never touch nor are touched by Blake's "desart wild," that random, prickly realm of exposure to heat, cold, hunger, and thirst, the desire within chaos where intermittent moments of violence, cataclysm, or union are separated by days of empty longing. Safe from the desert's abandonment, people live and die without ever realizing that their bodies are truly bound to other bodies.

Desert is the sacred space of wildness, the paradoxical place of separation and reunion. Dry, open land, the gospel's "place apart," is where we are *unjoined* from the profane world of distraction and appetite so that we can once again sit in ashes and abstinence beneath the tree of life. Sheltered by the umbilical axis mundi that roots heaven to earth, we may look up, see between its branches the stars of our desire, and learn unity from separation.

There, religions are born, mystics made. There, fasting the eye and spirit away from our appetitive regard for life, mindfulness and union become possibilities. Empty as the beggar's bowl, all irrelevancy stripped away, you are left with the nonnegotiable essentials. Yesterday's needs are replaced by today's utter physical dependency on the Creation. Longing for survival feeds questions of life, death, meaning, communion, sacrifice, and mystery.

In the Christian prototype for the encounter with wild, sacred space, Matthew's gospel says that the Spirit led Jesus, after his baptism in the River Jordan, "into the wilderness," which in the Bible means desert. There he prayed and fasted for forty days, faced his hungers and his demons, and turned aside the three primary temptations of civilized life: to seek ease and comfort above all else, to acquire wealth, power, and prestige at any cost, and to presume knowledge of divine will (or confuse it with one's own). With the trials over and Jesus ready to begin his public ministry as one who has encountered his weakness, poverty, and dependence on the Divine, the gospeler tells us that "suddenly angels came and waited on him."

Would angels be there for the rest of us too? How long, covered in the sackcloth of grass, thorn, and sky, before our desires and illusions fall to intimations of communion; before edges dissolve and we comprehend the mystic's dream of union beyond all boundaries and distinctions? Before we sense the very ground of being, feel beneath our feet the uncountable exchanges recorded in the earth's long thoughts? Before desire for a higher union reveals the illusion of self against the interbeing of life, the air of one body that moves in and out, eddying into creaturely existence here and there, changing seamlessly but still varied in the detail manifest in matter? Before we uncover a communion that was there all along, coherent in our breathing, that spirit of the sacred and the wild we carry within ourselves, the breath of prayer, of the contemplative beneath the Bodhi tree?

Fasting and praying in a barren place, we might find that we live in God's wildness after all. All we need is a body and time to breathe beneath desert stars. The antiphons of leaf and lung will take care of the rest. Unseen within our breasts, oxygen and hemoglobin work their flesh-and-blood spells. Heaven is lodged within the marrow of nature's unknowable depths, in the interstices of every particle in every organism, where blood and mitochondria, chlorophyll and chloroplasts provide the base rhythm for all philosophies, all gospels: breathe in, breathe out, sacrifice and receive, let all things go, let all return.

There are metabolic fires in the cells of our living flesh that bond our eating to our breathing as a prairie fire bonds earth to sky. The proteins, fats, and sugars we take in by ingesting the bodies and by-products of living things are metabolized in the presence of oxygen. That aerobic process is accomplished within each cell by energy-transforming organelles called mitochondria. Cells in our cardiac muscle are packed with mitochondria to fuel the high metabolic rate required to do the heart's work.

Hummingbird flight muscle has even more mitochondria, as well as more cristae, the folds in a mitochondrion's inner membrane, which facilitate the electron transport that ultimately makes energy available to cells. That electron transport chain, combining hydrogen with oxygen to generate the energy packets of ATP (adenosine triphosphate) in the cells of every aerobic organism, is the reason we breathe. When we inhale oxygen-rich air and feel a hit of energy, it is our mitochondria stoking our fires in a combustion that is seven times more efficient than the one that propels our cars.

"Return to me, with all your heart, with fasting." The lector read these words from the Book of Joel on Ash Wednesday, and as I walked forward to have my forehead smudged with the ashes of the previous year's Palm Sunday leaves, I couldn't help thinking of mitochondria. I had forty days of fasting ahead of me, time enough for the pull of mitochondria and the breath of prayer to show me why we locate desire in the heart.

The symmetry that joins our breath to our food binds us also to the plants that make oxygen and energy available to our mitochondria. The mitochondrion's counterpart in the cells of plants is another double-walled organelle, the chloroplast. Using water, sunlight, and the carbon dioxide produced in part by animal metabolism, photosynthesis within each chloroplast traps energy in the form of sugars, which in turn can be used by plants and animals to make ATP.

If animal life had somehow evolved without mitochondria we

might be less dependent on oxygen, but the truth is, were it not for the energy transfer trick of this organelle, all of us would be stuck somewhere back in the primordial muck. Evolutionary biologists believe that the advent of mitochondria was the adaptation that made multicellular animals possible in the first place. They point out that both chloroplasts and mitochondria look and behave like single-celled organisms living within larger, more complex organisms. Much like primitive microbes, both of these organelles reproduce via binary fission, manufacture their own proteins, and carry their own DNA completely distinct from that borne by chromosomes in the cell's nucleus. They may have started out as single-celled organisms that were subsumed by larger ones, or they may have gained entry voluntarily as parasites. Either way, as eater or eaten, these small beings eventually became so dependent on their hosts and vice versa that they evolved into indispensable players within the complex energy exchange of eukaryotic life. The history of our biosphere, from protozoa to dinosaurs to the freckled kid who stole your pencil case in third grade, has been dominated by organisms that depend on that barter. Among the passing myriad is a beetle whose illuminated mitochondrial pulsations illustrate how the primal longings for food and air overlap with a third: the desire for ecstatic union with the other.

On warm July evenings I sit on the deck of our cabin and watch the courtship dance of fireflies, a small beetle that generates soft pulses of light in specialized cells called photocytes. It is the most plaintive and romantic luminescence in this corner of creation. Each point of light hovering above the meadow throbs on and off like a tiny heart lit with its own captured morsel of the day's solar offerings. These are the males flashing "Where are you?" signals to wingless females perched here and there on grass stems. The female come-hither response is easy to pick out because they flash from a single, unmoving spot, allowing the male to home in.

Making all this light every evening takes a lot of energy, and so it came as no surprise when biologists found cells nearest the photocytes carrying a high load of mitochondria. The photocytes need oxygen to generate their glow, but the abundant mitochondria tie up virtually all of the locally available supply in the process of making ATP. The local shortage of oxygen creates a barrier or switch that plays a role in regulating the firefly's pulsations. Somehow the researchers discovered that ATP production in and near the photocytes is temporarily shut down by a puff of NO (nitric oxide), a neurotransmitter that inhibits mitochondrial uptake of oxygen. As soon as the available oxygen level rises in the center of the photocytes, they light up. Then, for reasons that remain unclear, the NO dissipates, the mitochondria get back to work hoarding oxygen, and the light fades out. Food, air, sex—all have their turn atop the order of longings that light and fade on a midsummer's eve.

A fourth kind of longing, the nostalgic yearning for home, for mother and motherland, is also borne in our mitochondria. Mitochondrial DNA (mtDNA) are passed on from one generation to the next by matrilineal succession. My mitochondria carry my mother's mtDNA and my children's mitochondria carry their mother's mtDNA. Fathers have had no say in the matter of normal mitochondrial genome mutation and evolution—which is worth some thought because mtDNA mutate at a much faster rate than other DNA. This continuity between mothers and mitochondria has the ring of truth if only because it is our mothers who feed and shelter us first and best.

As your prenatal home in the maternal wilderness, your mother's womb binds you genetically to every other member of the race. In the 1980s, two scientists, Allan Wilson and Rebecca Cann, used mtDNA to devise a family tree for *Homo sapiens*. After sampling mtDNA from mothers' placentas from around the world, they developed a computer model that used mutation markers to trace the branches of humanity back to a point of origin. That origin,

Wilson and Cann say, was a woman living in Africa approximately 200,000 years ago—one mother in our original motherland. There were, of course, other *Homo sapiens* women living at that time, but the branches carrying their mtDNA must have subsequently died out. The media gave the research some headlines, referring to "mitochondrial Eve," while competing scientists discredited Wilson and Cann's statistics. Since then, however, other researchers have improved upon the sampling method and statistical model, only to confirm that, indeed, our origins converge on a single woman likely from Africa, though she lived thirty thousand years later than Wilson and Cann's.

Yes, brothers and sisters, our very flesh and blood returns us to the milk of one bosom. Surprised to find that our hymns of one body are more than metaphorical, I have stood with my back to the altar at the cathedral—mindful of the holy interchange of eating and energy, the ashes of respiration, the ashes of decay, the mystery of our mothers' blood—and held the sacramental cup. The congregation flows out of the pews like blood cells along arteries, then down along the nave toward the eucharistic moment where we, kin in our mitochondria, in our sin, and in our sanctity, come together in the blood and body of the crucified man-god whose incarnation makes us one in a real and sacred communion. And we sing, "Lamb of God, who takes away the sins of the world. Have mercy on us." What mercy we may have we share.

The same goes for our sin, and these days, traces of our most persistent sins are showing up in mothers' milk and in mtDNA. Sandra Steingraber, a mother and ecologist who writes about our transgressions against the healthy exchange of energy, oxygen, and water between Earth's bodies, calls the womb "our first habitat." In two books, *Living Downstream* and *Having Faith: An Ecologist's Journey to Motherhood*, Steingraber calls us to look at frightening truths to which we have for fifty years been closing our eyes. She is that all-too-rare an individual, a scientist whose moral courage and respect for the Creation have thrust her, honestly, eloquently, and courageously, into the public forum. Surviving cancer, Steingraber took inspiration from one who did not—Rachel Carson, the original American voice crying in the befouled wilderness. Carson made her plea in 1962 during the advent of the age of poison and with her book *Silent Spring* brought the perils of industrial and agricultural toxins into North American consciousness. Eighteen months after the book's publication, she, like tens of thousands of women in recent decades, died of breast cancer. Steingraber makes her plea for sanity in a time when many people are so dazed by science and technology that they can no longer see the bizarre logic that has us poisoning our food and water today and then regulating and medicating the results tomorrow.

If we ever doubted the body's ecological interbeing with the air, the water, the earth and its organisms, toxic breast milk and mutant mtDNA should be enough to set things straight. Once breast milk—the most intimate and wholesome form of nourishment available to us, our first bond with another body, the birthright of every placental mammal—becomes the most contaminated substance in nature, the time for repentance and transformation is at hand. Once mtDNA—the matrilineal blessing of our evolution, the physiological thread of our communion—becomes a vehicle by which a mother's genome passes on mutations triggered by organochlorine pesticides and other contaminants, the days of fasting and sitting in ashes are upon us.

A woman like Sandra Steingraber is small compared to the pesticide and pharmaceutical corporations, the vested interests of industry, academia, and government. Small like yeast, like the "yes" of one woman allowing her womb to bear the promise of redemption into the world. In *Having Faith*, Steingraber talks about the placenta and calls it "a biological mystery. It is an evolutionary shape-shifter...the flat cake that feeds us all...a blood-drenched forest. It is the sapwood of pregnancy."

The first time I took a good look at a placenta was at the unplanned home birth of Sage, our third child, whom Karen pushed out into my trembling hands one cold October night as I kneeled on our kitchen floor. Later, when things calmed down and Cathy, a midwife friend, arrived to take charge, I needed something to distract me from the panic that was starting to settle in my knees. That was when Cathy asked me if I wanted to look at the placenta, which didn't seem like a good idea at the time but turned out to be just what I needed.

There it was in a large stainless-steel salad bowl, a flat and round piece of tissue shaped like a cake or a loaf of peasant bread. The umbilical cord, pale blue and ropy, extended from one side. Cathy reached in to pull the caul, or amniotic sac, back into position, forming again the translucent tent that had sheltered Sage for nine months. Complete, save for the small opening through which she had just minutes earlier made her entrance into the world of our kitchen. Most remarkable of all, though, was the inner face of the placenta itself, the firmament that our daughter saw suspended above her as she floated in amniotic fluid. I remember especially its arteries and veins radiating from the cord in twelve shades of purple, blue, red, and burgundy, like branches from a trunk. And there were tiny white spots like points of light here and there between the rippling bloodways. A tree beautiful in its limbs and the stars beyond. We come to our being beneath a tree of life that feeds us, and when we look overhead we see the night sky between the branches.

*Placenta* is from the Latin word for "flat cake," and in German the word is *mutterkuchen*, "mother-cake." Most mammals know that this birthday cake is meant to be eaten, and there are accounts of placentophagy among the women of traditional cultures around the world. The practice is enjoying a small and marginal resurgence today among young mothers who have enough pagan courage to embrace the wild-mother urge as a way to health in body and spirit. They know that the placenta's abundant hormones and antibiotic properties can help prevent hemorrhage, heal the uterus, and cure postpartum depression. Midwives at home births have stopped hemorrhages by having mothers quickly eat some of their placenta. Women who experienced severe depression for weeks and months after their first birth have eaten their placenta at a subsequent birth and reported greater health and well-being throughout the postpartum phase.

Not surprisingly, our squeamishness about such abandonment to natural instinct has sent modern placentophagy underground. Women quietly exchange ideas and recipes (the blender seems to often play a role), and submit anonymous but proud reports to newsletters and websites. Although Karen attends home and hospital births regularly as a doula or birth assistant, and takes great pleasure in helping women locate the primitive mother within, her own births have never given her the kind of trouble that would compel her to try the mother-cake. During her last pregnancy, however, she read somewhere that mothers who couldn't bring themselves to the task were taking their placentas into Chinese herbologists to have them dried, ground up, and made into capsules. After she was asked to leave our local herbologist's premises, Karen gave up on that idea, brought her placenta home, and placed it back in our freezer where it stayed until we could bury it on our next trip out to the Land.

We usually have one or two placentas in our freezer at any given moment waiting for burial. Karen cannot bear to see them discarded, so if the mother whose birth she is attending has no plans for the placenta, she brings it home with her in a plastic bag. In the predawn hours I hear the front door unlock, her footsteps across the floor and down into the basement, and then the muffled *whump* of the freezer lid falling back into place.

Since the first time I made the mistake of thawing something that I thought was a roast, I cannot go to the freezer without thinking of birth and afterbirth. Karen says that a placenta has to be eaten or honored and so our placenta grove grows summer by summer at the Land. Some time in May I will dig new holes on the edge of the raspberry patch. Karen will plant the winter's offering, light a smudge of sage and sweetgrass, and then I will fill the holes with black prairie earth and new canes. In time, the chloroplasts in the raspberry leaves will receive the nutrients once held in human mitochondria. By July, if there has been rain, the raspberries will ripen and we will eat them by the red, sacramental bowlful.

# EL MARAHKA VI

*We shall not cease from exploration*
*And the end of all our exploring*
*Will be to arrive where we started*
*And know the place for the first time.*

—T. S. Eliot, "Little Gidding"

L aurens van der Post once stood in the shadows of Kalahari Desert scrub and watched a Bushman mother hold her newborn son up to the stars. She was asking for their blessing so that he might grow up to become a great hunter. She knew her boy, like all people, belonged to the stars. And of course she was right, to the extent that the atoms that make up our flesh and blood were once carried in tiny bits of dust formed around stars in the Milky Way.

Exile—the delusion that while we belong to nothing, everything belongs to us—is so much a part of the human condition today that we have difficulty imagining an existence unmarred by its attendant longing and restlessness. We might as easily imagine what it would be like to live in the body of a fish. I don't know if I have ever returned the gaze of a person whose spirit is completely at home. I have come across half-shadows of the ideal, perhaps, from time to time: an old rancher I met once on the east bench of the Cypress Hills, a Grey Nun happy amidst the dying in a small-town hospital, a Cree elder holding his audience within the spell of an ancient story. But for a model of man truly free of exile, I have to

resort to people I have met in books. I am thinking here especially
of van der Post's descriptions of the Bushmen of South-West Africa
(now Namibia). During the 1950s, van der Post lived and traveled
with Bushman family groups in the Kalahari Desert, a parched anvil
land hard enough to take the sun's unrelenting hammer. He was a
longtime friend of Carl Jung, which may explain in part how he
came to see the Bushman as an incarnation of the two-million-year-
old man living inside all of us. When one Bushman met another,
his greeting—translated rather poorly I suspect as "I see you, I see
you"—was an acknowledgment that the spirit within one body recognizes and mingles with the spirit within another. Here is a passage
from van der Post's *Testament to the Bushman*:

> The essence of this being [of the Bushmen], I believe, was his sense
> of belonging: belonging to nature, the universe, life and his own
> humanity. He had committed himself utterly to nature as a fish
> to the sea. He had no sense whatsoever of property, owned no
> animals and cultivated no land. Life and nature owned all and he
> accepted without question that, provided he was obedient to the
> urge of the world within him, the world without, which was not
> separate in his spirit, would provide. How right he was is proved
> by the fact that nature was kinder to him by far than civilization
> ever was. This feeling of belonging set him apart from us on the
> far side of the deepest divide in the human spirit.

Van der Post learned from the Bushmen that the stars are hunters.
Hunters in a desert and, if you are at home in the desert, free of
exile and its child, nostalgia, you will be able to hear their cries as
they chase their prey across the firmament. I can't hear the hunters
because I am a person of the Word, a son of Jacob, for whom the
desert is barrenness and exile. One day I may yet meet the other, the
one who is at home in the world. And if we do meet, we will wrestle
and then embrace, and he will ask to be let go, but I will ask for a

blessing first. He, born of the line of Isaac's wilder son, will ask if I know who I am and on hearing my name give me another, predict my ascendancy, then bless me after all as I let go and hobble away with my wounds, knowing that I have seen the face of God.

It is a story "figured in the drift of stars," but studied in the tents of our sheltered faiths:

*And behold, Yahweh placed twin sons in Rebekah's womb. They wrestled with one another even as she carried them within. One son, it was said, stirred whenever she walked near a place where men studied the Torah; the other jumped if she passed by an idol to the old gods. She felt their jostling again the day she squatted in the tent stained the color of dried blood. And the ruddy one prevailed and emerged first, covered in a mantle of hair, and they called him Esau, ready-made. His mother took fright at his coloring, for it reflected the glow of the tent walls like a blood curse that would not wane with the moon, that stayed as a reminder of the old way of service to many gods.*

*Esau, admoni, ruddy like Mars, the planet of his birth, made Rebekah think of Adam, the red-skinned first man made of blood and earth. He was a warning made flesh, an Edom, a man out of Eden, like Cain, destined to spill blood. The second-born brother was named Jacob, "one who gripped the heel of his brother," and he would become a dweller of tents, a scholar, a farmer, and a founder of nations. The boys grew and their father, Isaac, son of Abraham, favored Esau for he knew the hunt and was a man of the field. Jacob, absorbed in his studies, earned the favor of Rebekah, the fettered one, for she saw in him the promise of a civilized people bound to the written word and their faith in the one God. Rebekah saw Esau and knew he was crude, wild as the beasts he hunted, a man of the moment who kills with his own hands and eats unclean food without washing or a thought for tomorrow.*

*Once, Esau came home from a long and fruitless hunt. He was exhausted, near starvation, and stumbled into Jacob's tent where the smells of lentil stew hung in the air. Esau said to Jacob, "I am near death's door. Let me eat of the red stew there and I will live." But Jacob answered, "I will give you the red stew, but first sell me your birthright."*

*And Esau, "Here am I dying—what use to me is my birthright?" Jacob, the scholar in the tents, made his starving, half-wild brother swear to the terms and then gave him the stew and a rusk of bread. He watched Esau eat hungrily and made plans for his inheritance.*

*Later, Jacob married to the approval of his parents. Esau brought shame upon Rebekah and Isaac by taking two Hittite wives. Still, Isaac loved Esau for he was the son who brought him the savory wild meats he enjoyed. And it came to pass that when Isaac was old and his eyes growing dim so that he could not see, he called Esau to his side and said, "Behold now, I am old. I know not the day of my death. Take your weapons, your quiver and bow, and go out into the wild to take me some venison. Make me the savory meat that I love and bring it to me that I may eat and that my soul may bless you before I die."*

*Now, Rebekah, the fettered one, heard this and spoke to Jacob when Esau went off into the country to hunt. "You must be the one to receive your father's blessing," she said. "Do as I tell you and your father will anoint you, not your heedless brother. Go and fetch two kids from the goats and I will make a savory dish of them that you may serve your father in Esau's place. Then he will eat it and give you his blessing before he dies."*

*And Jacob said, "Behold, my brother is a hairy man and I am smooth. My father will feel me and know that I have tried to deceive him, and I shall receive a curse and not a blessing." Rebekah answered by covering Jacob in Esau's clothes and by wrapping his hands and neck in animal skins.*

*Dressed in animal skins and Esau's clothing, which smelled of the hunt, Jacob went to his father bearing goat stew spiced to taste of wild meat. And finding Isaac, he said, "I am Esau, your firstborn. I have done as you asked. Arise and eat of my venison so that your soul may bless me."*

*Isaac was suspicious and recognized Jacob's voice. "Come nearer," he said, "that I may feel you and tell whether you are my son Esau or not." Jacob came forward and his father felt him, held him close, and said, "The voice is Jacob's, but the hands are the hands of Esau." Again, he asked, "Are you my very son, Esau?"*

*And Jacob answered, "I am."*

*Then Isaac ate the stew and drank the wine Jacob had brought. Afterward, he said, "Come near now and kiss me, my son." As Jacob came near, Isaac smelled Esau's clothing with its scent of campfires and wild grass. Then he blessed the wrong son, saying, "See, the smell of my son is as the smell of a field which the Lord has blessed. Therefore, may God give thee of the dew of heaven, and the fatness of the earth, and plenty of corn and wine. Let people serve thee and nations bow down to thee: be lord over thy brethren, and let thy mother's sons bow down to thee."*

*Jacob left with his stolen blessing and Esau arrived back from the hunt and prepared his venison stew. He went before his father, Isaac, and said, "Let my father arise and eat of his son's venison that his soul may bless me."*

*And Isaac answered him, "Who art thou?"*

*"Your firstborn son, Esau."*

*Isaac trembled exceedingly and said, "Who? Where is he that has taken venison and brought it me and I have eaten it all and blessed him before you came? He is the one blessed."*

*And when Esau heard these words of his father he cried with a great and exceeding bitter cry and said to his father, "Bless me, even me also, O my father."*

*And Isaac said, "Thy brother came with subtlety and has taken away your blessing."*

*And Esau, "He has supplanted me these two times: he took away my birthright; and, behold, now he has taken away my blessing. Have you not reserved a blessing for me?"*

*And Isaac answered and said to Esau, "Behold, I have made him your lord, and all his brethren have I given him for servants; and with corn and wine have I sustained him: and what shall I do for you, my son?"*

*"Have you but one blessing, father? Bless me, even me also, O my father." And Esau lifted up his voice and wept.*

*And Isaac answered, "Behold, thy dwelling shall be the fatness of the earth, and of the dew of heaven above; and by thy sword shalt thou live, and shalt serve thy brother; and it shall come to pass when thou shalt have dominion, that thou shalt break his yoke of thy neck."*

This paraphrased story, from Genesis 25–28, so powerful in its allegory and prophecy, concludes with Esau threatening to kill Jacob and the two brothers leaving home in opposite directions. Decades pass, Esau living in Edom and Jacob in the Paddam-aram where he names some places and sets out begetting the descendants that Yahweh promises will be as numerous as specks of dust on the ground. Then, in the thirty-second chapter of Genesis, Jacob suddenly sends messengers to Esau, hoping to reconcile with his brother. Terrified that Esau may still want to kill him, Jacob panics when he receives word that his brother and four hundred men are already on their way to meet him. He decides to conciliate by sending forward lavish peace offerings and a message in which he refers to himself as Esau's servant and to Esau as his lord. What follows is one of the most enigmatic and symbolic set of verses in the whole of the Pentateuch.

Jacob has stayed behind on the shores of the Jabbok River with two wives, two slaves, and eleven of his children. At nightfall, he sends the lot of them across the river with all of his possessions. He stays by the riverbank and spends the night wrestling with someone—a man, a spirit, or Yahweh himself, the text leaves it for us to decide. By daybreak, Jacob has a dislocated hip,[1] but demands a blessing from his nameless opponent, who says:

*"Let me go, for day is breaking."*

*But Jacob answered, "I will not let you go unless you bless me."*

*"What is your name?"*

*"Jacob," he replied.*

*"Your name shall no longer be Jacob, but Israel, because you have been*

*strong against God, you shall prevail against men."*

*Jacob then made this request, "I beg you, tell me your name."*

*"Why do you ask my name?" came the answer, and he blessed Jacob then and there.*

After the two wrestlers disengage, Jacob names the place Peniel, which means "face of God," and fords the river to face his half-wild brother.

Hebrew and Christian exegetes usually interpret this story as Jacob wrestling with God or with an angel, but it seems to me that to arrive at such a conclusion you have to put on a pair of glasses that blinker you to the language and narrative context while twisting the passage into something that supports the usual ecclesial and moral agendas. Jacob's wrestling occurs within a complex narrative and has to be seen in relation to the events that it follows and precedes. Here is a man whose ascendancy as the patriarch of a great tribe is founded upon blessings and birthrights he swindled with God's apparent approval or forbearance. He is convinced that the rightful recipients of this legacy are going to kill him in the morning. Stripped of his family, slaves, and possessions, he spends a restless night on the bank of a river, the very threshold that separates him and his wilder brethren. Whoever he wrestles with on that sweaty, fear-filled night, either awake or in his dreams, the experience shows him something of the face of God. He comes to the new day a new man, strengthened though wounded by the ordeal. How can anyone in Western civilization read this and not catch the earmarks of an archetypal rite-of-passage narrative from the heroic tradition?

Biblical commentators and systematic theologians look always for meaning that corroborates Judeo-Christian themes and schemes of God's intervention in history: choosing a people, making covenants, and handing down laws that demand fidelity and purity from adherents. A square peg like the story of Jacob's wrestling at the riverside has its corners whittled off until it fits one of the round holes of orthodoxy. It becomes a spiritual test for the father of the great nation, a holy confirmation of his fitness as patriarch, because, like Moses, he saw God and lived.

On the other hand, should we be surprised that five thousand years of shaping religions with the written word and every other possible appropriation of wildness has made us forget where the ancient scriptures came from, forget that we descended from mythmakers and storytellers who lived and hunted by the grace of the land? Genesis is a collection of written-down stories based on the oral tradition of Bronze Age tribal peoples who lived four millennia ago in the Middle East. The stories are the fireside narratives of people who were still coming into their identity as agriculturalists. Many among them continued to supplement their diet with wild game, while tribes feared and hated in neighboring lands were undoubtedly living even closer to the old ways of spear and bow. Jacob's, and therefore Israel's, story of ascendancy is the saga of a people emerging from their hunter-gatherer past, leaving Eden below the horizon of their history. Esau and Jacob wrestled in the womb to set the stage for the story's epic tensions and betrayal. How can we hear of Jacob wrestling on the night before his reunion with his twin brother, the one who eats wild things, without thinking again of that primordial struggle between the hunter and the farmer? Jacob, the patriarch of Judaism and of the Western tradition of monotheism, was wrestling with the archaic hunter in his own soul and, by extension, within the soul of our civilization.

Take another look at that dialogue at the end of Genesis 32. The sun rises over the River Jabbok, illuminating two figures locked in the embrace that bore them through a night of battle but now looks less combative in the light of day.

"Let me go," says the hunter, "for day is breaking."

The farmer, civilized and always looking out for a better deal with creation, replies, "I will not let you go unless you bless me."

Then the hunter asks the farmer if he knows who he is. "What is your name?" he says.

"Jacob," comes the reply, meaning the one who gripped the heel of his twin brother (*Ya'aqob*, from "heel," *'aqeb*, or "to supplant," *'aqab*).

The hunter, still in the arms of the farmer, renames his partner Israel ("may God show his strength") and prophesies that he will prevail against men. The farmer then begs the hunter to give his name, but he replies with a question, "Why do you ask my name?" before giving the requested blessing.

The two disengage, but the archetypal farmer, Jacob, is wounded. He will no longer walk the free gait of original man. He limps away and names the place of his wounding Peniel, which means "face of God." Then he hobbles across the river to meet his brother, a hunter he betrayed many years before. He goes forth expecting the bitterness and vengeance he deserves, but instead finds reconciliation and peace.

> He himself went ahead of them and bowed to the ground seven times, until he reached his brother. But Esau ran to meet him, took him in his arms, threw himself on his neck and wept as he kissed him. (Genesis 33:3–5)

Embraced by the one he usurped, Jacob lives the truth of the previous night's dream and feels once again that he is in "the presence of God." He says,

> "Please accept the gift I offer, for in fact I have come into your presence as into the presence of God, since you have received me kindly. So accept the gift I have brought for you, since God has been generous to me and I have all I need." And he urged him, and Esau accepted. (Genesis 33:10–11)

The language of this archetypal reconciliation here in Genesis makes it impossible *not* to reflect on Jacob's entire path as second man, appropriating his brother's birthright and blessing, struggling through the long night of civilization, recognizing finally the face of God in his brother now at some distance from his roots, and then begging to be blessed by all that is primary and ancestral and holy.

Considered this way, the story of Jacob and Esau becomes a powerful myth that traces the path we took in forsaking our original lifeways and driving out our wilder, preagricultural brethren only to discover that the betrayal, subjugation, and disenfranchising leaves us wounded, longing to be blessed, and in need of a new identity that will place us once again in the presence of God as we knew it in Eden.

Laurens van der Post saw the image of God on the faces of the Kalahari Bushmen he traveled with. He believed that hope for modernity consists in religious reconciliation of this great divide in the human spirit. Here he is again in his essay "Witness to the Last Will of Man":

> It is only now that we have lost what I re-found in the Kalahari in the nineteen fifties when, for months on end, I moved through country no "sophisticated" man had ever set eyes on, that I realize in full what it meant and did for my own senses, brutalized by years of war. It was as if I had been in a great temple or cathedral and had a profound religious experience. I returned to the world, knowing that unless we recover our capacity for religious awareness, we will not be able to become fully human and find the self that the first man instinctively sought to serve and possess. Fewer and fewer of us can find it any more in churches, temples, and the religious establishments of our time, much as we long for the churches to renew themselves and once more become, in a contemporary idiom, an instrument of Pentecostal spirit. Many of us would have to testify with agonizing regret that despite the examples of dedicated men devoted to their theological vocation, they have failed to give modern man a living experience of religion such as

I and others have found in the desert and the bush. It is the last temple on earth which is capable of restoring man to an objective self wherein his ego is transfigured and given life and meaning without end.

Looking back with a nostalgia that I am powerless to describe and which often wakes me aching in the night and walks like my own shadow at my side, I must testify with all the power and lucidity of expression at my command that this lost world was one of the greatest of such temples, in which the first man and the animals, birds, insects, reptiles and all, had a glow upon and within them as if they had just come fresh and warm from the magnetic fringes of whoever made them. He and they were priests and acolytes of this first temple of life and the animals dominated his stories, his art, his dancing and imagination because they followed neither their own nor his will but solely that of their creator.

Follow, I would add today, the first man in ourselves, as well as in the rainbow pattern of beasts, birds and fish that he weaves into the texture of the dreams of a dreaming self, and we shall recover a kind of being that will lead us to a self where we shall see, as in a glass, an image reflected of the God who has all along known and expected us.[2]

Van der Post is saying, I believe, that our modern religious and cultural obligation is to reenter the myth of Jacob at the riverside so that we can reengage our legacy and culpability as the second sons of creation, and hold on for life until the wrestling becomes an embrace in which we can face and see clearly all that we have subsumed and overtaken—not for guilt or blame, not for that pointless wringing of hands, but for the greater spiritual reckoning that dawns when the sun lifts over the horizon, spills across the river, and shows us that we are in the hands of our ancestral brothers, the first ones who, nearer the Genesis point, bear the face of God and the original blessings we need and must beg for now more than ever.

# SHELTER 7

———————————————————•———————————————————

The surface of a good tipi pole should feel as smooth as the skin on the underside of a woman's arm. Any rough spots will eventually wear holes in the canvas as it rubs against the pole. Using axes and drawknives, we began trimming branch stubs and sharp snags off each of the poles, feeling with our hands for smoothness and then sanding from one end to the other with fine sandpaper. While we worked we talked about alternative sites for the tipi, about the way a tipi liner helps to direct airflow upward and out the smoke hole, and about plans for a late summer weekend when, after the poles had cured a bit, we would gather to raise the tipi for the first time.

The week we raised the tipi, the woodpeckers returned. I awoke on August 1, the feast day of Lammastide, to the queer chatter of a hairy woodpecker just outside the cabin window. He was past our scrawny apple trees, riding up and down on his invisible roller coaster between the cabin and the first coulee to the east, shouting hallelujahs to the morning. Already the woodpeckers were celebrating the decline of summer and the approach of autumn when the woods are free of warbler song and theirs again to declaim. The sun had a new slant, its powers waning enough for birds, birdwatchers, and pagans to notice.

Nine hundred years ago, a monk in Gloucester woke on the first of August to a dream about the death of England's king, William the Red, son of William the Conquerer. It was the year 1100 and the English peasants were starving. Many had been cleared off their land by the king's men. Hearing of this portentous dream, the abbot of Gloucester sent word to the king to warn him. William, who was hunting in his new forest game preserve, recently cleared of peasant farmers, laughed at the monk's warning and went on his merry way. Moments later, the story goes, he was killed, shot through by his brother's arrow.

Stories of a king who is sacrificed to restore health and harvest to the land run throughout the mythologies of both pagan and Christian farmers. The notion that the grain must die so that we may have life ties our Eucharistic celebrations to agricultural pagan feast rituals. Lammas, or "loaf mass," was a medieval Christian feast day that adopted practices and myths from the Celtic Lughnasadh celebration. Lugh, the Celtic god of the sun, was thought to be dying or losing power by the time of first harvests in late summer. The feast of Lughnasadh honors the sacrifice made by his mother, Tailtiu, who died of exhaustion preparing the land to plant the year's grain. Lughnasadh and Lammastide paid tribute to the earth and its gifts, but also to the people who sacrificed themselves to grow food for their families and communities. As the Celtic people took on Christian ways, they kept their annual appointment with Lugh and Tailtiu on August first by placing on the altar loaves of bread baked from flour ground with the season's first-harvested grains.

We kept Lammastide at the Land by roasting cobs of corn over the fire pit. Karen and the girls made corn dolls using dried apples and leftover corn husks. We stared into the fire as darkness fell, but nobody danced in circles or rode on the backs of birds far above people singing as they gathered hay in the fields. We lacked the "mirth of those long since under earth":

> In that open field
> If you do not come too close, if you do not come too close,

On a summer midnight, you can hear the music
Of the weak pipe and the little drum
And see them dancing around the bonfire…
…Round and round the fire
Leaping through the flames, or joined in circles,
Rustically solemn or in rustic laughter
Lifting heavy feet in clumsy shoes,
Earth feet, loam feet, lifted in country mirth
Mirth of those long since under earth
Nourishing the corn.[1]

The day after Lammastide, friends and family began arriving to help raise the tipi. About forty-five people, every man, woman, and child a descendant of the keepers of such traditions, except for Grace, that is, who drove down the valley from Pasqua Reserve for the day. Mike shifted into engineer mode and studied his plans and drawings for the tipi installation, before relaying instructions to a small army of unskilled helpers. Door pole to the east, this pole goes on the north perimeter, this one on the south. Once we had the main tripod bound together and hoisted aloft, the meadow was a different place. Form had arrived where a moment earlier the wind rode alone on the unseen.

Grace, ever patient, chuckled at our calibrations and measurements; this was not the way she raised tipis, but she had worked with white people before and nothing surprised her. She winced when we used a staple gun to attach the colored ribbons to the fine tips of each pole. We were, to be sure, an unceremonious bunch, about as purposeful as a group of Sunday picnickers in the park. People were scattered all over the hilltop meadow: women talking in groups, toddlers in the grass nearby, teens on chairs by the cabin, men at the tipi site doing their best to recall sheepshank and half-hitch manoeuvres, other people laying out a potluck supper, one taking photographs from across the coulee, another off to one side playing a drum softly and singing a wordless chant. It was the hottest day of the year. By late afternoon, the sun had heated the air to 104 degrees, and all but the keenest tipi helpers were heading for water and shade.

After supper, the covering went on the frame of poles like a well-trimmed sail up a mast. The meadow changed a second time. Dusk brought darkness to the valley, relief from the scorching sun, and long shadows cast from a dwelling as native to these hills as little bluestem and long-tailed weasels.

Two weeks after the tipi raising my father showed me some photographs he had taken that day. Neither he nor his ancient camera make any claims to photographic excellence, but one of the images of the tipi at dusk is accidentally and remarkably poetic. It is a time exposure that didn't quite work—the kind of blurred image you often throw away as you flip through the stack of prints back from the photo lab. The sky is softly aglow with a spectrum of color running from amber to smoky blue, and, within this muted wash, the tipi vibrates, a triangle of pale earth tones anchored to the burnt-umber foreground, where dark figures seated and standing join the shadows lain upon the land. Because of the time exposure and possibly some camera jiggle, there seems to be no real edge between the human bodies and the sky. Amber light invades their outlines, softens the boundaries, and gives each a bit of fire from the heavens. The mood this creates in the shot is somber, contemplative, graceful—everything that we were not on that sweaty August afternoon.

The nearest shadow in the picture is that of a woman who appears to be toting a small baby on her back, though no one at the gathering had a child that young. Another figure is a gray blur bending over to touch the ground in front of the tipi door. Everyone else is standing or sitting in the grass in relaxed postures, facing the tipi. But, if you look closely at the surface of the tipi, you can just make out the faintest tracings of a body in motion: two arms holding something and two legs with bent knees, striking a posture that brings to mind dancing figures painted on cave walls by neolithic artists. I am fairly certain that this was Kate, our oldest daughter, drawing one of the flap ropes aside to open the smoke hole for the very first time. Above the moving figure, the ends of the tipi poles fly up in a radiating fan of fine lines, shadowy wisps that disappear into the tinted gauze of a cirrus-covered sky. Across the tips of the poles, three distinct white streaks—perhaps scratches or some other artifact of the photographic process—run across the sunset like the arcways of parallel meteorites.

My father tells me that he held the shutter open by hand for a count of four. One, two, three, four—just enough to find a chink in time that let us see the ones long since under earth, the old ones somewhere deep within ourselves.

# EL MARAHKA VII

———————————————————•———————————————————

In van der Post's novel *A Story Like the Wind*, there is a Kalahari Bushman named Xhabbho. He is innocent, unselfconscious, yet wise and adept. His utter abandonment to laughter, his religious attention to the little god praying mantis, and responsiveness to the "tapping" in his chest show him to be at home in his body and in the desert, his senses and faculties fully conversant with the greater mystery in which he is immersed. The Bushman would have had difficulty understanding notions of nostalgia and the divisions implied in concepts of exile, home, and wilderness. To him, there was the desert and the unknown world beyond.

Before agriculture gave us the means to appropriate nature's gifts, including our own languages, on an ever-increasing scale, to live was to dwell within a fully animate mystery of processes and interchanges. Participant in some but not all of these reciprocities, we still could not in any significant way control or manage them. This terminology—immersion, animate, reciprocity, interchange—comes from David Abram's phenomenological model of the life-world in which our species evolved, body and spirit as one, over hundreds and thousands of years. In *The Spell of the Sensuous*, he details the immersion of premodern people in the medium of creation, animated by other intelligent creatures and by gods, which they identified and participated with, spoke and listened to, experiencing their being through their senses in a unified stream of life and spirit flowing between and among creatures on the wind that quickened everything. With the presence of spirit as all-pervasive and available as the air, religious practice was an exchange of giving and receiving. There was a time, suggests Abram, when we all, by receiving the tastes, smells, textures, sights, and sounds of creation and giving back in kind, participated in a reciprocity that served the health of the individual and of the community as a whole.

This, I know, sounds like yet another romantic reduction of the good old days before we all got greedy and walked out of Eden with hoes in our hands, but Abram's theories, taken as he offers them in page after page of detailed, clear-headed argument backed up with rigorous research, cannot be dismissed as New Age twaddle. So, what does he say changed things? What calamity or opportunity drew us away from this animistic participation in "the more-than-human world"? Abram argues convincingly that the introduction of a new form of magic overthrew the sensory magic of our unselfconscious immersion in the Creation. Today, we take this usurping sorcery for granted as an essential part of the mind's encounter with phenomena. It is, perhaps, the most powerful appropriation of all and it is the one I am using here and now to transmit ideas and thoughts with black marks printed upon paper. Here is part of Abram's account of how the written word knocked the wind out of the solar plexus of human culture:

> Only as the written text began to speak would the voices of the forest, and of the river, begin to fade. And only then would language loosen its ancient association with the invisible breath, the spirit sever itself from the wind, the psyche dissociate itself from the environing air. The air, once the very medium of expressive interchange, would become an increasingly empty and unnoticed phenomenon, displaced by the strange new medium of the written word.[1]

The Hebrew scriptures, and the Exodus saga within it, contain some of the world's first stories written in a nonrepresentational text. Archaeologists speculate that writing may have started, however, as a way of keeping track of agricultural surpluses for storage and trade. Alas, our first writers were accountants and not poets. Once the growing of food had spawned a complex economic system of resource stockpiling and commerce, farmers and traders had to invent bookkeeping. They needed ways to record this more complex use of nature and so began making marks on clay tablets, walls, sheepskin, and tree bark. The rest, indeed, is history. The bards and storytellers among the ancients, it seems, dismissed writing as a prosaic tool at best, the passing fancy of bean counters. But there has always been a record-keeping streak in people who converse with God—a need to say, "Yahweh spoke to me here"— so the people Yahweh chose for his monotheism project took up the stylus or the chisel to mark the major events in their history.

It comes as no surprise that a text as old as the Exodus story has a verse or two missing. God only knows what it was that "He knew" when, according to that broken verse in early Exodus, He finally decided to answer the cry of His people. But who can resist guessing? Maybe He knew that writing, like agriculture, would play a role in drawing humanity further from the gates of Eden, to an exile and a restlessness that in a few short millennia would foster both the dramatic tragedies of a Sophocles and the historic tragedies of empire-building, the redeeming sacrifice of a Christ and the death-dealing enterprise of Christendom, the glory of Gothic cathedrals and the horror of the Crusades, the poetic vision of Milton and the moral blindness of kings, the theophany of Rembrandt and Michelangelo and the evil of the Inquisition, the promise of the Enlightenment and the disappointment of democracy, the creative fire of Darwin, Teilhard de Chardin, and Mozart and the consuming fire of Nazism, unfettered international capitalism, and industrialized agriculture.

Why choose the Hebrew people? Because they were ready.

Having left the hunter-gatherer's Eden, the Hebrew people adapted quickly to agriculture and became aware of a new distance between themselves and the rest of the Creation. The Genesis myths express this beautifully: they had seen their own nakedness. Having wrestled with the archaic hunter within and come away wounded, they hobbled across the river and into their destiny. One shift away from nature led to another, and suddenly they were keeping their stories not in the landscape but in sacred scrolls, which allowed them in their exile and restlessness to, as Abram says, carry their homeland with them. And so it was the convergence of three crucial factors that chose the Hebrew people: agriculture, the alphabet, and enough oppression and exile to bring their spiritual longing into focus.

Abram claims that the alphabet removed us from ourselves, creating an interior, deeper exile, placing us at a reflexive distance from the other. He credits the formation and spread of the Greek alphabet in the fifth and fourth centuries BCE with completing our alienation, creating the necessary abstraction and reflexive thinking that brought us the categorizing knife of science via Socrates, Plato, and Aristotle. But two hundred years before the age of Greek philosophers, great Hebrew prophets were writing texts of consolation for their people exiled in Babylon.

There seemed to be an explosion of prophets in the Middle East from the time of Elijah through the seventh century BCE. The countryside was at times crawling with "wild ecstactics" from outside the Yahwistic tradition (and therefore pagans to the Hebrew way of thinking). Elijah himself is said to have slaughtered more than four hundred of the prophets of Baal on that fateful day atop Hakkarmel. The moaning and dancing depicted in that story from First Kings refers to the common practice of prophets of all traditions who used music, mime, and dance to induce altered states of consciousness in themselves and their adherents. The Hebrew word for *prophet*, whether it was a freelancing ecstatic or Isaiah himself, is *nabi*, which derives from the verb for "to be beside oneself."

The prophets and poets of this time were all beside themselves, and they were writing to unify and console people who were likewise exiled in spirit, if not also exiled in body. The great poet of exile is second Isaiah, the mysterious author of the final twenty-some chapters of Isaiah, known collectively as The Book of Consolation. Theologians have speculated that the unnamed author who supplemented the pre-exile chapters written by the historic Isaiah with these poems penned during the Babylonian exile may have been a woman. They point to the feminine imagery of nurturing, birth, breasts, motherly affection, and consolation as proof and say that her gender explains the assiduously maintained anonymity under which the verses were written.

Whoever she was, the poet we call second Isaiah put down some lines so lovely, so inspired, that on their own they compensate for some of the magic we lost in taking up the pen. In some passages, it is as though she is consoling the whole human race in its departure from innocence and the embrace of the Mother, reminding us of all we once knew in our flesh and bones without ever having to be told.

This is from The Jerusalem Bible:

> A voice commands: "Cry!"
> and I answered, "What shall I cry?"
> —"All flesh is grass
> and it's beauty like the wild flower's...
>
> Who was it measured the water of the sea in the hollow
>     of his hand
> and calculated the dimensions of the heavens,
> gauged the whole earth to the bushel
> weighed the mountains in scales,
> the hills in a balance...

The poor and needy ask for water, and there is none
their tongue is parched with thirst,
I, Yahweh, will answer them
I, the God of Israel, will not abandon them.

I will make rivers well up on barren heights,
and fountains in the midst of valleys;
turn the wilderness into a lake,
and dry ground into a waterspring…

No need to recall the past,
no need to think about what was done before.
See, I am doing a new deed,
even now it comes to light; can you not see it?
Yes, I am making a road in the wilderness,
paths in the wilds.

The wild beasts will honor me,
jackals and ostriches,
because I am putting water in the wilderness
(rivers in the wild)
to give my chosen people drink…

"Listen to me House of Jacob,
all you who remain of the House of Israel,
you who have been carried since birth,
whom I have carried since the time you were born.

"In your old age I shall still be the same,
when your hair is grey I shall still support you.
I have already done so, I have carried you,
I shall still support and deliver you…

Does a woman forget her baby at the breast,
or fail to cherish the child of her womb?
Yet even if these forget,
I will never forget you.

The monotheistic path cleared by the prophets from Moses to second Isaiah and beyond came to fruition among people whose new estrangement from nature had them wondering if they *had* been forgotten. Meanwhile, the experience of the mind and spirit in exile was bearing other fruit, particularly in Greece, as the fathers of Western science and classical philosophy put pen to parchment. In fact, in all agricultural civilizations where writing had taken hold, east and west, there was a period from roughly 800 to 200 BCE when philosophers, prophets, and spiritual thinkers of every faith and discipline were stepping into the first light of the world's wisdom literature. This era, pivoting on the axis of the year 500 BCE, is what Karl Jasper has named the Axial Age, or *Achsenzeit*, as he calls it in the opening chapter of *The Origin and Goal of History*. Much of the written wisdom of humankind was recorded during that time— the Hindu Upanishads, Lao-tzu's Tao Te Ching, Plato's dialogues, Isaiah, Jeremiah, and other books in the Hebrew scriptures, and the teachings of the historical Buddha, Confucius, and Zoroaster.

If you scan through the teachings attributed to prophets from the Axial Age, certain themes recur. There is much said about the self, or consciousness, or the soul in relation to the body, which implies a certain division or exile, and at the same time there is an exhortation toward completion and wholeness, which implies a preference for union.

ॐ

This from the Upanishads:

> In bodies bodiless,
> In things unstable still, abiding
> The Self, the great Lord all pervading, —
> Thinking on Him the wise man knows no grief.

> This Self cannot be won by preaching,
> Not by sacrifice or much lore heard;
> By him alone can He be won whom He elects:
> To him this Self reveals his own true form (*tanu*).

Here, in the Upanishads, the universe is made by the word Eternal:

> This universe is a trinity and this is made of name, form, and
> action. The source of all names is the word, for it is by the
> word that all names are spoken. The word is behind all
> names, even as the Eternal is behind the word.

The Tao Te Ching, in particular, speaks to the need for oneness:

> Being one with the Tao is to be at peace,
> and to be in conflict with it,
> leads to chaos and dysfunction.

And from the Tao again:

> The virtue of Tao governs its natural way.
> Thus, he who is at one with it,
> is one with everything which lives,
> having freedom from the fear of death.

Finally, here is an excerpt from one of the original Buddhist *suttas* that the five hundred *arahants* ("fully enlightened beings") chanted together in unison to indicate their approval for its inclusion into the written teachings of the Pali Canon. Theravada tradition has it that the enlightened ones had gathered at the Sattapanni Cave in India to hold the First Buddhist Council in 544 BCE, just three months after the death of the Buddha:

> The body, monks, is not self. If the body were the self, this body would not lend itself to dis-ease. It would be possible (to say) with regard to the body, "Let my body be thus. Let my body not be thus." But precisely because the body is not self, the body lends itself to dis-ease. And it is not possible (to say) with regard to the body, "Let my body be thus. Let my body not be thus."

These are the written teachings that agricultural people, newly distanced from nature and from their own bodies, needed to hear, 2,500 years ago. They still make sense today for those of us hobbled by the wound of Jacob. To a mid-nineteenth-century hunter on the Kalahari Desert or on the North American Great Plains, though, the great wisdom of our prophets would have been as unintelligible as the wind has become for us.

# SHELTER 8

---

*We only live, only suspire*
*Consumed by either fire or fire.*

—T. S. Eliot, "Little Gidding"

## FIRE

Civilized people don't do their own killing, have no patience for death and its surly companions. Sustained by viands cooled in the frozen-food section or misted in the dewy produce displays, we dine as far as possible from the death toll, pretend we can live without killing. It goes on in secret, the other side of truckloads, spattering unseen fields with deaths unpropitiated and unceremonied, more by far than if we had the courage to feed ourselves.

The eater is refined too, elevated beyond any thought of the incremental injuries and uncounted violence exacted by mere living. All here arrive and depart in messy, wrenching moments and in between the furnace is stoked in a long and gory string of immolations not especially ameliorated by switching from flesh to grass, for it is all grass anyway. Someone small and many legged begins eating the lettuces and that's the end of him. And who, anyway, died to suffer the garden, the field, the hive? Even summer's sweetness comes upon the deaths of workers. When the goldenrod bloom we take honey from the bees, carry the dripping frames up to the cabin. A few of them follow us, find their winter's store, begin the job of bringing it back. Dozens die in the effort, drowned in pools of gold, pinched between frames or fingers. Children, only half-tutored in the lie, notice the carnage early on, imagine bloodthirsty farmers amok in the countryside. A daughter eats the honey on her morning toast and asks, "Is every day a killing day?" In the garden, she rescues purslane and sow thistle and scowls at my hard-hearted ways.

"All things, O monks, are on fire," said the Dhammapada. George Herbert, holding fast to Christian love, asked,

> My God, where is that ancient heat towards thee,
> Wherewith whole shoals of martyrs once did burn,
> Besides their other flames? Doth poetry
> Wear Venus' livery?

Venus was no prude. She kept Cupid at her side and never shied from the eros of divinity. Her question? Can we recall what it was to be not man apart but man within? Sex, said a wise priest, "is the most powerful force on the planet, the best of all fires, the most dangerous of all fires...We wake up in the world and in every cell of our being we ache...sensing that we are incomplete, unwhole, lonely, cut off, a little piece of something that was once part of a whole."[1]

The trail this side of Eden is strewn with the cinders of mis-begotten ignitions; the morning sky smolders and yet we go on tossing sparks on the commons, from the air around us to the nucleus within, all tinder, all tendered whenever gain strikes the flint of desire.

The worst of lovers we are, all hands and mouth, demanding without giving, indulging unleashed lusts, unfasted appetite, consuming a bounty, a work, a glory, and a wisdom too great for the eye. Proverbs are lost and unlearned where no one wants to go anymore, in the chaos of a dry, empty land of thorn and thirst, where desire sleeps alone. Buffered behind parapets and strip malls, safe concubines to one another, we tell stories, say prayers toward the same creation of, serving of, loathing of self.

The holy longing has ligaments in its flesh that bind together kin in kindness, a latent adaptation, waiting to be tried, though prophesied by the wise who were tested in deserts. "Kindness is my religion," they have said. Who would have predicted, considering oxygen and hydrogen on their own, that binding the two would make the planet's defining magic: ice and vapor, freshet, river and sea. Tributaries bind earth to sky, every river has its head in the clouds, and there is no greener green than the *viriditas* that lights a hillside after rain falls upon the cruel kindness of wildfire. What miracles would we see if we ever burned that braver fuel, that wild and holy kindling native to the heart's candled organelles, the inner membranes of outer desires that allow us to step, reach, lift, reap, and sow with these kind limbs?

Beyond the mystic longing, the fuel for metamorphosis, there is its chastening reply, the pain that heals. Flesh taken meets flesh given, making sacred, whole and holy once again. Let yourself be consumed, transpose the misbegotten yearnings—roads through wildwood, dams over river's roar, windrows scorched across the greed-wrought fields—and attend to the other in that deeper eros of sacrifice.

First on the bonfire: our pretended innocence. The city takes shelter within the colonized corpses of the truly innocent and then takes their voices. Those bearing the yoke of life and death for us—the wilder ones beyond the walls who suffer our taste for the good life—carry our sins, do our sweating and bleeding for us. We, the chosen ones, unhurt, unhurting, have been singing stolen songs of innocence for twenty centuries. Our god does the sacrificing now, and all he asks for is a weekly ritual of remembrance. So why, we wonder, is all this debt piling up?

Poured upon pretended ignorance, our arrogance makes the most volatile of fuels. Chart the trajectory of a miracle, say you know the mind of God, believe that science will come through with a cosmic write-down of our debt, and then wait for the comeuppance. This mystery we walk amidst bears just enough predictability to tempt blasphemers.

Toss it all on the pyre; comfort, hardest to give up, burns the brightest fire. Let us dance to our upholstery gone to ashes. Light candles after dark, take hoe in hand, turn waste into soil. Volunteer for less of everything except sweat; be satisfied with the development of our souls.

This, then, a prayer for a holocaust of the sham nursery outgrown: cushioned and cabineted, in which men have calibrated the flight of angels with Meccano sets. The blackened earth will birth richer stories, truer dreams. No longer to debauch but to serve the child, covering the lost and loveless with clothes from adult shoulders, then turning themselves bravely out to the cold of night and the heat of day in places where the long truth and real drama survive dormancy, dry as husks, chafed as the skin of lizards, waiting through the age of self-obsession for a few naked ones who can raise an honest song or a story to the power of a cleansing, fanning wind.


# WIND


The wind has not left us, still breathes upon our sin. The odd mystic, some mothers, most children, feel its grace. A mother who knows the little death of birth, who labors outside the shelter of spinal taps and Demerol, lets the natal spirit gust over her. In the final minutes, the infant head pausing at the burning threshold, she may sink into her body's fatigue, nothing left to give. The doctor calls for more Pitocin, prepares his tools. A midwife, knowing, says, "Touch your baby." Fingers reach the wrinkled brow, a low and throaty cry takes the room, and the child rides out on a wave before the wind.

Have you seen a small child out walking in wind? Seen her feel a surge of air at her back, hear the roar in her ears, then stop to totter in its grasp? Her arms rise up, she rocks back on heels, closes her eyes, and begins to smile. Given away freely and possessed by air, she knows the oldest kind of joy.

The bought and paid for speak of freedom and give nothing away. Confound an economist, escape prediction, and you will have entered the kingdom's present mystery. Give without hope of return. Listen to the wind. It will always urge in directions away from appetites and into the hands of others. So conscripted, we may remember real innocence, embrace wildness.

The storm blew down my father's tent, snapped poles, turned deck chairs upside down. To me, it was an assault from a dark, chaotic realm. My smallest daughter laughed and then wriggled into the secret world beneath a wind-turned chair.

# EL MARAH KA VIII

---

If there is any magic remaining in the everyday rituals of modern life it is in the power of the written word. Scrawl a few marks on a strip of paper and, depending on its details and who you are, money and property will change hands, marriages will be made, laws will be enacted.

When the four young pagans who live under my roof need some guidance, Karen and I, the omnipotent lawmakers, will sometimes remind them of a set of ordinances that has come to be known as The Family Book of Rules. *Take muddy shoes off at the door. Make a mess, clean a mess. Hold the door open for the person behind you. If you feel the urge to hit someone, go get a parent.* Our youngest child, the only preliterate in the household, is starting to sit with books and "read" to herself now. She scribbles "poems" on scraps of paper and then recites them for our benefit. She still has the illiterate's native capacity for learning verses, though, and prefers the stories we invent at bedtime to any in a book. She has developed her own way of carrying the family rules in her mind by making them into songs. Still, while she skips blithely away from a morning's disarray singing "make a mess, clean a mess," the magic of writing has its hold even on her, as though she senses that the authority of the household code arises from its permanence in being written down, suspended in a book.

When language is converted to text it is removed, says David Abram, from the natural, sensuous flow of time, conscripted more completely as a tool of reflexive, abstract thought. The wild utterances formed in a union of flesh (throat, mouth, tongue) and spirit (the breath of the speaker and its source, the air, which then receives and reverberates with the sounds), once they are written down are corralled and transfixed within the magic of phonetic glyphs on the page.

As Abram suggests in *The Spell of the Sensuous*, this new form of magic gave us a potent new lever for our reflexive thinking, but it came at the expense of the original immersed-in-nature innocence of oral culture. Stories and laws written down have a power to persuade and influence great numbers of people across geographical and cultural boundaries. Ideas and entire religions suddenly became transferable in time and space. Judaism, and its precocious offspring, Christianity and Islam, have their roots in writing. Moses is the father of religious writing, having brought the word of God to the Israelites inscribed on two stone tablets. In the twenty-fourth chapter of Exodus, Moses heads up Mount Sinai and spends forty days and nights with Yahweh. Yahweh Himself inscribes in stone the law that becomes the new source of wisdom and truth for the exiled Israelites. Their tribal forbears, rooted in the land and fully conversant with nature, had always looked to creation itself for their guideposts of wisdom and truth. But pagan ways die hard, so while Moses is up the mountain, the Israelites become increasingly restless and turn to their pre-Yahwist gods and idols. Moses returns, hears the chanting, sees the Israelites dancing before a golden calf, and goes into a rage, smashing the stone tablets and chastising his people. Now, at this point, Moses could have just recited the law for the Israelites and hoped for the best. But he knew that spoken words would not be enough to control this headstrong tribe. So he starts up the mountain again to talk things over with Yahweh, who tells Moses to cut another set of tablets.

Read this piece of Exodus carefully and you will notice a strange inconsistency that seems to shift the responsibility for writing down the law from God to man. The first set of tablets were inscribed by the finger of God: "These tablets were the work of God," according to Exodus 32:16, "and the writing on them was God's writing."

The second set of tablets is cut by Moses, and Yahweh says at first that He will "inscribe on them the words that were on the first tablets" (34:1). Later, however, we find Yahweh telling Moses to do the writing: "Put these words in writing" (34:27), He tells Moses, who then spends forty days and nights inscribing the words of the Covenant onto the new stone tablets.

Why the shift? What happened between verses 1 and 27 of chapter 34? What happened was that God revealed a new set of divine attributes, which become central to Judaism and Christianity both in their full flower. In much of the Old Testament, the God of the Israelites operates in the mode of the competing agricultural pagan gods—exacting tribute and loyalty, meting out vengeance and punishment in anger against enemies and transgressors. But here, in the closing chapters of Exodus, the central story in the progress of monotheism, God shows a brief glimpse of the compassionate, forgiving face He will ultimately adopt full time once the people have matured and risen above their polytheistic origins. After Moses cuts the tablets but before he receives and transcribes the words of the Covenant, Yahweh, quite out of the blue, makes the astonishing proclamation that He is "a God of tenderness and compassion, slow to anger, rich in kindness and faithfulness, for thousands he maintains his kindness, forgives faults, transgressions, sin" (34:6–7).

Along with the necessary guidance of the written law, which will act as "a portable homeland," to use Abram's phrase, the God of Moses offers something to the Israelites and to all exiled peoples that is just as important if not more so: a divine example of and injunction toward compassion. When Moses returns down from Sinai the second time, bearing tablets he has inscribed himself, he is transfigured by the encounter with God in His full glory: "The skin on his face was radiant after speaking with Yahweh. And when Aaron and all the sons of Israel saw Moses, the skin on his face shone so much that they would not venture near him. But Moses called to them and Aaron with all the leaders of the community came back to him; and he spoke to them" (34:29–30).

You can't blame them for being careful. After all, the first time Moses came down the mountain with stone tablets he threw a fit and just about smashed them over their heads. Now he comes down with more tablets, looking stranger than ever. But they see that he is not angry this time, that he has become a living reflection of God's glory. Part of that glory, formed in the two-thousand-year journey of the Israelites from the moment Yahweh first spoke to Abraham, through Jacob's wrestling by the river, through the exodus and the struggles of the prophets to return the people to their God—part of this long ascent out of agrarian pagan worship to monotheism is an incremental revelation of God's compassion, glimpsed at certain moments of prophetic insight punctuating the overriding perception of God as punitive and jealous. We know that the three streams of monotheism that sprang from these old stories have had scant success in following the injunction to be compassionate. Hebrew, Christian, and Muslim people have written in blood the history of failing to be as forgiving as the God they serve. Three millennia after receiving the wisdom of Sinai, each of these religions is still struggling to redress that failure, perhaps more so in the case of Christianity, by virtue of its claim that this promise of compassion was fulfilled, enfleshed in Christ.

There is a story in the New Testament that illustrates the power of compassion to heal a wounded community. Like chapter 34 of Exodus, it, too, shows God and man writing on the earth. It is an account of Jesus confronted with an adulterous woman, and it appears only in the gospel ascribed to "John," who some Biblical scholars have called "the beloved disciple," for no one really knows who wrote the anomalous, lyrical, and sometimes cryptic verses in this part of the testament. The story opens John's eighth chapter as a portico on one of the most powerful pronouncements credited to Jesus: "I am the light of the world; / anyone who follows me will not be walking in the dark; / he will have the light of life."

But before making this bold revelation, Jesus gives a dramatic demonstration of the properties of this light he brings to the world. The scribes and pharisees—local skeptics bent on proving Jesus a fraud—drag a woman into the temple, a woman they claim to have caught in the very act of adultery. Jesus, showing remarkable restraint, never asks them how it was they came to witness her sin. The accusers refer to Moses's law and its injunction to condemn such a woman to death by stoning. "What have you to say?" they ask Jesus, thinking they have caught him in a bind between his ideals of nonviolence and forgiveness on the one hand and the unquestionable authority of the Law on the other.

Jesus says nothing at first but bends down and begins to write something on the ground with his finger. Though I had probably heard this piece of the gospel read dozens of times from the Sunday pulpit, this odd gesture of writing on the earth never seemed particularly important until the spring of 2001, when twice in the space of two weeks the opening verses of John's eighth chapter surprised me with fresh insights. The first time it was at Mass, a Sunday in early April, with the children wrestling beside me in the pew as I tried to hear the gospel reading. It was a warm morning, the sun making short work of the snow and quickening the mud in gardens and parks all around the cathedral. We had walked to church through streams of earthen scent. Maybe someone had left a door open or maybe it was on our clothes and in our hair, but as the reader began the gospel I could smell again the good aromas of life returning to the city after a winter of deep snows that started at the ingress of November and never let up right through the weeks of Lent. There is a catch deep within the nostrils that comes with such a smell, and it always reminds me of the salty tang that fills the air in a room where a child has just been born. Mud, like afterbirth, reeks of vernal energy and innocence.

By the time the reader had finished the gospel, I knew that Jesus had touched the ground to locate innocence and the energy of compassion within the earth, within himself, and within the "guilty" woman standing there before him. Bending low, he placed himself beneath the gaze of everyone watching, accusers and accused, and he touched the earth, the ground of being, the humus that makes humility and, therefore, forgiveness possible.

Not long after that realization I was sitting in a packed hall to hear a favorite theologian, Father Ron Rolheiser, talk about spiritual restlessness and the importance of pondering as a route to compassion. Ten minutes into his lecture, much of it covering familiar territory from his book *The Holy Longing: The Search for a Christian Spirituality*, he began describing Jesus' encounter with the accused woman in John 8. I have done my best to recall the meaning if not the words of what Rolheiser had to say about this moment in the New Testament:

*The pharisees bring the woman in, but Jesus refuses to look at her and begins to write on the ground. Now, what is happening here? Even when they ask for his interpretation of the Law, he does not look up. He refuses to look at the woman in her guilt. He writes with his finger in the dirt the first time and then looks up at the accusers and says that any one of them who is without sin should be the first to throw a stone at the woman. Then he bends down again to write in the dust a second time. The others leave one by one until Jesus is alone with the woman. Then he finally looks up at the woman and says, "Woman, where are they? Has no one condemned you?" She answers, "No one, sir." And Jesus says, "Neither do I condemn you, neither do I, now go and sin no more." You see, he refused to look at her in her guilt and only when he could see her in her dignity did he look up at her.*

*Only God writes with His finger on the earth—as the author of creation. And he writes twice. What we have here in the gospel of John is an allusion to another time when God wrote twice with his finger—in Exodus, with Moses on Mount Sinai. That time, too, it is what happens between the two writings that is important. You remember what happens to the first set of stone tablets with the Ten Commandments? Moses flies into a rage and almost breaks them over the heads of the Israelites. Then he goes back up the mountain to talk to God, get some advice on what to do with these sinful people. But God surprises Moses. Instead of promising vengeance and retaliation, the kind of sacral violence seen elsewhere in the Old Testament, God says that He is the God of forgiveness and compassion and chastises Moses for "stoning" his people with the stone tablets, for using the Law to judge. That is why Jesus wrote twice on the ground before he could look up, see the woman in her dignity, tell her to go and sin no more. He was remembering and reminding us that God is the God of compassion and forgiveness.*

This continuum, from the Hebrew scriptures to the Christian gospels, of teaching compassion to a recalcitrant people who are all too willing to face others in their sin and pass judgment, traces the development of an ethic that agricultural and industrial civilizations have always needed, but sporadically applied, to keep the peace. At our current distance from the humus of our origins, our need to bend over and finger the soil that contains our health, our humility, and our compassion is greater than ever. It's a long way to stoop now, but to remain upright in the face of our great sin is to abandon the life-giving humus of creation in favor of the deadly hubris of our ill-advised judgments and desires.

# SHELTER 9

---•---

The animals that once lived in this valley are returning, and cottagers and acreage dwellers now report regular sightings of cougars. Last winter a black bear came up Echo Creek, wandered into a farmyard, and received a bullet for his trouble. The skin of the last bear to be seen in our part of the valley now adorns the wall of the cottager who shot it from his patio eighteen years ago. The last buffalo to walk this way was shot by its owner. A large bull, he had walked through the six-foot fence of a bison ranch fifteen miles upstream. The rancher tried to turn him back with horses and enlisted the help of a champion steer roper. When the lasso touched the bull's haunches he turned and went straight for the horse and rider. That put an end to the rodeo. The next day someone found the buffalo heading east along the river in our part of the valley. A mile or two downstream of us, not far from a place everyone around here calls Skinner's Flats, they shot him, hoisted the body up with a front-end loader, and skinned him. He might have hurt someone, they said, and he was legally the rancher's property, an asset on the way to becoming a liability.

Ravens, too, are returning to the valley in great numbers after a century-long leave of absence. No one has them pegged yet as asset or liability so they are thriving largely unnoticed. A few days after the tipi raising, I was in the meadow when I heard the call of a raven coming from somewhere along the hillsides in front of the cabin. I looked east and saw one, then two more, their lamp-black wings flapping like rips in the sky. Their rollicking flight carried them slowly—ravens don't hurry unless they have to—against a west wind and finally above the meadow. After a few rowdy croaks they fell silent and detoured to circle the tipi like bored teenagers on the prowl. Then one of them let out that strange call you will sometimes hear them make up north in springtime. It is unlike any other bird vocalization, a low-pitched bell-like *bong* that rings in the air. As the note reverberated against the hills, the middle bird did a barrel roll. Then the three of them circled again just above the tips of the poles where the colored ribbons rippled in the breeze. They flapped there, almost hovering for a moment, and then cupped the wind again to make altitude and carry on up the valley.

The next morning, getting ready to go back to the city for a few days, I went out to the tipi to close the door and smoke flaps. There was a long smear of whitewash on the south face of the canvas, directly beneath the tip of one of the highest poles. I walked around the tipi and found two more smears, each below pole tips. Yes, I know—raven is back.

Of course, a smear of shit or the yowl of an unspecified creature will seem more menacing to a tipi dweller in the middle of the night. A young couple from the city asked us if they could overnight in the tipi while we were away. The woman had slept there a few days earlier and wanted to try it again this time with her partner. Later we heard that they didn't make it through the night. Sometime in the hours before dawn, a big wind flew in from the north plowing across the lake and up our slopes. With the tipi poles creaking and the canvas flapping, the two in sleeping bags within wondered if it might fall down on top of them. Then they began hearing strange and loud animal sounds coming from just outside the door. This went on for some time, a caterwauling of something near death or ecstasy, until the man decided he had had enough and stepped outside with his flashlight to investigate. Seconds later he rushed back in through the door-flap and said they had to leave at once because some large animal had "left its mark" by defecating on the tipi.

Did you hear that, Raven, you terror of the night?

# EL MARAHKA IX

---

Trodden into the ground of El Marahka and many other altars on many other hilltops, the dried meal of human blood rests alongside the dust-borne disease of shepherds, farmers, magistrates, and clerics. There for reference, it is a record of sin piled upon judgment succeeding more sin. The trick of life on two feet is not to remain upright too long—a good crouch better than a bad stand. The body bent, fingering the soil, may find kingdoms or at least *kin* and *kindred*, the truth of words whose roots are tangled in oldest English, the speech of ancestors who lived, ate, warred, and died by kind. To a husbandman on the Sussex Downs, *kind* was a sorting tool: corn from barley, ewes from rams, tribe from tribe. A way of uniting kin to kin in native bonds, but dividing too, carving *other* out of *brother.*

Hunters who were long in the soil before the plowman's blood never breathed these words, nor *wild.* No need of such sorting tools to wield against any who walked, crept, swam, flew with them within the earth's dreaming seasons. Even breath, they knew, cannot be withheld, belongs to the all within all, to the sacral touch between beings, between the eater and the eaten. Theirs was a giving to small violences within, large ones without, in a commensal dinner in which all gave in requisite and reciprocal sacrifice. In leaner seasons, hunger preyed and the small and old ones gave first. In plenty, gratitude drew the breath of creation and fasting summoned the caress of the Divine.

Those first to travel with the hoofed and horned from pasture to stream, take shelter in the fold against the daily relinquishments, were the first to scorch flesh upon piled stone. They knew they'd taken from other mouths and had their debts to pay. Later came the seed gatherers who pinned their stories to the earth with new tracks. Stories of an exiled Israelite fostered out of the desert's grain-fattened kingdom who saw his tribe in Pharaoh's thrall and, breaking it, then bound themselves to Yahweh by the orders of Leviticus:

*Sons of Israel, you are to take an animal out of the herd, from the flock, a male without blemish and immolate it on the north side of the altar, before Yahweh and the sons of Aaron; pour out its blood on the borders of the altar, then quarter it and arrange it, head and fat as well, on the wood on the altar fire. Wash the entrails and legs in water and then burn all of it. This holocaust will be a burnt offering and its fragrance will appease Yahweh* (Leviticus 1:1–13).

Then came orders for consecrating young pigeons, oblations of wine, wheaten flour, incense, or of unleavened bread sanctified with oil; orders for communion sacrifices, sacrifices for the sins of high priests that require a young bull, for the sins of the whole community, for the sins of community leaders, for the sins of individuals; for reparation; for ordination rites; and then strict observances on the fruits of land and sea, separating the ritually pure from the ritually impure, "clean" from "unclean." *And*, Yahweh said, distinguishing the Israelites from those who sacrificed pigs or handled snakes, *eat and touch the dead bodies only of ruminants with cloven hooves, all others are unclean and detestable; in water only creatures with fins and scales, all others are unclean and detestable; of the insects only migratory locust, solham, hangol and hagab locusts, all others are unclean and detestable; of the birds here are those that may not be eaten, that must be held detestable: the tawny vulture, the griffon, the osprey, the kite, several kinds of buzzard, all kinds of raven, the ostrich, the screech owl…several kinds of heron, hoopoe, and bat…Any small beast that crawls on the ground is detestable; you must not eat it. Anything that moves on its belly, anything that moves on four legs or more—in short all the small beasts that crawl on the ground—you must not eat these because they are detestable. Do not make yourself detestable with all these crawling beasts; do not defile yourself with them, do not be defiled by them* (Leviticus 11:1–43).

The Leviticus knife goes on sorting sacred from profane, setting apart first fruits for consecration, slaughtering, appeasing, expiating, atoning by day, by week, and by season. And then quarantining all that might take flesh or life away from the tribe: the leprosies of existence, and the mysteries of woman, blood, and semen. And so it was the weeds that follow our appropriations took root in the soil beneath altars. Snakes and lizards became the creatures of unholiness; the wild became the home of Azazel, the demon who dwelt beyond the exertions of God's glory. On the tenth day of the seventh month, the Day of Atonement, the people were to pile their sins upon the head of a live goat and then send it off into the empty land, bearing a year's residue of transgression away into a demon wildness.

# SHELTER 10

———————————•———————————

The night I saw strange sights through the tipi smoke hole I couldn't fall back to sleep. I lay there and watched the wheeling, placental heavens slide eastward minute by minute, hoping to recover the dream or hallucination or whatever it was. By morning I was wondering what mescaline might be like.

Three days later I heard a car door slam and looked up to see a stranger walking my way across the meadow. He was in his late sixties or early seventies, dressed like a banker on vacation. As we walked down to look at the tipi, he told me about the time he tried peyote during a religious ceremony conducted inside a tipi. It was 1957, early fall, and his newspaper editor had sent him to Red Pheasant Reserve to write a feature on two Saskatchewan psychiatrists who were trying to record the ceremonial use of peyote. These doctors, Abram Hoffart and Humphrey Osmond, were the first to use LSD and mescaline to treat schizophrenics and alcoholics. They had captured the attention of Aldous Huxley a few years earlier during his own investigations into therapeutical and religious use of the drugs.

In one of his letters to Huxley, Osmond included a verse in which he coined the word that would eventually come to define not only the drugs themselves, but an entire generation of young people dreaming of life beyond the walls of rationality. The word *psychedelic* entered our lexicon in a letter mailed by Osmond from Weyburn, Saskatchewan:

To fathom hell
or soar angelic,
just take a pinch of psychedelic.

Some of the trips Huxley wrote about in *Doors of Perception* came from mescaline he obtained from Osmond in 1953. In the book he goes on at length and with obvious enthusiasm about the "Native American Church," a religious movement in North America that he believed combined the best of Christianity with the traditional spiritual practice of indigenous people. Huxley gives examples of rituals in which contemporary American Indians "sacramentalize" their own traditions, blending Christian and pagan ways.

There are people, among both Christians and those who practice the spirituality native to this continent, who would be offended by such a mixing of the two religious traditions, even without the use of hallucinogens. It comes from a certain desire to have our attentions to God and spirit fixed in time, stay as pure as they were in Grandfather's day, that golden age when religious practice was ideal and unchanging. But a religion is alive and organic like a language or a form of music. As long as people practice its ways, it is by necessity and use changed and renewed—alive. For it to remain the same, people would have to stop using it, speaking its words, playing its melodies—but once that happens, it is dead.

The science of cosmology tells us that anything in the universe that appears to be standing still is an illusion of our narrow outlook. We think of Christianity as a fixed entity that sprung to life one winter's day in Bethlehem and then moved inexorably throughout the world obliterating all indigenous traditions in its path. But even at its origins, Christianity was a fusion of ideas and philosophy from at least three different civilizations.

Starting from its core as a Judaic offshoot arising amidst the prophetic traditions and history of the Hebrew people, Christianity only came into its own after Saint Paul applied Greek ideals of egalitarianism and moral reason to the story of Christ's life and divinity. Then, as the new faith made its way around the Roman Empire, it began to acquire the organizational structure and sense of order that, like a good Roman bridge, has stood up under the multitudes of believers passing from century to century. Today's postcolonial critique points to that streak of Roman imperialism in Christianity as the evangelizing impetus that ran roughshod over local pagan religions as the faith moved outward through the world. True enough, Christianity has drained much of the soul and sensuality out of our religious contact with the earth. On the other hand, it is always easier to love a religion when its priests are dead and gone. Many of the agricultural pagan traditions that existed in the Old World, as rich as they were in celebrating the bonds between humanity and the rest of creation, accessed spiritual energy in ways that we could never countenance today. Violent and terrifying rites, sometimes involving rape and human sacrifice, were not spiritually uplifting for the animals, slaves, and tribal enemies dragged to the altar. Those practices are gone and not missed; others, the more benign, somehow survived, incorporated into the evolving, subsuming juggernaut of Christianity. There is precious little in Christian practice that is not derivative in one way or another. The church calendar consists of feast days overlaid upon the ancient celebrations of Europe's earliest indigenous religions.

We are powerless before the flow of spiritual genes from one tradition to another. Longings of the spirit, like longings of the flesh, are blind to boundaries. While some people will busy themselves purging and segregating, there are always others, often indigenous people, celebrating God's presence in the world in a cross-fertilizing flow of belief and practice that is as natural to religion as it is to flowers. There is great solace in knowing that in the end Rome always loses its grip on its outposts. Despite its best centralizing exertions, the Church has been able to prevent neither the influence of the local, the marginal, and the indigenous upon the unfolding of Christianity through time nor the exuberant growth of new liturgical and devotional practices that spring forth whenever the mustard-seed truths of the gospel story reach the native soil of this place and this time.

# EL MARAHKA X

———————————•———————————

Who can say when the blood of a child first sprinkled an altar? Long before Leviticus, before Abraham found the ram, back in the mythic shadows of Cain and Abel, the first iron weapons came out of the hearth and the fighting with seasons and soil placed tribe against tribe in more than ritual battle. Floodplains birthed nations and then empires, suckled new warriors hungering for the next valley. Hunting tribes fell like grain at harvest, the deltas and river bottoms gave up their tilth, and the gods of the warrior-farmers tallied the sum and demanded human flesh in return. Look to the altars of any ancient farming people and you will find the stones clotted with the blood of the expendable ones: women, children, slaves, and enemies. One blade or another brought death: entrails on the altar or the threshold, your enemies' or your brother's; villages ran with gore, tents and rooftops smoldering from the last raid while every household braced for the next. Blood and revenge the norm; civilizations utterly unacquainted with peace. Daughters raped and sons killed before their bones had matured, while tribes, nations, and empires rose, clashed, and fell across the Levantine plains. Prayers begged for vindication and vengeance, and God's shield against enemies: *Bless my people, O God, and curse the Amorites, Edomites, Canaanites…heap hot coals upon them, plunge them into the deep, never to rise again…let their tents be deserted, their campsites a graveyard.* Facing the Edomites in the Valley of Salt, David lifted this song:

Who will lead us to Edom
to breach the city wall?
God, will you still hold back?
Will you desert our camp?

Stand by us against the enemy,
all other aid is worthless.
With you the battle is ours,
you will crush our foes. (Psalm 60:11–14)

Hatred sent outward, kinship inward, the two forming a tribal lever fulcrumed upon the sacrifice of young lives. This passed for honor, as it still does wherever people quench fear and hatred with blood. And the wild creatures, clean and unclean, stand further off as another kind of enemy, the untouchable others from an alien realm.

During the long centuries after Elijah's time, hatred of the other became a communal sin too great to bear on the back of a goat. Jesus was born amongst a people who had survived generations of displacement and foreign occupation, who had been handed over in blood from empire to empire: Jerusalem under siege, laid waste, the people exiled, then returned, the temple destroyed then raised again, Judea with its own coinage, a brief theocracy, then the Persians arrived with fresh horrors, and after that the Greeks who abolished the practice of the Jewish faith and made sacrifices to Zeus in the temple, then another siege of the holy city and suddenly the new hated occupants are speaking Latin and worshipping renamed gods of war and harvest who demand new land to feed the hordes at home across the sea. The Hebrew people, inured to the latest colonizers—the curiales, the procurators, the consuls—grumbled but kept their heads low when the centurions passed by, saved their rancor for the Samaritans and other uncircumcised neighbors. To the Roman tetrarch the Hebrews were a tractable people, a little strange in their lawbound worship of a single god, but on the whole pliant. Small rebellions and tax revolts were easily tidied up with public executions.

"Are you not the one who started the revolt and led those four thousand cutthroats out into the desert?" asked the tribune of his prisoner.

"I?" said he. "I am a Jew and a citizen of Tarsus." Then he turned to the mob and spoke in their Hebrew tongue, telling them how he had once dragged the People of the Way from synagogues, flogged and imprisoned them, how on a trip to Damascus to get more prisoners a light blinded him at midday and a voice called out, "Saul, why are you persecuting me?" and how he converted then and received his mission to evangelize the pagans. And then he turned to the court and saved his skin by claiming Roman citizenship.

"I am a Roman and cannot be flogged." And it was true. Paul was a Romanized Jew, trained as a pharisee but in love with Greek culture and language. Who better to spread the news that God's incarnation has dissolved all former distinctions among tribe, nation, and faith?

Paul took up the tentmaker's trade, became a traveler offering shelter threaded together by his own zeal, the truth of God, and some of the most inspired letter writing in Western civilization. His epistles, a new faith promulgated in writing, went to backsliders around the empire, encouraging the faithful, refreshing memories with the words and promises of the one who faced imperium with a mustard-seed kingdom where the fallen can stand again:

> In the Creator's image there is no room for distinction between Greek and Jew, between the circumcised and the uncircumcised, or between barbarian and Scythian, slave and free man. There is only Christ: he is everything and he is in everything. (Colossians 3:11)

Here he is exhorting the Ephesian converts to embody a new unity, the all within all:

> Bear with one another charitably, in complete selflessness, gentleness, and patience. Do all you can to preserve unity of the Spirit by the peace that binds you together. There is one Body, one Spirit...one God who is Father of all, over all, through all and within all. (Ephesians 4:2–6)

And here he reassures the good pagans of Galatia:

> Before faith came, we were allowed no freedom by the Law; we were being looked after until faith was revealed. The Law was to be our guardian until the Christ came and we could be justified by faith. Now that that time has come we are no longer under that guardian, and you are, all of you, sons of God through faith in Christ Jesus. All baptised in Christ, you have all clothed yourselves in Christ, and there are no more distinctions between Jew and Greek, slave and free, male and female...(Galatians 3:23–28)

I remember once seeing a young mother, a descendant of buffalo runners, sitting with her son on a city bench waiting for the bus. Her toddler son saw a caterpillar. Drawn to the fuzz wiggling above concrete, he reached down to see how it might feel. His mother slapped his hand, scolding, "No! Dirty. Don't touch!" In the boy's recoil I saw the old knife of Leviticus flash again. Paul's mission to the uncircumcised could not dispel the taint of former laws: clean, unclean, sacred, profane, chosen, unchosen.

The raw, unappropriated spirit of creation breathed the entire living cosmos into a dethroner of princes, an exalter of the lowly who was born blessed and cursed, marked by a star to be baptized in the river by a wild man, an eater of locusts, before he went forth to lose and find his way in the wilderness. Then, in the hands of angels, to Galilee and three years of touching the unclean, consorting with sinners, drawing in dirt, healing, blessing, and teaching circumcised and Samaritans, beggars and tax collectors. This was the Spirit at large in history, a lion of God loose in the village who chose to lie down like a lamb, surrendering to human will. And in that submission the ways of man were overthrown— this time not merely the grasp of mankind upon creation but of creation also upon mankind, fulfilling the desire not of one belly but of the entire, star-blown nature of things, the heart of matter giving itself over to human acquisition in a drama of sacrifice that reconciled all to one, surpassing a point of conscripted otherness beyond which we must regard life either as a unity, the all in all of Paul's epistles, or as meaningless enmity between self-interested and discrete particles.

> Water and fire succeed
> The town, the pasture, and the weed.
> Water and fire deride
> The sacrifice that we denied. (T. S. Eliot, "Little Gidding")

More than merely upright and reluctant to stoop far enough to grow our own potatoes and retain at least that agricultural bond to the source of our humility and compassion, now we private kings of postmodernity imagine ourselves afloat in some nether region above the earth where sacrifice is not only unnecessary, but abjectly foolish. We are the civilization that gave up on sacrifice in despair as the rate of our consuming eclipsed our capacity to ritualize any reciprocal offerings, forbearance, or self-denial. Renewal will come when our appropriation of nature creates enough scarcity, disease, and ecological dysfunction to cleanse the land in cataclysm. Then the sacrifice will come all at once, passing like wildfire through a prairie that has not seen grazing in many years. Religion is a prescribed burn; Christ an incendiary. "I have come," he said, "to bring fire to the earth" (Luke 12:49). The wild man who was his herald and dwelt in the desert like the old ones living on what he could hunt and gather preached of *metanoia*, change of heart, and said that one would come who baptized "with the Holy Spirit and with fire" (Matthew 3:11).

It was a message out of wilderness, the prickly place where we are outside the comfort of our tools and taking. The same pre-Advent message of repentance that each generation needs to hear anew: we who have lost touch with the original covenant with God must now put on the hair shirt and immerse ourselves in the wild, not to mortify the flesh or flagellate ourselves into a more pious, less material existence, but to take a pathway apart from the comforts of civil life, to experience solitude and elemental existence where the minimum is suspended in our utility, to fast from our appetites and conscriptions long enough to gain a sidelong glance at the unity within which we are more brother than other. True religious experience demands a level of self-sacrifice and exposure. Following the example of the prophets and mystics of all cultures and religions, we might begin to let ourselves be conscripted, begin to walk the pathways of transformation.

In the Christian gospels, talk of change, conversion, renewal, and transformation is often associated with talk of the Kingdom of God or the Kingdom of Heaven. In what are regarded as some of the most inscrutable parables ascribed to Jesus, he compares the kingdom to a mustard seed, to yeast, to a treasure found in a farmer's field, and to a pearl of great price. Some of the metaphors speak of hidden powers of transformation—the tiny mustard seed that becomes a great tree and shelters all the birds of the air, the small measure of yeast that leavens the flour into nourishing food. Other images speak of hidden riches that can only be discovered by giving up all of one's material possessions. These parables taken together show the two sides of experiencing kingdom or participating in the transformation of a family, a community, an ecosystem, or a nation: the Kingdom of God is a great power for renewal hidden in the smallest particles of the Creation, but to unearth that power and let its leavening work among us we have to give up our desires to possess and allow the kingdom to possess us instead.

Preoccupied with possessing heaven, Christians have become blind to the Kingdom of God in their midst. The pharisees asked Jesus when the kingdom will come and his reply seems calculated to bring the spiritual seeker down to earth. All religion, and Christianity in particular, goes astray on the assumption that the ultimate dimension of reality is only and always elsewhere, in an afterlife, a messianic realm, or a golden age yet to come. "The Kingdom of God," Christ says in the Gospel of Luke, "is among you."

Where? In all that remains beyond our grasping. In a tree's branches vibrating with the migrant songbirds of a May morning. In the fierce bond between a nursing mother and her child. In all that serves the innocent and the excluded ones: children, the poor, the aged, the endangered. In the wild, transformative energy of sacrifice, when we bend over and ground our work and our choices in the kingdom truth of making the first last and the last first. In the ongoing creation of this cosmos, a movement that our species is privileged to sense and even join insofar as we will hand our lives over to the power dwelling in a mustard seed.

All within all was wind and fire rushing in upon our private realms, a wild truth that would have to be quarantined. New scribes, the magistrates of Christendom, seized the story of renewal, justice, and love on earth and made it safe: the tame promise of righteousness buying heaven in the next life. The Christ, sequestered, housebroken to our desire for comfort—without flame, without spirit—became for most believers a personal virtue voucher to be claimed and redeemed at the soul's coming out. Reassured but unresurrected, the faithful over the centuries have always wanted to dampen the holy wind down to whispered expiations of private sin, the cosmic fire down to flickering votive candles lit for pennies a prayer. Even so, the Word prevails, renews itself from time to time when the paschal wind blows into our shelter, lighting new fires, bewildering the world and uniting us with voices from the Spirit's holy depths. Every few hundred years something shakes ecclesial privilege and authority—something as large as the continental drift of civilizations abrading, crashing, rising, and falling or as small as a single, purposeful life. A rich young man strips off his embroidered finery, leaves his father's home, and walks barefoot into the countryside to serve the poor, start a new community of believers, or compose hymns to the universe. God be praised, it seems to happen often enough to keep us back from the brink.

Pierre Teilhard de Chardin, a priest and paleontologist whose mystical writings encompass a harmony between science and Christianity, once stood all alone in the Ordo Desert of the Asian steppes and said a Mass for the earth. It was 1923, a Sunday in August, the feast of the Transfiguration, and he had neither bread nor wine at hand, but he felt the urgings of his faith in Christ the all within all, the Word enfleshed in every iota of existence. At the rising of the sun he made his own sacrificial offering, holding up to God the world's attainments and diminishments borne within a single day. This was his offertorial prayer:

> Since once again, Lord—though this time not in the forests of Aisne but in the steppes of Asia—I have neither bread, nor wine, nor altar, I will raise myself beyond these symbols, up to the pure majesty of the real itself; I, your priest, will make the whole earth my altar and on it will offer you all the labours and sufferings of the world.
>
> Over there, on the horizon, the sun has just touched with

light the outermost fringe of the eastern sky. Once again, beneath this moving sheet of fire, the living surface of the earth wakes and trembles, and once again begins its fearful travail. I will place on my paten, O God, the harvest to be won by this renewal of labour. Into my chalice I will pour all the sap which is to be pressed out this day from the earth's fruits.

My paten and my chalice are the depths of a soul laid widely open to all the forces which in a moment will rise up from every corner of the earth and converge upon the Spirit. Grant me the remembrance and the mystic presence of all those whom the light is now awakening to the new day.

One by one, Lord, I see and I love all those whom you have given me to sustain and charm my life. One by one also I number all those who make up that other beloved family which has gradually surrounded me, its unity fashioned out of the most disparate elements, with affinities of the heart, of scientific research and of thought. And again one by one—more vaguely it is true, yet all inclusively—I call before me the whole vast anonymous army of living humanity; those who surround me and support me though I do not know them; those who come, and those who go; above all those who in office, laboratory and factory, through their vision of truth or despite their error, truly believe in the progress of earthly reality and who today will take up again their impassioned pursuit of the light.

This restless multitude, confused or orderly, the immensity of which terrifies us; this ocean of humanity whose slow, monotonous wave-flows trouble the hearts even of those whose faith is most firm: it is to this deep that I thus desire all the fibres of my being should respond. All the things in the world to which this day will bring increase; all those that will diminish; all those too that will die: all of them, Lord, I try to gather into my arms, so as to hold them out to you in offering. This is the material of my sacrifice; the only material you desire.

Once upon a time men took into your temple the first fruits of their harvests, the flower of their flocks. But the offering you really want, the offering you mysteriously need every day to appease your hunger, to slake your thirst is nothing less than the growth of the world borne ever onwards in the stream of universal becoming.

Receive, O Lord, this all-embracing host which your whole creation, moved by your magnetism, offers you at this dawn of a new day.

This bread, our toil, is of itself, I know, but an immense fragmentation; this wine, our pain, is no more, I know, than a draught that dissolves. Yet in the very depths of this formless mass you have implanted—and this I am sure of, for I sense it—a desire, irresistible, hallowing, which makes us cry out, believer and unbeliever alike: 'Lord, make us *one*.'

Because, my God, though I lack the soul-zeal and the sublime integrity of your saints, I yet have received from you an overwhelming sympathy for all that stirs within the dark mass of matter; because I know myself to be irremediably less a child of heaven than a son of earth; therefore I will this morning climb up in spirit to the high places, bearing with me the hopes and the miseries of my mother; and there—empowered by that priest-hood which you alone (as I firmly believe) have bestowed on me—upon all that in the world of human flesh is now about to be born or to die beneath the rising sun I will call down the Fire.[1]

Any priest who calls down holy fire, takes the Word out of safe chambers, and proclaims it as the Divine that dwells within all matter is going to be muzzled sooner or later. Teilhard scared the pants off the scribes in charge of bridling the wild truth of the incarnation. By 1926, his Jesuit superiors forced him to abandon teaching, exiled him back to China, and issued an order prohibiting him from publishing anything other than strictly scientific literature.

Pantheist, syncretist, heretic—these were the terms leveled against him at the time, and though he died in 1955 and the censorship order was lifted decades ago, Teilhard's books, none of which were published while he lived, continue to stir strong feelings from the defenders of the faith.

His humble aim in his science and writing was to be one atom within the infinite and thereby lend the small weight of his soul to the task of creation, the unfolding of the cosmos. In his cosmology we are all the blessed, particulate matter of a unified and emerging universe in which spirit and flesh are fired together as one radiant, luminous phenomenon. Reading that offertorial prayer, I thought of some of the people alive at the time who were included in his evocation of the "whole vast anonymous army of living humanity." On the morning of Teilhard's eucharistic feast for the cosmos, even as the lonely desert-bound priest held up the earth and its people to God, Einstein was at work at the University of Berlin, Gandhi was at his loom pondering the civil disobedience of his *satyagraha*, Monet, ancient and nearly blind, was painting blurry pond lilies in Giverny, and Hitler was recruiting thugs for his Beer Hall Putsch, launched three months later.

But there were others stirring too, the human atoms forgotten and unknown to history. On that August morning of 1923, there was a young mystic coming of age on the far side of the planet— one whose life, like Teilhard's, was eventually to form a bridge across rivers running between old worlds and new ones, between science and faith, between protestant and Catholic, and between the post-Enlightenment culture of modernity and the realm of eternal mystery. I know a little of his story only because his son and granddaughter let me read a sheaf of pages written in his hand at the end of his days.[2]

He left behind no volumes of theology, no trail of miracles, or sect of adoring adherents. All I have to go on is the foolscap memoir of a man I never met and the testimony of those who remember him with admiration and love, but it is enough to make me wonder if he was not one who lent the expansive force of his soul to the new Genesis of Teilhard's dreams, and, what's more, if he was not one of that stranger, rarer breed—a follower of Christ, a Christian worthy of the name.

The memoir bears an epigraph from Psalm 71: "Forsake me not, / now that I am old and gray, / Till I proclaim your strength / to this generation / and thy power / to all them that are to come." It begins with an image of the boy and his mother hiding out in a shepherd's hut to get away from a meddlesome grandmother. He was the youngest child of the vicar of Wicklewood, a cleric whose Victorian faith was an intellectual appendage, a professional and cultural necessity. After a first wife died in childbirth leaving five children for the vicar to raise, he married the boy's mother, the daughter of a prominent Cambridge don, the master and vice-chancellor of Caius College. The vice-chancellor's wife did not think the vicar a fit husband for her daughter and so the marriage took place in secret while she was vacationing on the Continent. Even after the boy was born, his grandmother harried her daughter, insisting that she abandon the marriage. The shepherd's hut was the place where he and his mother came to "accept the hard things in life, and to know there is a godward side in other people."

The boy grew up in a rural vicarage on three acres of land in East Anglia near a private game park. In early years, he played long hours with his half sisters in a place they called "the Dell," a portion of the garden where they hid among ivy-covered stumps, climbed mossy-limbed trees, and spoke with fairies who lived in the shady recesses. Wicklewood was, as the name implies, a place with a long history of spirits and enchantment, the kind of landscape that leaves its traces on a child's soul.

For his first nine years, there were the five other children to enliven the household—four half sisters and a half brother—but then one day everything changed. His half siblings had become too great a load for their new stepmother and so his father sent them away to an orphanage in Wales. Overnight the hallways and gardens fell silent; he was suddenly the only child of two middle-aged and bookish parents. For the rest of his life he would struggle to forgive his father for this unaccountable decision.

Having judged the village school unsuitable for their son, his mother and father had always taught him themselves. When he turned ten, however, they decided he needed a little more in the way of education and arranged to send him away to boarding school at Norwich. War had broken out across the channel and England was in upheaval. In his child's understanding of events, the war had forced him away from his parents and into this strange environment so unlike home. At school he became utterly despondent, weeping for days on end and refusing to eat. As much as anything he missed the Dell and the games he had continued to play alone in the enchanted lands of Wicklewood. The boy who came home for school holidays was drawn, withered, and pale enough to make his parents send for the physician. The doctor, who knew something of the family story, prescribed a strange therapy. He instructed the vicar to build his son a hut in the garden where he was to live quietly and independently, coming and going as he wished. It was as though the doctor believed the boy should be allowed to begin life all over again on his own. Even more surprising was his parents' assent to the plan. His father built the shelter with a wooden frame, a solid roof and canvas sides, two of which were generally left wide open though could be shut tight in bad weather. It was eight feet wide by twenty long—a kind of longhouse in the garden.

And so the boy lived there in a solitude that turned out to be a saving grace. As an old man he reflected that during this phase of his life, with the war just ending as he came into adolescence, he was being drawn by the hand of God into a deeper interior life. He had long hours of quiet every day. Spontaneously, without any knowledge of what he was doing, he took to daily periods of meditative stillness. Two or three times a day he would go to favorite places in the woods or slip into the vaulted silence of the empty church. Often he would climb to the top of the church tower, peek out from behind the stonework battlements, and survey the parish of Wicklewood. In all of these places he would sit in untutored contemplation, a natural apprentice to the mystic way of the desert monk. At the time he made no association between his quiet practice and prayer, nor did he give much thought to the God of his father's church. He simply knew he was seeking beyond himself for something he thought of as the compelling and hidden reality behind the life available to his senses.

From his garden hermitage he would go off on daily excursions deep into Kimberley Park, the private reserve near the vicarage. He stole through the locked gates and moved beneath the trees unmolested. Gamekeepers and others he came across never spoke to him and came to regard him as just another feral creature loose in the sanctuary. Animals and plants were his only companions. Finding nature's multiplicity all around, he became accustomed to moving slowly as he made his way from hermitage to woods or church and back again. As he sat in the shadow of oak and beech trees, birds and squirrels would approach and sometimes run across his shoulders. One cold night a mother partridge brought her brood of new hatchlings into his hut and took shelter under his bed.

With time in the hermitage, the boy grew stronger, wiser, and healthier. He came to realize that he was by stages discovering a new realm of reality behind the material world, that this other life is God and that even as he sought, he too was being sought. Once on his wandering through Kimberley Park, he came across a small spring in a shaded copse. Nearly covered in thorns and bushes, it was a basin of clean sand with water bubbling to the surface at several points. Later, he was to learn that the spring had once been a spiritual place beloved to Lady Kimberley who named it Mary's Well.

During this period, an uncle gave him a microscope, an instrument that opened up another gallery in his mind's developing regard for living matter. Entering the kingdom of the minute, with its stunning symmetry and microcosmic dramas, he grew all the more convinced that there must be a Person behind such concealed marvels. It was the beginning, too, of his education as a biologist.

Eventually, his health restored, he returned to school in Norwich. This time, however, rather than board at the school, he was placed in the care of a kind and patient woman who fostered children to provide for her own young family. In the shelter of her love and once again in the company of many children, he felt his humanity expand, his unease in society fade. At sixteen, he graduated and entered Caius, his grandfather's college at Cambridge, where he became a student of biology. Throwing himself into science in general and entomology in particular, at the same time he began to read books on the mystic and ascetic life. These he received from a poor and elderly aunt who he had begun to visit in his college years. She had been disinherited from his father's family for her conversion to Roman Catholicism, but her faith and devotion amidst poverty, isolation, and infirmity inspired him along with the stories he read of saints and monks.

Moving into postgraduate studies in entomology, he gradually became disenchanted with the reductionist outlook engendered by his studies at Cambridge. The demons of existential angst come quickly to an earnest young man who finds himself pulling bugs to pieces day after day. All that had once inspired him as wholeness and mystery was now laid bare on the dissecting table, separated into lifeless categories. In despair and thinking of suicide, he went to see a blind grocer friend who shared his interest in spiritual matters. While the grocer worked, he helped tidy the shop in silence. Then, perhaps sensing the young man's unease, the grocer asked, "Have you ever thought of taking Jesus for a friend?"

He did not answer—the question seemed so odd, disturbing.

Leaving the shop, he spent the night praying and pondering the question. What if it were possible that the Creator who had made all of life, all of the creatures of his childhood at Wicklewood, could be interested in him personally? Could even be considered a friend?

Over time he came to think of that question from the grocer as the moment of his conversion, or at least its beginning, for it was a long and gradual process marked by struggle, doubt, uncertainty, and failure. He was to meet other friends, including a Franciscan monk, who became for him the incarnation of God's personhood, the living, personal manifestation of divine attention.

In time, he graduated with his doctorate in entomology, met a woman, and married. They started a family, and he took a job with a pesticide company that was developing and testing chemical products to protect military rations from insects. Later, he was transferred to another branch that was devising new commercial insecticides. He hated the idea of killing so many creatures needlessly, but the income was enough to support his young family and the work gave him opportunities to study a variety of insects. When war in Europe became imminent for the second time in his life, he and the rest of the senior staff were given an agreement to sign, which said that in event of war they would be switching their research to the development of poisons to be used on the battlefield. The work would have exempted him from active military service, but he refused to sign the papers. Not long after, he was let go. He was thirty-two years old, unemployed with a wife and three small children to support.

He had for some time been pondering the possibility of becoming a priest in the Church of England. After praying and talking with his wife, they decided he should enter theological college. She went back to work as a teacher and while he undertook an accelerated study program, they lived on her income as well as a small legacy that fell into their laps right when they needed it most.

Toward the end of his studies, the Second World War began, but
when his conscription papers came he registered immediately as a
conscientious objector. Upon graduation, he was offered his choice
of two parishes: one in Bedford and the other in southeast London.
It was 1939 and Bedford was the quieter place: little poverty or
social strife, and safe from German bombing raids. The decision
had been made for him. He took the more dangerous and troubled
parish in southeast London. They lived there for the duration of
the war, ministering to the wayward and hungry of east London
on a salary of £28 a month. Meanwhile, the "Battle of London"
reached its peak in their neighborhood. One day he came home
from early weekday Mass to find their street cordoned off by the
bomb disposal squad. His wife was away visiting relatives with their
two youngest children, but he'd left the oldest boy asleep in bed.

"My son's in there!" he told the constables, but they wouldn't
allow him in the building. He backed away and snuck down a lane
and into the rear of their home. The boy was still sound asleep
beneath a pile of blankets and in their rear garden, ten paces from
the kitchen door, was the unexploded bomb. He took his son from
the house and called in the disposal squad.

When the war ended, he and his wife began thinking of emi-
grating to Canada. Friends and relatives warned of hardship and
isolation and said that such a move would not be in the children's
interests. He went to a religious community in Mirfield to pray over
the matter and in the middle of the night heard God telling him not
to be afraid of going to Canada. Soon after that, the opportunity
came. A town named Broadview in the province of Saskatchewan
needed an Anglican pastor. Never questioning the call, the mystic
of Wicklewood packed up his family and set out for the New
World, assured of God's care.

At the time of Teilhard's consecrating Mass, millions of
Europeans had already awoken to such stirrings, the Jacob ethos
deep in the blood, dreams of a wilder land comingled with the

will to possess or convert. Arriving on the plains of this continent they came face to face with Esau. There the myth carries on—the wrestling, an ambivalent embrace, leaving us hobbled on the shores of the river that runs between first and second man.

# SHELTER 11

A week after the tipi was dismantled for the winter I walked out at sundown to see what kind of mark it had left on the meadow. Standing just outside the circle of flattened grass I thought of older rings I have walked among on prairie hilltops. Though the land was dark, the sun, just below the western horizon, lit up the sky so that it looked like the shade of a lantern. An infinite gradient of blues, ranging from softest azure above the sunset to a deep cobalt in the east, overarched the valley. I stepped into the circle and felt at once a calling within myself, that same need for the tipi to show me something again.

An owl hooted softly from somewhere to the east. I often see great horned owls come out to perch at dusk on a hilltop snag I erected years ago to mark the tragic death of a cousin. So I looked that way instinctively, without thinking, and as I lifted my head a coyote yipped once and something fell out of the sky. Right above the snag, due east of the tipi circle, something was slowly falling from the heavens. It was brighter than a full moon and half its size, a ball of blue-white fire, the color and intensity of a welder's arc. It fell and fell, sparkling at its edges, drawing a long, ragged tail behind it, until it disappeared behind the far hills, extinguished like an ember tossed from a celestial bonfire.

There was to be one more message from the tipi, a gift of its sheltering that was forewarned but not foreseen. Mike called to say that he and Lorran were expecting a third child to be born the coming spring. There was no doubt in their minds that it was the tipi, that they had in fact conceived the first night they slept in it. I laughed, remembering Grace's warning, and then thought of Mike and Lorran's old Teutonic surname—*Wild*. Sometime next May, when the coulees ring again with towhee song and the Saskatoon bushes blossom, a little more Wild will be born.

# PART TWO

---•---

# FROM
# MOUNT
# CARMEL

*Wherever ye turn there is the face of God.*
THE QUR'AN

# WILD GRACE

———————————————————•———————————————————

The land falls away from us here in a theater of grass not quite as ancient as the sand and clay beneath it. The sun is aloft, but we're waiting. Karen, who walked up here with me an hour ago, sits quietly in the refuge of her thoughts on a flat boulder just downslope. My thoughts are ranging away from here too far to embrace the peace that I have felt before on this hillside. A trip that was supposed to be a spiritual retreat now feels like a flight into bewilderment.

We made our arrangements weeks ago, knowing Karen would need a respite from the work it takes to get four children pointed in the right direction at the end of summer. Music and dance lessons, basketball registration, school supplies and clothes to buy. One child starting high school, one in elementary school, one still homeschooling, and one just weaned—sometimes Karen feels like she's packed fourteen years of child rearing into thirty days.

August rolled on by with me lost in my own projects, oblivious to the bedlam downstairs. I've been preparing a submission on the birds and plants that would be affected by a dam proposed for one of the continent's last great stretches of wild prairie river. Six days ago I was on the river with a good friend, Rob, his son, Orion, and my son, Jon. We had some weather so the boys learned the rough side of canoeing in a long day of trudging the shoreline, rope over shoulder, head down, hauling a loaded canoe into driving rain and a headwind too stiff to paddle against. Things cleared the next morning and the wind came round. Lashing the canoes together and hoisting a sail made of tarp roped to cottonwood staves, we ruddered our way down the river through five-hundred-foot-high cliffs and badlands, sagebrush flats, cottonwood groves. Later in the day we saw a bull snake, prairie falcons, and several eagles, both golden and bald. As evening drew on and we neared our campsite, a pair of golden eagles flushed some geese from the river right in front of us. The larger eagle, the female, rose into the air and then stooped on the panicked geese, knocking a single bird down to the shore. We drifted by in silence, watching her wrestle the goose into submission while her mate waited nearby. A foot on the goose's breast, she ripped at it, tossing feathers into the wind and checking now and then on her audience. A piece of down landed in Jon's hair without his noticing.

That night we camped on a large sandy island with cottonwood forest at our backs. With supper over and the boys in the tent, Rob and I reclined by the fire to drink tea and watch the night sky. A strange glow that was not lightning throbbed on and off a couple of times to the west. It might have been artillery exercises at the military range twenty miles away, and I said something about almost having forgotten the world beyond the valley. That was enough to shift our talk to the second most popular topic for discussion around the campfire on canoe trips (the first being bears). Anyone who has lived by canoe and river for a few days will recognize this kind of palaver: *What a great day it was... You know, I could live like this all the time... I guess this is what it was like for the Indians before we made a mess of things...* Rob had just followed through with the next sentiment—*we deserve to live like this more of the time*—when a plow wind blew in from nowhere, extinguished our fire in a single stroke, and flattened the tent with the boys inside.

As we ran to the tent to rescue our sons, I heard a strange sound coming from the water's edge, a hollow *ka-dunk, ka-dunk, ka-dunk,* rhythmic but getting quieter with each iteration, as though receding from us. A canoe might make that kind of sound, it dawned

on me, if it were tumbling along a beach and off into the darkness of a storm. I ran blindly in the direction of the river, chasing
the sound through utter blackness. I reached the river just as the
sound stopped. It had to be somewhere in front of me in the water.
Rob arrived with his lantern, swung the beam across the churn-
ing surface of the river, and there it was, a few feet offshore, half-
submerged and floating away in the shallows.

After we had hauled the canoe out of the river and beaten a path
into the shelter of the cottonwoods, where we were able to anchor
the tent with lines, the message settled into my thoughts: *This, too,
was part of the old life in such a place.*

It was a kind of rude grace, that storm in the midst of utter
tranquility and comfort, a small comeuppance that has lingered in
my thoughts this week when we are all of us wondering about the
messages borne in a sudden moment of violence. The day after
we got off the river and returned to city life, the calendar flipped
over to Tuesday, September 11, 2001. Now on this hilltop, five
days later, there is a tranquility again, but it feels wrong, dishonest.
Waiting at home there are facts I can't retreat from: in particular,
four children I am rearing in a world that is beginning to harvest
the fruits of its long fear of the pagan and the wild.

Disasters abound. I heard an ecologist say recently that we will
lose 50 percent of the continent's biodiversity in this century. A
farmer whose sons have given up their dreams of ever living on
the land told me last month that he thinks the seed and chemical
companies will have complete control of prairie agriculture within
twenty-five years. And now political and religious leaders are trying
out old words like *crusade*, hoping they might stimulate the righteous hatred that fuels vengeance.

Escape bears its own despair. At dusk the earth will look like a
good place to rest, as it has to others on this hilltop. Now, while
the sun still shines and the wind blows over this upland, I am
having trouble recalling what it is in our faith in God and heaven

that cannot be taken, owned, or earned. A sound floats by on the breeze, a rolling *groa-oa-oa-oa-oo-oo*, the edges softened by distance, the rhythm like a thumbnail drawn across the teeth of a comb. Hearing this, the call of migrating cranes so far overhead I cannot see them, I believe in their journey miraculous and wild from northern marshes to southern ones a thousand miles away, and I can at least imagine the possibility of such unfettered truth in the human longing for spirit.

Grace, as tent-flattening storm, the cry of cranes, or the still voice whispered in the prophet's ear, is a kind of sympathy expressed between Creator and creature. Saint Paul used the Greek term *charism*, meaning "a gratuitous gift," something that can never be taken or appropriated. Church doctrine says that grace belongs to the "supernatural order" of things. That may be, but it spills over into the natural order and touches us from somewhere within the fierce heart of wildness.

A few feet behind Karen and me on the top of the hill there is a statue of the one who is "full of grace." Here she is known as "Our Lady of Carmel." This is the Mount Carmel in my corner of the Americas, a hill of remnant grassland perched atop the watershed I think of as my home range. Christians have been busy renaming heights of land "Mount Carmel" since they first jumped off the boats and walked uphill. This Mount Carmel, a graceful rise of mixed-grass prairie 1,987 feet above sea level, is a mountain only in our fondest imaginings. From the top, though, a pilgrim gains the view that made its namers think of alpine. Four hundred miles of skyline encircle us here, all of it arcing around farmland that, before a colony of German settlers arrived with their plowshares, was one small cove on the northern coastline of this continent's inland sea of grass. Only the crests, this one and its outliers, have kept their pelt. The native grass in small tatters now, I can make out in the middle distance gray remnants, two or three acres here and there, where the slope was too steep, the soil too stony, for the plow.

Mary wasn't the first virgin to honor this prominence with her spirit. Local legend suggests that a girl named Hattie McKay may have died here 130 years ago—before anyone claimed the hill for Our Lady of Carmel. In Hattie's time, the generation that preceded the ones who turned the sod wrong side up, this hill had other names. An early map calls it "Keespitanow Hill," a story calls it "Big Butte," a local history says "Round Hill."[1] Sir William Butler, romancing his way across the Great Lone Land with an eye out for anything that might make a good chapter in his memoir, conceived the hill's name in phonetics that would roll off the tongue of a Victorian reader:

> The hill of the Wolverine and the lonely Spathanaw Watchi have witnessed many a deed of Indian daring and Indian perfidy... Alone in a vast waste the Spathanaw Watchi lifts his head, thickets and lakes are at its base, a lonely grave at its top, around four hundred miles of horizon; a view so vast that endless space seems for once to find embodiment, and at a single glance the eye is satisfied with immensity. There is no mountain range to come up across the sky-line, no river to lay its glittering folds along the middle distance, no dark forest to give shade to foreground or to fringe perspective, no speck of life, no track of men. Nothing but the wilderness. Reduced to its nakedness, space stands forth with almost terrible grandeur.[2]

Butler published his florid travelogue in 1873, a year after Hattie died, but the hilltop grave he mentions could not have been hers. An old Métis plainsman, Isador Dumas, interviewed in 1928, recalled the day in 1872 when he built a coffin for Hattie. Isador and a friend, Alexander Ablais, dug a grave and buried her at the base of Mount Carmel. Hattie, or Henrietta McKay, was a Catholic—"Irish," says one of the accounts, which is the word that local histories will sometimes use to avoid the less appealing term *half-breed*. There were no Irishmen in this region before 1890, not full-blooded ones anyway; McKay is a common Métis name, and Fish Creek was a Métis settlement just up the river from Batoche. The story goes that she refused to marry an "Englishman," the euphemism for *Protestant*. Her parents were insistent for some unspecified reason. She may well have carried his baby, though the gloss of local legend carries no hint of that. Whatever its cause, her fear of life in his hands grew until she lit out for the hills one morning.

The first discalced Carmelite, first unshod Christian hermit in these parts, Hattie took refuge in the wild anchorage offered by a height of land her native flesh knew to be blessed and holy. Hers was the same half-wild impulse that sends us out to the country beyond our scribed and sheltered lives, looking to be saved but not safe, gone to thunder, bewildered by wind, hobbling on stones as old as starlight. But the Word had already diminished the oral tradition of her ancestors, suspending her somewhere between the old truth carried in narratives known and remembered in the heart's love of stories and the new sorcery of scripted truth. None of it bore the grandmother's warnings she needed, the injunction against eating water hemlock or camas bulb. Or had her *kōhkom* taught her the dangers of such plants and she sought them out at the foot of Keespitanow, choosing to return to earth rather than surrender like settled territory signed away in treaties? Either way, the death-from-life distilled within roots and leaves bore her down to the wet, rebirthing greenery that skirts this hill in spring.

Where are you now, Hattie McKay? They've searched this hillside over and your small bones are gone away. Did you whisper prayers to the one who is filled with grace, the patroness of all virgins who'd rather die than fall into the grasp of the unholy? *Hail Mary, full of grace*…words that spring to the lips of every

Catholic in times of fear and bewilderment.

"This is the first Sorrowful Mystery—The Agony in the Garden," my mother would announce before we launched into the first ten Hail Marys as my father drove the Dodge at five miles per hour into the oblivion of a January blizzard. To this day I associate Mary with bad prairie weather. We'd pray the rosary until a light from a farmhouse appeared and then my father would get out of the car and vanish into the white swirl while we chanted another decade from the backseat. Too many moments later he'd reemerge, open the door, and shout above the howl, "Okay, they can take us in. Let's go," and we'd follow him across the snow toward the yellow light that meant sanctuary from the storm.

Fear marks most of my early memories of the Virgin Mary. I remember hearing adults talk about her appearing to children at a "grotto." Steering clear of grottoes was easy in a prairie town, but the plastic figurine on my mother's dresser vexed me. As a small child given to nightmares, I'd often end up in my parents' bed before daybreak. One morning, I woke to find myself alone in the room—just me and the figurine, which seemed to be shimmering on the dresser. I stared at it, frozen in dread, and then the damn thing moved, just a little, a trick of the half-light and my imagination. I threw off the covers and bolted from the room, never to sleep there again.

I was terrified, in the way only a child can be, that I would be chosen for a visitation. Right now, on this hill named for Elijah's mountain, I wouldn't mind a sign of some sort. A little reassurance would be appreciated. I settle in next to Karen on her boulder and wrap an arm around her small form. We've decided to wait for the sun to set. There's dust in the air from harvest so it should be a good show. Holding on to the woman who long ago decided she can put up with my ways, I am thinking of all that has fled embrace: Hattie and her people, the surviving wildness, the spirit of rural life. Most remote of all, though, are the mystical forces of redemption and prophecy carried forward in our traditions of Mary and Elijah. This has not been a week for hope. You wonder if we have a prayer. Maybe that's all we have.

# PILGRIMS

---

The first time I came to this hill, I hitchhiked. I was planning
to be away for several days, staying at the Benedictine abbey
a few miles east of the shrine, so I wanted to leave the car behind
for Karen.

On the highway north of the city I watched trucks and RVs
go by my outstretched thumb for a half an hour before a big blue
Buick with a lawnmower handle sticking out of the trunk pulled
over. The driver was an Indian man, about my age, alone. He was
heading up to Gordon Reserve in the Touchwood Hills and could
take me as far as his turnoff. Music from a country station played
low on the radio, and three ribbons dangled from the rearview
mirror: black, white, and red.

"You ever been up to Gordon?"

I said I had once, to do some walking in the hills, and then asked
him if people on the reserve had seen any cougars this year.

"Oh yeah—a few. Cougars, bears, elk, even wolves now and
then."

He told me about a large black bear his neighbor had shot.
"Fifth largest on record for the continent, they said."

What about ravens?

"Yep—lots. I never saw them in the hills when I was a kid, but
now they're all over the place."

Eagles?

"Lots," he said, "even in summer."

We passed a new buffalo ranch, one of many to arise in recent years, and he told me about a friend at Gordon who keeps bison.

I asked about construction on the Touchwood Reserves—wondering if more work was underway to improve living conditions. He said they had telephone service now and there was a new pipeline being built to introduce modern water and sewage systems. They had always used cisterns. The reserve is seven by eight miles, but most of it is bush so almost everyone lives along a narrow strip that follows a couple of roads. There is a small piece of farmland on the top, enough to keep two band members busy. Most members live in towns and cities, he said. If they all wanted to come home at once, there would be nowhere to put them. The band council is working on a land claim, though, so they may get more room eventually.

He'd lived in the city with his family for years—until 1987. He still wonders if he should have stayed there, at least until the kids finished their education. "When we moved back they started getting in trouble a bit. Too many people just let their kids run here and there and do whatever they want whenever they want, but we had a curfew, a time they had to be home in bed." Now his oldest ones are back in the city taking university classes.

Then he told me about a recent car accident on another one of the Touchwood Reserves. It had been in the papers the week before. A carload of young people, a bridegroom and his friends, on the way to a wedding in a brand-new sport utility vehicle. They rolled it on an open stretch of road. The RCMP said it rolled so many times the passengers were tossed out of the windows in every direction. They found seven people in the ditches and fields: five dead, two in critical condition.

"I used to do some hiking myself." He smiled, remembering something. "There is this guy from Gordon who goes hiking every summer all over the States. In the spring, he just walks out to the highway, puts out his thumb, and heads south. He travels all summer long and then returns in time for winter."

"Why *Gordon* Reserve? Doesn't sound like the other reserve names."

"It was the name they gave our chief when he signed the treaty way back; they couldn't say his real name and it translated into English badly—'Walks-on-four-claws'—so they called him Gordon.

"My mother was Métis, from Manitoba, and a Catholic. She told us the Catholics were kind and good people and they didn't swear. She never had a chance to go to school so she wanted us kids to go to a Catholic school, residential school."

I asked if it was any better than the Anglican school on Gordon Reserve where children had been molested and beaten for decades.

"It was the same—barbed wire, like we were in prison, and we were. We did all the farm work for them, it was a lot of work. Every night I could hear screams coming from down the hall. If some kid wet the bed, they'd tie the soaked sheet around his head and make him go to the mess hall like that. Oh, shit, yeah, we saw those priests kissing the little girls all the time, right in front of us. They didn't care. They knew we couldn't do nothing about it. The nuns sometimes too—took boys back to their rooms. But they were only human—everyone's got sexual urges, you know. We always wondered though—you know, those nuns were always so fat and then the next year they'd come back skinny again. That place closed down in the 1970s. It's a place for bad kids now, eh? But they were doing some construction out behind that old building and they found a bunch of graves—little ones, unmarked graves."

I asked him if Christian missionaries ever show up at his reserve these days.

"No—well, just those ones from the city who tell people if they donate to some church it'll save their souls."

He pulled over and stopped at the place where he had to turn east off the highway. I stepped out of the car, thanked him for the ride and conversation, and watched him disappear up the gravel road that leads to the Touchwood Hills.

Forty-some motor homes, semitrailers, and half-tons whizzed by before a mud-spattered truck slowed to a stop on the shoulder. I threw my pack into the back and jumped into the cab, nearly sitting on an enormous set of binoculars.

The driver, a man of ample proportions, apologized for the gear strewn across the seat and began to talk. He uses the binoculars to keep an eye on his cattle. Four hundred head, mostly on a pasture run by a friend who lives on Kawacatoose Reserve.

But cattle are just a sideline for him—he's in the construction business, owns his own company. Specializes in water and sewage projects on reserves. Doing one on Kawacatoose right now, in fact. Been working for Indian bands for twenty-five years now. It's good— they get to know him, and he always hires local reserve labor when he does a job. Been working on reserves all over the north too. His operation comes to a reserve completely self-contained, a complete camp, water, housing, food, and power plant—the whole shebang. Comes in, hires local workers, does the job, and pulls out.

"City people don't understand the conditions on some of these reserves—you just don't until you see it yourself. Up on that reserve by Carrot River, the kids there act like they're scared of you. They run off and hide in the bush. Everyone there lives in twenty-by-twenty-four-foot homes. You wouldn't believe the conditions there—it's backward, real backward. They were using cisterns all full of crud on the bottom, three inches of it and then that'd get all stirred up every time they refilled it. And the violence they live with. Gave a band councillor's daughter a lift into town once so she wouldn't have to hitch a ride. That girl was nice, just a real nice kid, y'know, and she said she'd been raped eight times by men on her reserve. She was thirteen. They shoot ducks all summer long on that reserve. There's a smokehouse behind every home. They live on smoked duck meat. Had some. Tasted pretty good.

"Shame about that accident up in the Touchwood Hills. Five kids killed. A terrible thing, to lose that many young kids at once. But they say that the mother who owned the car—it was new, eh—she got a notice in the mail a day or two after the accident, telling her the car was being recalled for a steering malfunction. Makes sense—it was eleven-thirty in the morning. Sure they were kids, but they probably weren't drinking at that hour."

And we talked about farming practices. He doesn't use sprays. Doesn't have to—he's only growing cattle feed. Still, he won't go anywhere near the stuff. "The guy that owns this land here, he doesn't use artificial fertilizers, just takes all the manure from his cattle corrals and spreads it over his fields. Now, look over there on the other side of the highway. That guy uses fertilizers and his crop's nowhere near as good. Nowadays guys will come and haul your manure away for nothing. The day's coming when you'll be able to sell the stuff by the ton. People are realizing they can't afford all these inputs—chemicals, nitrogen, and all that. They're afraid that all this continuous cropping is wearing the land out. Some are going back to a fallow rotation. This guy on the right over here— he's going organic. One more year and he'll be certified. Lot of guys going organic these days. There's an engineer who farms organic not far from here and he's a vegetarian. Won't eat anything unless he grew it himself. Doesn't trust the system. And that's an engineer. Oops. *(Turns the radio volume up a notch.)* That's Shardelle—she's a local girl. That's her new song they're playing."

A few miles roll by as he tells me how he met the woman he lives with. He knew her and her husband. They had four children together. "The husband was a good guy, heck of a plumber. He could do anything with his hands, but as soon as he had twenty dollars in his pocket he'd go and get drunk. She told him it was her and the kids or the liquor. After a while he started in on the kids whenever he was drinking. Finally had to go and get her and the kids one day. The guy was drunk in the basement with a rifle, shooting up through the main floor and the kids were all looking for a place to hide. Yep, on a Friday you're footloose and single and on Monday you've got a woman and four kids to look after. Didn't have much then. Lived on a little farm, kept some cattle, pigs, chickens, grew a garden. The kids seemed to thrive on it—they all grew up good. One girl's a secretary in the city. One of the boys has been working with me on construction for fourteen years now. Not sure how people do it in the city—couldn't live there a week. Found a fawn by the farm a few days ago—figured someone had shot the mother, so I took it in and got some milk formula from a guy who farm-raises whitetails. But she just wasn't a thriver. Died after a couple days. Damn they're cute. I fed deer all last winter. Put out a barley trough for them and they left my hay bales alone. Lots of other guys had trouble with deer spoiling their bales, but I didn't get any of that."

On the roadside again afterward, I stared at the pebbles and weeds and found the forewing of a blue butterfly no larger than the nail on my little finger. There was a dead bumblebee too and a fritillary of some kind. Savanna sparrows fluttered across the highway to declaim their buzzy quatrains from fence posts. Barn and tree swallows swooped overhead. On the road, young people in sports cars, retired folks in camper vans, farmers in half-tons, and families in minivans all sped on by, following the same shallow orbit to the horizon. Two hours passed before a white Dodge utility van slowed to a stop. It was a meat wagon heading back to the processing plant in a town up the road.

"Just returning from a delivery. Saw you when I was heading south and thought you might never get a ride."

He pointed to a buffalo herd in a roadside pasture. I asked if the buffalo ranchers get more income from the hides and skulls or for the meat.

"Oh, the meat, for sure. We do a lot of buffalo these days, more of it all the time."

He went on talking about the price dropping to parity with beef and told me a story about a fellow from one of the local reserves who'll bring in a buffalo or two now and then. They slaughter the animals, carve and package the meat up for him, and then he goes back to the reserve with his pickup truck and one guy stands in the back handing out the brown-paper packages to folks as they drive up and down the roads. I asked how they kill the buffalo and he said they use a gun, same as for cattle, only larger calibre, a 30.30. I thought about asking him if anyone makes kosher buffalo.

Talk turned to the five kids from the reserve killed in the accident, and then he dropped me off on the west side of his town, in view of the abattoir. "Provincially Inspected Custom Killing," it said in two-foot-high Helvetica type.

In five minutes I was picked up by a truck driver hauling a semitrailer load of new minivans bound for dealers along his route. He would be home that night after fourteen days and 120 hours of hauling. He didn't mind working for the car dealers, though you can't trust them—"they're the worst gougers you'll come across. But they get it at the other end too. Quite a change from working on reserves. Used to haul for construction companies building sewage and waterlines on reserves. Some reserves have lots of money and the people are just like you and me, but other places there's no money and things get rough. This one place, they smashed every piece of glass on every vehicle in the construction crew. Don't know if it was kids or what, but the old folks weren't friendly either. Didn't seem to care about getting water. They were used to things the way they were. That summer a man on the reserve took his rifle and shot his neighbor just like that."

Then he mentioned the five dying in the rollover. Buffalo never came up.

The last mile slipped by in silence before we stopped at the turnoff to the abbey where I was to stay. I thanked the driver, jumped out of his truck cab, shouldered my pack, and started to walk with a warm wind at my back.

# AT THE RIVERSIDE

---●---

As altitudinous as it feels when you are here, the "climb" that leads up Mount Carmel hardly merits the word. Even for my flatlander thighs it is an easy skip along either a gently sloped trail through the woods, marked at intervals with the fourteen stations of the cross, or a steeper, shorter route up the patch of prairie on its southwestern side. Today we followed the way of the cross spiraling up the flanks of the hill, around the shaded north face through hazel and poplar bush. Some of the larger trees succumbed during a recent windstorm, prostrating themselves before the fieldstone monuments that hold the images of Christ's Passion.

Sitting here in front of the hilltop shrine on a rock formed in Devonian seas, I can feel the wind taking command again. Toward the horizon, though, there is a haze hanging in the air, making it impossible to see most of the church steeples that dot the countryside. Likely dust from harvest, which is all but finished now in the second week of September. At every turn of the compass the inland grain terminals, new concrete titans astride the wounded earth, rise through the haze that covers Saint John's, Saint Bernard's, Saint Anthony's, Saint Joseph's, Saint Augustine's, and Saint Peter's—churches raised in the early twentieth century by German Benedictines. I point out to Karen Our Lady's Church at the nearby hamlet of Carmel. Farther off to the southeast we can just make out the top of Saint Peter's Abbey where we stayed last night.

A century ago, the Benedictine brothers stood on this hill and faced this same direction. Scouting for land where they could build a colony centered on an abbey—what was to become the northernmost Benedictine monastery in the New World and the first in Canada—they saw fertile grassland running to the horizon, dotted with sloughs and lakes, and a small creek running south. All of it virtually uninhabited, for the Cree, Saulteaux, and Nakota had been moved onto reserves twenty years earlier. Within a few weeks, the monks and priests were living in tents alongside the creek, a muddy stream named the Wolverine—an animal that we often think of as a symbol of the wild, though in the hunters' stories of this continent it has represented gluttony. Each time they entered the tent chapel they would bless themselves with creekwater held in a limestone basin that one of the fathers had dug out of the hillside and placed upon a tripod of poplar staves. The German-Catholic colonists were already arriving, filling up the countryside and building the town of Muenster (German for "monastery") beside the Wolverine and its new religious community. They came, knowing that the Benedictines were there ahead of them, putting together an outpost of agrarian Christian civilization that would make the wilderness less daunting, more familiar. It was a model the order had applied across Europe on both sides of the Rhine for nearly fifteen hundred years, since Saint Benedict smashed the temple to Apollo upon Monte Cassino and replaced it with the monastery that launched the Western monastic tradition of rural religious community.

Once, in the library at Saint Peter's, I came across the legends of Saint Boniface, another Benedictine afoot among the unbaptized. In the stories, he walks into pagan Bavaria with a great ax and fells Thor's sacred oak with a single blow. The scruffy barbarians convert holus-bolus as the rabble atop Cassino and Hakkarmel had centuries before. Boniface marches on throughout the Germanic countryside baptizing pagans for twenty-five years until one Pentecost

Sunday a band of Frisians slay him in the act of reading scripture to his latest converts.

There was no converting of savages nor martyrdom to pagan knives for the men who built Saint Peter's Abbey beside Wolverine Creek. Themselves the descendants of the wild Bavarians Christianized by Saint Boniface, they managed to keep apart from the government's program of civilizing the people of the plains. Still, there was this hill to sanctify in the name of Christ as their founder had at Monte Cassino centuries ago. No pagan shrines to smash this time. In fact, a crude cross made of poplar limbs greeted them on the hilltop the day the Benedictines arrived—placed there by mixed-blood Christians who had been calling the place Mount Carmel since Hattie died twenty years earlier.

Not long after the abbey was built and the village of Muenster anchored to its side, the lay and religious members of Saint Peter's Colony set out to make Mount Carmel into a fit shrine for Catholic pilgrimage and devotion. Once they took possession of the land containing the hill, part of which was donated by the original homesteader, the colonists over the next twenty years erected the monuments typical of Catholic pilgrimage sites the world over.

As shrines go, this Mount Carmel would not be considered impressive: a small, open-air chapel with limestone walls, fourteen art deco stations of the cross mounted on fieldstone cairns, and, on the summit, a statue of Our Lady of Carmel and the infant Jesus on a high concrete pedestal. Its spiritual significance and appeal comes in large part from the care invested in the place by all the hands and feet of those who over the years have hewed the stones, mortared the monuments, trimmed the bush, and served the coffee, turkey sandwiches, and saskatoon-berry pie—doing the work that would allow them to return on other days to walk the trail of sorrow and kneel before the mother of God.

The annual pilgrimage honoring Our Lady of Carmel is held here every July just as the saskatoon berries are ripening. The year I went, little squalls of rain came intermittently from the west throughout the pilgrimage Mass. No one complained, for most gathered there were farm people who had been praying for moisture since spring. They sat on the hillside in lawn chairs and on blankets, some with umbrellas, most making do without, all facing the grotto where the abbott presided over Mass. When it ended, everyone gathered at the base of the hill to share a lunch and visit a while before returning home to farm, town, and village. A small devout crew remained to follow the stations of the cross together. By that time I was in the woods on the south side of Mount Carmel, with an ice-cream pail hooked onto my belt, picking saskatoon berries that I swear were swelling as it rained.

I was well hidden beneath poplars and an understory of saskatoon bush, but only a few paces from the fifth station of the cross. In the absentmindedness of berrypicking, with rain running down my hands and rinsing the purple juice from my knuckles, I listened to the murmuring approach of the pilgrims. Verses of their song drifted along the pathway and reached my ears, mingled with the patter of the rain hitting leaves and the sharp *kersnap* of an undaunted least flycatcher:

> O thou mother, font of love
> Touch my spirit from above,
> Make my heart with yours accord.

All day I had been feeling aloof at the ceremonies, a little uneasy in my status as stranger and observer among ardent believers, many of whom had been making this pilgrimage since early childhood. I knew I did not belong, yet I was once again possessed by something I feel from time to time when I'm at Mount Carmel or the abbey itself. There in the rain-drenched bush, I think I understood the feeling for the first time. I saw that it is in places such as this, among the Benedictines and the community they serve, that the riverside longings of Jacob, in fear, remorse, and hope, find expression as we assess the wounds of our estrangement and search for ways to reconcile, which is ever and always to come into the presence of God. From here I can believe in a more expansive way to spirit, one big enough to include all movement that is truly *re-ligious*, that is grounded in the search for the tie that binds: self and other, civilization and wildness, rural and urban, orthodox and reformer, pagan and Christian.

As the procession came to the fieldstone station near me, I drew back into the shadows and watched. I recognized the leader, Brother Basil, whom I am accustomed to seeing on a tractor seat and dressed in jeans, shirt, and ball cap. Instead, he was looking sharp in a fedora and cassock. When they had finished reciting the prayers for the fifth station and moved on up the trail a ways, I slipped out of the woods and fell into line. Coming to the next station, Basil turned, saw me, and asked if I would read the prayer:

> Lo, we have seen him, and there is no beauty in him nor comeliness; he is despised and the most abject of men, a man of sorrows and acquainted with infirmity. His countenance is as it were hidden, whereupon we esteemed him not. His appearance is inglorious among us. And yet he is the beautiful one above all of humanity, and by his bruises we are healed.

# FRESH WOUNDS

⸻ • ⸻

Autumn is the season of dispersal and drift. Here on the leeward side of Our Lady, there are spiders ballooning away, lifting into the golden air on gossamer strands fired by twilight. They are prayers made visible, or questions drifting from Creator to created and back again.

It is a movement that happens in the sweat lodge on hilltops just like this one. On his day of atonement, a man crawls into the lodge's dark womb. He is broken, spent, from years of indulging every appetite and now he comes desperate for help. Having served nothing outside of his own hungers and thirsts, he has wagered and lost everything—health, family, community, hope. There he sprawls naked and bloated, prostrate before the assembled Grandfathers, the wise ones of granite and gneiss who have lived to guard the prairie world and prang the plow and who now lend the orange glow of their primordial, igneous heat. He wants answers as much as he wants another drink, but all that he receives, after the prayers and chants lifted upon the burning air and scorching waves of steam, are more questions. Through the one who pours water, the Grandfathers speak: "Why are you here? What will be your walk in this place?"

The stones on this hillside and every other one murmur these same questions. As we truck minivans to market, butcher farm-raised buffalo, build sewage systems on reserves, drive into the city to retrieve a lawn mower, we remain deaf to their whispers. Then one day we're called into the morgue to identify a son or daughter killed in a rollover on the way to a wedding. That is when we hear the Grandfathers: "Why are you here? What will be your walk in this place?"

Each of us answers day to day, year to year, in the choices we make, in all that we do and leave undone. Just now, though, on this rock at the foot of Our Lady, as we wait for the sky to darken above the aggrieved nations of this continent, the questions seem directed at our entire civilization: Why are we here? What will be our walk in this place?

That crucifix of poplar logs was raised here in Hattie's time by people who risked much and crossed oceans to find a land that had not yet been yoked to human will. Knowing they could die of hunger, cold, or a dozen other perils, they came anyway. Christianity, needing resurrection after resurrection, has hung the Divine in the world in every one of its advances. On these northern plains, the desperate and the foolhardy led whole ecologies, landscapes, nations, and cultures up to the heights of Golgotha to be scourged and condemned, mocked and pierced through to the miracle of their flesh and blood. Now that so much is in the tomb, we beat our breasts and wonder why the antelope and sage grouse are disappearing, where the prairie crocus bloom has gone, who to blame for residential schools, how our farm communities will survive. In resignation and despair we give up on our dreams of renewal in wildness and turn away to walk the road of easy consolation. We forget why we came in the first place.

I do not know what new life is fermenting within all that has been tilled into the soil of this continent, but I wonder if its green shoots will show first here, at its marginal center. Our hothouse civilization will wither on the vine sooner or later, leaving this land to the hardy, half-wild perennials who persist yet in places such as this where people still have a chance of learning the answers to those questions. Midwives, hunters, shepherds, and saints are the ones who foster the seed bank that bears humanity forth from the collapse of one civilization to the rise of the next. When it comes, and come it must, who will we huddle next to if it is not these quiet ones who still know how to moderate the mysteries of life and death? Here, in the center of the continent but far from its centers of power and privilege, we have a disproportionate share of North America's pagan stock—folks who have chosen to dwell beyond the walls of the polis. Saskatchewan is the most rural province in Canada. Thousands of Indians, farmers, and ranchers still live in the countryside, and even our towns and cities are filled with the recent refugees of rural living, people who can show you how to net fish under the ice, butcher a hog, plant barley, dig a root cellar, witch water, deliver a breech calf, skin a beaver, bury the dead in winter.

As nonindigenous people leave to take up the comforts of large urban centers in the east and west and the birthrate meanwhile rises among indigenous and mixed-blood peoples, we are distilling down to a population of those who can't leave and those who want to stay, and we are beginning to see in each other's faces features much like our own. No telling yet what it is, but something new is rising in this convergence. I remember Father Ron Rolheiser saying once that God sends us wild men and women when we need them. Saints, he said, like Francis of Assisi, head off into the countryside, dream their dreams, and we receive a new spirituality that sustains us for seven hundred years.

What if the missionaries had it exactly backward and they were sent to the New World not to convert but to undergo conversion and convergence? We are fascinated to hear of those early missionaries, Spanish and French Jesuits, who "went native" when they arrived in the Americas—partly because we see it as an anomaly in the main narrative, but also because we wonder if it was a better way to God, if it contains a mythic truth we need to walk in this land.

The standard myth of our colonial adventure clatters from our tongues unredeemed by forethought. You hear it from mouths, both indigenous and nonindigenous, the base narrative that runs beneath our everyday discourse, our political wrangling, and our regard for past events and present tensions: White men ventured across the waters to a land where original hunting peoples lived an Edenic existence. Missionaries, conquistadors, sailors, criminals, peasants, and religious outcasts made the crossing first, drawn by a longing for riches or paradise of one kind or another. And then they stormed the gates and yanked the citizens of Eden into the fallen world where they have ever since been forced to live by the sweat of their brow—vanquished people in a vanquished land.

No myth can end that way, like a railway trestle halfway across a canyon. There has to be a coming round again, to where the end meets the beginning. More than tragedy for an indigenous utopia, the coming together of the children of Jacob and the children of Esau is spawning something that we cannot see in our lament for lost ecologies and lifeways. The wounds are still too fresh, the graves too recently filled, to say what it means to live among people who by the reach of their narratives and religious practice remain so much nearer the unappropriated wildness that animates the Creation.

Something pagan in the souls of our immigrant ancestors longed for this world and its unfettered energies. The braver sons of Jacob came, believing they would tame the land and convert the heathen, but it was the wildness of this place that woke them in the middle of the night and stirred within them a restlessness to emigrate. The more comfortable and civilized stayed behind. My one grandfather came here as a teenager with dreams of deer on the heath and fish in the creek. The rest of his eighty-three years he dedicated to one stretch of the valley, hunting, fishing and trapping, running cattle, smoking fish, raising pigs and honeybees, making whiskey. He set foot outside the watershed but once and that was to retrieve some cattle mistakenly shipped to the stockyards in a distant city. I have a photograph of a brother he left behind in Scotland, taken when the man was in his retirement. A banker all his life, he is wearing a tweed suit, vest, and tie and standing in his Edinburgh garden among the dahlias and Canterbury bells. Though he is my great-uncle and clearly has the outsized ears and legs I inherited from my grandfather, there is a gulf between my heritage and his that blood cannot span.

We, the grandsons and granddaughters of immigrants, are the inheritors of a longing that has not quite gone away. We feel it yet when we sit on hilltops like this one. It pulls us into the tragedy and poetry we've spun from the history of our colonizing. It is there in our spiritual curiosity, drawing us to places where the Grandfathers can murmur their questions to us; there making the hairs on your neck tingle when the radio tuner stops on the community station long enough for you to hear a drumbeat and voices chanting in the high-pitched tones of an intertribal song; when the scent of sage and sweetgrass from an old woman at the end of the pew mingles with the candle wax and incense smells of the sanctuary.

We arrived on these shores longing for bewilderment, starved for mysteries not yet translated, creatures unnamed, gods untaken. Having all but forgotten the animals in our beginnings, in our stories, and in our bellies, we played out the drama of Jacob and Esau. Birthright swindled from starving hunters, blessings gained in pretense and cunning from the blind generosity of creation and Creator, we banished Esau with the power of the ink-borne animism whose fresh tracks are printed now all over this world no longer new. It wasn't guns and steel and tall ships that separated the hunters from their land and its spiritual power. It was the new power of the word, the inevitable and inexorable transformation unleashed by men wielding texts, sacred and profane, that has sent the children of Esau into bewilderment, tasting the dust of exile the Hebrews tasted first—the long cycles of oppression and estrangement, of broken covenants, of spiritual longing, of leaving

Creator and tradition only to return again. Together we have been riding a tidal wave of human inquiry raised by the tremors that ensued when people of the word, convinced of their rights under gods of heaven and science, fell upon the shores of this planet's last great store of natural and spiritual riches.

The children of Jacob have come lately to the riverside in guilt and fear, our dreams of renewal and prosperity turned to nightmares of wrestling with ancestral spirits, the hunters' guardian. Plundered gold and silver may have financed the centuries of war among the colonizing empires, but the fight that defines us now is our ambivalent embrace of the people whose blood has known these hills and plains the longest. We can no longer let the missionaries do our spirit grappling for us.

Wounded and wiser, Jacob hobbles across that river, looking for reconciliation and bearing the gifts he has always given to Esau. In his brother's arms he hears the hollow ring of his apologies and learns that his gifts have always exacted a price:

*Accept as gift this word, this text that translates mystery, that cannot be divided from the other tools that it has spawned and which you have already taken as your own. It was your accepting these other gifts that silenced the voices of your land. The spirits that once spoke in the voices of buffalo, rock, and river have been harnessed to grander schemes, shunted, without ceremony or sacrifice, into service of human desire. By this river, in your embrace, we are coming to see that spirit and matter are confluent. We have been naively unleashing the spiritual energy contained in matter, digging minerals from the earth, pulping trees into paper, burning fossil lives of ancestors. Your forbears were intimately familiar with these energies in the personages our forbears dismissed as totems and idols for the primitive and superstitious—Bear, Eagle, Sun, Moon—the many faces of the One particularized in creatures and manifestations that mediate between human desire and the rest of creation. Where the wisest of your people and ours once proceeded with due respect and caution in dealing with the spirit in matter, most of us now are crude and unsophisticated in our encounter with the powers of creation. If we now seem to cling to you in our dreams it is only because we are beginning to see that ours is a culture inflated on illegitimate access to the resources of this land, and that the modern cult of materialism has been fattened on energies unleashed in the misappropriation of the natural wealth of these continents. The consequences of our unholy confiscation are falling nearer to our own doorsteps all the time and we are now getting glimpses of the disarray that attends upon the passage of so much energy through so few hands.*

Pentecost happens in that embrace. Brothers may reconcile, see the face of God in one another, when they remember their beginnings in a single womb, within the maternal axis mundi, the place where there is always a mother brooding over the troubled world with unfailing love, humility, and faith.

I follow the wind as it shudders through the short-cropped grass beneath Our Lady of Carmel, until my eyes come to rest upon the remnant blossoms of low everlasting, a plant that grows in frowsy circles on this hilltop. Eternal flowers—remember that, Holy Mother? It took an Indian to charge you with the energy of a Tonantzin, turn you into Our Lady of Guadelupe, empty a cloak full of roses before the archbishop, and burn a new image of your grace, with brown skin and a shimmering robe of stars, upon the walls of the cathedral.

Don't leave us now, Mother of the Wind, at shrines like this. Take us with you into the upper room where you are always welcoming the Pentecost, always undergoing the winds of translation, receiving the fire of a new spirit, and then emerging with yet another name, another story.

# SONGS

———————————————•———————————————

*You are not here to verify,*
*Instruct yourself, or inform curiosity*
*Or carry report. You are here to kneel*
*Where prayer has been valid.*

—T. S. Eliot, "Little Gidding"

That first hitchhiking trip to Mount Carmel I stayed for several days at Saint Peter's Abbey nearby. Evenings I would join the brothers in the chapel for vespers, struggling gamely to follow the rapid shifts in tone that often play within a single syllable of Benedictine psalmody. *Psalm* is thought to have roots in the Hebrew word *zmr*, which means "plucked." They were written as true lyric poems, meant to be accompanied by the plucking of a lyre. One-third of the psalms are orphans, the identities of those who recorded them perhaps lost in the transfer from oral tradition to scripture. A few are thought to have been written down by Moses, Solomon, and an assortment of other figures, but half of them, at least seventy-three, were written by David, the shepherd who became king.

Among the first songs to be exiled in the word, the psalms were for a time drawn back into the oral tradition when Saint Benedict made them part of the order's liturgy of the hours, the daily sequence of devotion that consecrates every hour to God. According to Father Andrew Britz,[1] the Benedictine priest who edits the intelligent and scripturally radical newspaper Saint Peter's produces, their tradition of psalm singing began with Benedict encouraging his monks, many of whom could not read, to commit the 150 psalms to memory. Particularly devoted monks were known to recite the entire psalter daily. I had trouble remembering page numbers whispered to me by the sympathetic brothers sitting behind me in the pews.

As my time at the abbey passed, though, I became more comfortable with the psalm singing, and by week's end the pattern was familiar and reassuring. Each night the poetry of shepherd-kings lifted to the clerestory, chanted first by one whose voice resonated with ancestral undertones that have drifted from culture to culture, religion to religion, and continent to continent. Each psalm begins with an introductory tone from the organist followed by the chanting of one of the monks who acts as the cantor for the week. The organ falls silent and he picks up where it left off, singing a first line from the psalm. Then the others join in, reciting the verses until the psalm is through. The cantor during my first stay was one of the older men in the abbey. As he stood to sing he held on to the supports on the pew in front of him with hands that have been used for harder work than turning pages, and he raised his head slightly, closing his eyelids beneath a brow furrowed by more than contemplation. His lips parted and a voice escaped that was oddly pleasant and mournful all at once. Listening to the first line of the psalm—one of the suffering servant poems—filling the chapel space and reverberating in my own breast, I was distracted, thinking, "That voice, what *is* it about that voice?" Then it came to me: the wind powering his voice was vibrating at a low frequency, but the sound was dampened in his head, giving it a raw drone, a muted cry. It was that "voice like a bee up a flue" again, from half-pagan Celts singing tragic tales at fireside, the same one I've heard on old bluegrass records. It crossed the Atlantic in the memories of peasants and survives even today, albeit under a layer of Nashville varnish, in the "hurtin' songs" of this continent's rural music.

After the cantor plucked the bittersweet chord of one who has lived, spoken, sung, cried, sinned, and begged forgiveness, the rest of us on his side of the chapel joined in, adding our voices to the ancient communal song-prayer. A fine moment of communion it was, for the mere addition of our voices said, "Yes, brother, we hear you, we've been there too."

The body of the psalm is sung in antiphon, the two sides of the chapel chanting in serene, even tones back and forth to one another. The pews on either side face inward in ranks, like the two galleries of a parliament. Abbeys did it first, says Father Andrew. The barons of Britain adopted the design, literally, when they began using the confiscated Chapel of Saint Stephen, Westminster, as their House of Commons.

A good deal more peaceful than a House of Commons, a Benedictine chapel at vespers becomes a place of contemplative group prayer. Directing our voices inward, there is no escaping the sense of singing to and being sung to. At times, when all the voices align well, as they usually do when singing the doxology used at the end of each psalm—"to the God who was, who is, and who *shall* be, forever and ever, amen"—you can hear and feel the roomful of men inhale and exhale as one. Their breathing for a moment falls into the rhythm of meditation, and it is possible to imagine a holy spirit shared among us.

The poetry in the psalms, even in translation, is concrete and vivid, a verbal ligature binding human desire, joy, anger, and sorrow to the mythic and heroic elements forged in man's relationship with God. Long after you've left the chapel, snatches of verse stay with you, and your mind runs with rivers that clap their hands, deer that long for flowing streams, and a god who rides on the wings of the wind. The words of Psalm 126, with its dee-dah-dah, dee-dah-dah rhythm, took several days to fade from my memory.

They go out, they go out, full of tears,
carrying seed for the sowing;
they come back, they come back, full of song,
carrying their sheaves.

It is so easy to let the images and the aesthetics of evensong wash over you when you know you will be going home soon to places where no one sings daily psalms. For those who stay, there must be times when the liturgy of hours grinds along from day to day in numbing tedium. The mind drifts away from prayerfulness, the body waits for the familiar closing.

Toward the end of vespers, when stomachs are growling in anticipation of supper (will it be roast chicken with mashed potatoes and turnips, perhaps beef, peas, and scalloped potatoes? Raspberry crumble for dessert?), the monks sing "Mary's Magnificat," a song of praise, humility, and submission before God. The words of this canticle come from the first chapter of Luke's gospel. Mary has already had the visit from the angel Gabriel telling her she will bear a son whose kingdom will have no end. After an initial bout of resistance and incredulity that might be expected from an unmarried girl who hears that she will soon be impregnated by the Holy Spirit, Mary comes around. Just before Gabriel leaves, she gives her "fiat," saying "let it be done." Some time passes—Luke doesn't bother to say how much—and then Mary goes to visit her cousin Elizabeth.

Despite her old age, Elizabeth is preparing to birth a son of her own, the one who later becomes John the Baptist, the voice crying out in the wilderness. On Mary's arrival, the cousins embrace and Elizabeth, "filled with the Holy Spirit," exclaims, "Blessed are you among women, and blessed is the fruit of your womb." She tells Mary that the child in her own womb leapt for joy at their greeting. Mary's joyful reply, what we call the Magnificat, is not so much a speech as it is a song:

My soul proclaims the greatness of the Lord
and my spirit exults in God my saviour,
because he has looked upon His lowly handmaid.
Yes, from this day forward all generations
will call me blessed,
for the Almighty has done great things for me.
Holy is His name
and His mercy reaches from age to age
for those who fear Him.
He has shown the power of His arm.
He has routed the proud of heart.
He has pulled down princes from their thrones
and exalted the lowly.
The hungry He has filled with good things,
the rich sent empty away.
He has come to the help of Israel His servant,
mindful of His mercy
according to the promise He made to our ancestors
of His mercy to Abraham and to his descendants for ever.

There is an exultation in these lines that bursts forth like daffodils on sun-warmed soil. In his own "May Magnificat," the Jesuit poet Gerard Manley Hopkins asks why that month was given to Mary and his answer extrapolates the rising abundance within her until it fills all of creation:

Flesh and fleece, fur and feather,
Grass and greenworld all together;
Star-eyed strawberry-breasted
Throstle above her nested
Cluster of bugle blue eggs thin
Forms and warms the life within;
And bird and blossom swell

In sod or sheath or shell.

All things rising, all things sizing
Mary sees, sympathising
  With that world of good,
  Nature's motherhood.

Their magnifying of each its kind
With delight calls to mind
  How she did in her stored
  Magnify the Lord.

Well but there was more than this:
Spring's universal bliss
  Much, had much to say
  To offering Mary May.

Some versions of the "Magnificat" begin, "My soul *magnifies* the Lord." The same phrase in Hopkins's poem applied to nature and its fecund growth in spring makes me think of all the stories and rites of fertility goddess worship that predate Luke's gospel. *The Jerusalem Bible* includes a note pertaining to the "Magnificat" that suggests the song may have such earthy antecedents. In a sentence that shows well the intellectual courage of the people who worked on this translation—J. R. R. Tolkien among them—the editors say, "Luke must have found this canticle in the circles of the 'poor,' where it was perhaps attributed to the Daughters of Zion. He found it suitable to bring into his prose narrative and put on the lips of Mary."

That phrase, "Daughters of Zion," has various applications in Jewish tradition, but one of them seems to be linked to thinly veiled fertility rites that persisted into the Christian era. The "circles of the poor" have always found ways of keeping an ember or two from the old pagan fires alive and hidden away from the rabbis and priests who would rather see them extinguished once and for all. The coupling of god with goddess, of man with goddess, or woman with god is an earth-renewal myth that has been seeded into every agrarian civilization. You find it even in the Old Testament in such places as the Song of Solomon, in which a shepherd-king becomes the living male eros in nature uniting with its feminine equivalent in a ritual that consummates and renews the Creation. Jewish and Christian scholars, unwilling to admit the song's pagan origins, usually categorize it as secular love poetry, a harmless nuptial song and nothing more. Even so, there have been times when Jews under the age of thirty have been prohibited from reading its verses.

There is a primitive energy in this song that comes through in even a casual reading. As a ballad from the oral tradition committed to paper in the way other poetry of its era was, it shares some of the traits of pagan narrative verse in which mortals tangle with gods and goddesses in love and war. The same elevated descriptive language is here, too monumental and grand to apply to an erotic encounter between mere mortals. Here is a piece from the fourth chapter of the Song of Solomon:

> How beautiful you are, my darling!
> Oh, how beautiful!
> Your eyes behind your veil are doves.
> Your hair is like a flock of goats
> descending from Mount Gilead.
> Your teeth are like a flock of sheep just shorn,
> coming up from the washing.
> Each has its twin;
> not one of them is alone.
> Your lips are like a scarlet ribbon;
> your mouth is lovely.
> Your temples behind your veil

are like the halves of a pomegranate.
Your neck is like the tower of David,
built with elegance;
on it hang a thousand shields,
all of them shields of warriors.

At the end of the preceding chapter, the female lover says, "Go forth and gaze, daughters of Zion, on King Solomon and the crown with which his mother crowned him on his wedding day, on the day his heart was overjoyed." As late as the second century of the common era, young men in Jerusalem joined in a remnant fertility ritual in which they sang this scrap of the song to fresh-cheeked maidens dancing in the holy city's vineyards at dusk on the Day of Atonement.[2] The Song of Solomon is a powerful display of the pagan eros that still drives our religious becoming. Its survival in the accepted canons of the Jewish and Christian faiths testifies to an energy that persists even within the heart of dogma.

No one is more dogmatic than the postmodern critics who use other people's myth research to deconstruct Christianity and Judaism and show them to be merely derivative faiths. The theory seems to be that if an established religion shares characteristics with its religious ancestors it has no claim to legitimacy. Modern "neopagans" seem particularly vulnerable to this line of thinking, in effect falling prey to the very notions of religious purity and magical origins that have vexed the monotheists for so long. How we distinguish them from the guardians of church doctrine I am not certain, for they seem to labor beneath the same belief that any legitimate religion must somehow spring forth ex nihilo. In an era when revelations come weekly on the wings of science, proving to us again and again that everything under the sun is a work in progress, that all phenomena develop from earlier forms, it takes an obdurate turning away from truth and reason to cling to such a flimsy article of faith. If we believe in a divine order or principle dwelling in the nature of things, then why among all that moves in the universe would the human path to spirit be the one motion that is somehow exempt from its evolutionary exertions?

Everything in the cosmos has ancestors or an elementary form to which its characteristics can be traced. Religious practice, too, is successional. The gifts of one generation are passed through to the next, reproduced, and eventually mutated into new morphologies, new strategies for life. Still, we are not surprised when we hear Christian historians deny the primitive derivations of the faith. No, they say, Mithraism and other cults stole their rites from *us*, not the other way around, and Mary has nothing to do with fertility goddesses. We expect that from ecclesial circles and perhaps at some level we recognize, too, that we need the doctrine guardians, else we would have no medium of tradition to grow and regenerate within. Doctrine is the membrane that restricts but must not entirely cut off the transport of material that nourishes and regenerates a religion. That material, the particulars of the human response to spirit here and now, is moved by the pagan energy that is the richness and vigor of religion in its long inheritance of crossbreeding and mutation from one tradition to the next.

In Luke's gospel, Mary's response, her "yes," is a blossoming, an enlarging of the Creation that in the "Magnificat" spills over into a song of praise that recalls the feminine force in the Divine long celebrated by the old religions in the name of Innana, Astarte, or Ishtar. Overcoming all resistance to the entry of love, she surrenders completely to the role of *Theo-tokos* (Greek for "God-bearer"), allows it to appropriate her, conscript her as a vessel of the cosmogenesis, in a gesture that echoes and magnifies all previous and all subsequent submissions. And in her assent, that womb force in God's spirit acting through her life subverts the established pattern by which man conscripts the material of creation. The story arcs in a trajectory that holy people of many faiths have found worthy of following: God's ever-present invitation to be taken by the spirit, once accepted, leads to a life of praise and fruitfulness. This is what both Christian and Islamic mystics have called The Way of Mary, for the mystic, too, aspires to become a God bearer.

As I left the chapel on the final night of that first visit to Saint Peter's I found myself thinking about the kingdoms far beyond the monastery walls where the powerful are still on their thrones and the poor are sent away empty-handed. I would be returning the next day to a life that often seems an affront to the hopes expressed in the psalms and the "Magnificat," to a culture that vilifies God bearers. And I realized, too, that while I may detect something of the wildness in religion flickering in texts such as the "Magnificat" and the Song of Solomon, in the end these are only shadows trapped on the page by the appropriating power of the written word. I cannot touch the wild energy that dwells within a faith by reading and analyzing its old songs. If it happens at all, it will happen beyond the confines of the word, where there is grass and wind, a height of land, the possibility of fire.

# SCAPULAR I

---•---

This Mount Carmel was sacred to unknown and uncounted cultures, one succeeding the other, long before Hattie and her people came to lift hybrid prayers to Jesus and Manito. No holy place was holy first to Christians. Underlying Lourdes there are offerings from earlier people whose ways to the spirit we now reconstitute in the Eucharist. I look overhead to the towering statue of Mary, her face peach-golden tones in the failing light. She stares down at me with heavy-lidded eyes, and in the glow of twilight she is the image of all the goddesses she has subsumed. Like the Carrera marble the Italian sculptor carved her from eighty years ago, she bears all the illusions of solid timeless truth but moves in fact in a continuing metamorphosis. Look closely at the mother of God and you can see her own mothers, the ancient fossil lives of former divinities, their calcified structures not completely obliterated by the heat and pressure of time within earth. They sparkle across her skin in crystallized splendor.

Fifteen feet above the crest of the hill, the highest point for sixty miles in any direction, Our Lady of Carmel draws enough fire from the heavens to require lightning rods. Two cruciform protectors flank the monument and a wire across the top connects them just above Our Lady's head. Following the rods down to their bases where they are grounded deep within the hilltop, I find myself sinking back into the gloom that five days earlier descended on the continent's once inviolable kingdom.

For all my railing against the barriers we've built to protect our civilization and keep the otherness safely beyond, on Tuesday morning fear and confusion entered my blood as it did everyone else's when the infidels came knocking on the gates. It wasn't so much the images of Manhattan people running for cover or even the footage of the airliners plunging again and again into the towers. What got to me was the sudden and visceral realization that it really takes very little to blow a hole in our walls if someone is willing to be the lightning rod and let the energy released in self-sacrifice pass through his body and detonate the frightful power of tribal malice; that the force of sacrifice can be as destructive when harnessed to hate as it can be creative when harnessed to love. And religion was right there in the middle of things. American fundamentalists shouting, "God has seen our depravity and given us a warning," Islamic fundamentalists calling for jihad, and conservative Christians dusting off their "just war" treatises. Meanwhile, secular liberals were blaming all religion and quoting lines from John Lennon's "Imagine," as though it might be a new divine revelation.

We headed for the refuge of Mount Carmel and Saint Peter's yesterday, happy to escape the glib talk of war and the braggadocio of opinion leaders who know just how to protect us from the heathens. The world looks one step saner from here. It always does.

I awoke this morning with moisture in the corners of my eyes. The lines of a psalm we'd sung at vespers last night were with me again. It was the old shepherd's prayer, the first psalm any Catholic learns: "The Lord is my Shepherd / there is nothing I shall want / He leadeth me to lie down in green pastures." Jewish and Muslim people know the psalm too. It has words that all Middle Eastern people of all faiths can agree upon, just as they all claim descent from the same religious shepherd, Abraham. Beneath the memory of the chanted verses there stirred to life a residue of the dream I'd awoken from. An Islamic girl, a child, was patiently teaching me to read Arabic characters. Each glyph looked like a living creature or a person holding a graceful posture. One, I remember vividly, was a body reclining in lush grass, the psalmist's green pastures. I puzzled over the figures, as if under a spell, and when I finally saw that they were not so much phonetic symbols represent- ing tongue maneuvers as they were living characters describing with flesh and blood shifts in tonality and song, the realization washed over me in such a rush of clarity that I cried. It all seemed unspeakably beautiful. As though my skin could hear and my eyes feel, I absorbed bodily the wild ululation of each script and tried to express the sounds myself. And then we laughed, the child and I, at my ineptitude.

Later, after morning Mass, I walked out to a tiny grotto the monks have built in the shadowy pine and spruce woods north of the abbey. I sat down in the chair provided and faced the shrine, a modest statuette of Mary enclosed in glass. With the events of the week running through my mind and the knowledge that there were generals now plotting further horrors to be committed some- where in the mountains of Afghanistan, I could muster little regard for the lineage of deities that have accompanied us to this moment in history. I closed my eyes to Mary's indifferent stare and listened to the soughing of the big conifers. After a few minutes the notes of chickadees and nuthatches rose above the whisper of the trees, approaching nearer until their buoyant sounds rang in my ears. With a canopy of insistent birdcalls right overhead and the thwir- ring of wings nearby, I opened my eyes slowly and found seven chickadees hopping from branch to branch all around me. Taking care to make no abrupt movements, I reached into a pocket for one of the almonds I sometimes leave in coats and shirts. Finding one, I took it out and began to break it up with a thumbnail. Immediately, one then two chickadees came nearer to watch. One landed on my shoulder, fluttered down to my open palm, and took a piece of almond. Within seconds there were birds perched on my head, my fingers, and my forearms, squabbling with one another, jumping in to take a turn at the food and then flying off to branches nearby to eat before coming back for more.

The birds of Saint Peter's Abbey have been doing this for forty years now, ever since one of the brothers coaxed one to his hand. An old chickadee might live ten years, so these ones have simply learned from their elders in an unbroken tradition based on a small covenant between monks and birds. Some of them retreated briefly to the shrine a few feet away to land along the fieldstone base. When my hand was empty, the seven chickadees flitted around the shrine and onto the ground beneath where someone had scattered sunflower and millet seeds. I took another look at the shrine. Brick sides painted the color of roses, the glass and wood on the front showing the wear of many winters. Inside the glass case, the statuette of Mary stands alone with hands folded in prayer. Someone took pains to glue small faux sapphires along the edges of her robe. She wears a crown and her eyes are dark brown. There are dusty plastic roses at her feet and outside the glass more artificial blossoms. At the top of the shrine there is a piece of plywood cut into the shape of a large crown on which faded blue lettering proclaims, "Hail, Queen of Peace" and then below, "In the end my immaculate heart will triumph."

At Mass earlier, with the brothers and a small gathering of guests and retreatants, no one mentioned the turmoil of the week until we prayed the prayers of intention. A mother in the congregation spoke up when the celebrant invited others to add their own intentions. She said, "For my daughter and her family living in New York—may they and others hurt by the attack survive this darkness, fear, and anger, and come to a place of compassion and forgiveness rather than vengeance. Lord, hear our prayer."

All week long the talk on radio and television has been of

retribution—striking back at the phantom enemy—but now that it is Sunday a subtle shift has begun. People, often Christian leaders, are talking for the first time about caution, restraint, forgiveness. The airwaves now carry messages from religious and secular intellectuals, saying that we need not retribution, but redemption, a triumph of civility, peace, and compassion over barbarity and death.

When some act of hatred and violence tears apart the fabric of life, we have to act in ways that make it whole again. That cannot be done with more hatred and violence, but only with gestures that will restore the proper, sacred-making role of sacrifice. In the weeks that followed, that meant a sacrifice of our own lust for retribution, of our desire to be God and pass out sentence and judgment because we cannot wait for peace to triumph. One end of the spectrum of religious experience conjured this evil—as it has before with the Crusades, the Inquisition, and the assault on indigenous peoples in the New World—but it is the other side of the spectrum that speaks the most sane and consoling words in response: *Let the one who is without sin be the first to cast a stone.*

Redemption, like the first chickadee coaxed to the hands of a monk, is something that comes over time, the hours, years, and generations of waiting and pondering. We cannot pull it toward ourselves and must always be patient for Creator and creation to do the work. In the end, the immaculate love at the heart of things will triumph.

# SCAPULAR II

*Three things of this world delight the heart: water, green things, and a beautiful face.*

—A hadith of Islam

If there are spirits on this hilltop, at least some of them speak German. And more than a few wore the brown scapular of Our Lady of Carmel while they lived and breathed. Some images of Mary in churches and shrines show her holding up something that looks like two small swatches of cloth strung together on lengths of cord or narrow strips of the same material. Here at Mount Carmel she holds one in her right hand and the child Jesus on her left arm appears to be playing with another. Easily overlooked, this detail binds the site and its devotees to a long tradition of Carmelite faith that reaches back to the original hermits on the Mountain of the Lord and even further to Elijah himself.

No one knows for certain how the Carmelites got their start on the original Mount Carmel. The oldest authenticated records of Carmelite ascetics come from the twelfth century. Some claim the order started much earlier than that and see it as a long succession of holy men and women who were followers of Elijah in the wilds of Hakkarmel. These have been called the Sons of the Prophets and in their broadest terms have been said to include the Essenes and even John the Baptist, whose exact whereabouts as he emerged from "the wilderness" have never been pinned down. There are vague mentionings in the written record that suggest some kind of religious devotion on Carmel well before the time of Jesus. Jamblichus, a Syrian philosopher writing in AD 300, claimed that Pythagoras, the pre-Socratic philosopher and mystic, once spent time in silent prayer at a sanctuary on Carmel during the sixth century BCE. Tacitus also wrote of a holy place of some kind on the mountaintop in the first century AD. Like Jamblichus, Tacitus never specified which god was attended there, though modern Essenes, for whom the mountain is also sacred, claim he was worshipping at El Marahka. It doesn't seem too much of a stretch to assume that before and after Christ, there were scattered religious zealots of various faiths living on Mount Carmel. As disciples of Elijah, they might have been Jewish first, later Essene and Christian, and later still Islamic. It was the rise of the Muslim faith, in fact, that eventually led Christian mystics back to the heights of Hakkarmel where they staked the claim that bound them to the way of Mary and the scapular.

When the scruffy warriors of the Holy Roman Empire poured down out of Constantinople and into Jerusalem in the penultimate year of the eleventh century, they were answering the call of Pope Urban II to reclaim the holy sepulchre (thought to be Jesus' tomb) from the hands of unbelievers. It was the beginning of Christendom's first large-scale imperialist undertaking and the launch of a one-thousand-year campaign against the religion and civilization it has come to fear most—Islam. Assured by God's own spokesman on earth that their service in the Crusades would grant them a place in heaven (much as Islamic suicide bombers are assured by their imam today), Frank and Norman hooligans flooded the streets of the Holy City with the blood of its inhabitants, Muslim, Jew, and Christian. They held the city for eighty-eight years before Saladin reclaimed it for the followers of Muhammad. There were other Crusades after that, more or less failed attempts to erase the Muslim infidel from Palestine. Islam at that time, though, was a superior civilization, in its arts and literature, as well as in its science and military force. The Muslim defenders looked upon the plow-boys and knights errant sent forth from the fiefdoms of western Europe as utter barbarians. They were not far off. Some historians now argue that it was contact with a more sophisticated civilization during the Crusades that finally pulled Europe out of the medieval world and into the subsequent centuries of artistic, scientific, and mercantile exploration.

A pattern was established here that Christendom has repeated in its ventures throughout the world. Supported by the church and its contorted notions of sacral violence, the soldiers go forth in rape and slaughter to claim a territory in the name of one who forbade his followers to raise a sword in his defense. Horrors, social upheaval, great suffering follow for decades, perhaps centuries until eventually there is a retreat of some kind, either in defeat or in finally recognizing the futility and immorality of the enterprise. Meanwhile, something else happens away from the battles and carnage, something that shows religion to be more than merely the regrettable tool of popes and princes.

With the sun a few degrees lower in the sky now, I notice a glint of water on the eastern horizon. It's the Wolverine, or at least I believe it is, running past Saint Peter's and on down from the northern limits of the Qu'Appelle watershed. At Mass this morning I was daydreaming as I stared at the river motif that runs through the stained-glass clerestory of the chapel at Saint Peter's. Though the church is quite new and follows a modern, almost cubist design, the interior has an airy, skyward symmetry that alludes to Gothic cathedrals. Brushed-chrome struts are splashed by blue light from the *River of Life* that meanders overhead in the vaulted ceiling. The stained glass, like the pipe organ behind the altar, was built and installed by one of the brothers with the help of local volunteers.

As I looked at the small shards of colored light that glow in abstract forms on the river of glass, as though they were adrift on its current, the stories I'd been reading about Hattie McKay, the Crusades, the scapular, and the origins of the Carmelites drifted through my thoughts. Then one of the brothers rose to give the first reading. The words of the text came in waves, and I felt within me an alignment, like metal filings before a magnetic field, as the brightest, sharpest remnants from all those stories flowed in a kind of patterned chaos until, off into the distance of our history, I began to imagine I could see one of the rivers of narrative that bind human spirituality to the wildness of creation.

In the weeks that followed, as Christian leaders prepared to wreak vengeance upon the unholy ones who brought terror into the very temples of international trade, I headed upstream, following the meandering history of the Carmelite scapular back to its indeterminate origins in medieval, post-Crusades Christendom. I set off with hopes that I would find a spring at its source offering clear drafts of wisdom. Instead there was the murkiest of bogs, but I waded in anyway.

At my shoulder as I read was the same question that now seems to loom over every church, mosque, and synagogue. It will be asked a thousand times in the privileged and shocked nations as we try to fathom what would make a small band of Islamic men launch a countercrusade against the powers of modern Christendom. You can phrase it many ways, but it comes down to this: Why does religion divide when it should unite?

There may be no definitive answer, but I wonder if this question, too, is part of the divorce between monotheism and wildness. It is a primary division that has us now blaming religion for everything that is wrong with the world, from racial intolerance to mental illness, from war in the Middle East to environmental destruction on every continent. The evidence is damning enough and requires no litany here. The three faiths that arose in the Holy Land have at one time or another each been drawn into the darkest moments of humanity's passage, Christianity perhaps more so for its ascendancy in the past millennium. Responding to the latest round of horrors, those who are paid to broadcast their opinions have arrived at the obvious and logical conclusion, and advise that it is time to get rid of this curse. Others, staking out more moderate ground, are fond of saying they have nothing against private spirituality, but organized religion is an unnecessary and outdated cause of suffering that simply must go. None of this is surprising or remarkable, other than the widespread conviction that we have a say in the matter.

"No one has the luxury of choosing here because all of us are precisely fired into life with a certain madness that comes from the gods." Father Ron Rolheiser, in the introductory chapter of *The Holy Longing*, identifies spirituality as "something vital and non-negotiable lying at the heart of our lives." "Everyone," he writes, "has to have a spirituality and does have one, either a life-giving one or a destructive one…We do not wake up in the world calm and serene, having the luxury of choosing to act or not act. We wake up crying, on fire with desire, with madness. What we do with that madness is our spirituality."[1] Understood this way, the spiritual urge in humanity cannot but lead to some kind of communal, organized expression. People will always be inclined toward religion for, just as we are spiritual by nature, we are social. The first makes us long for consummation and the second makes us want to talk about it. For a wave to crest it needs an ocean of other waves: what Buddhists would call the *Sangha*, and Christians the Body of Christ.

We are no more able to rid humanity of spiritual longings than we are able to rid it of sexual longings. Both are part of the natural human experience of energies as wild as sunlight and rain. And, as students of the soul from Aristotle to Jung have observed, the two longings are faces of a single reality: a force of creation that rises in us, causing disorder if we express it badly or fall prey to delusions of possession, but always resisting our appropriations in the end. We recognize that the outcome of a single expression of sexual energy can weigh in as helpful, harmful, or neutral, while the outcome of *all* expressions of human sexual energy taken together is the lead point of a branch of our evolution as a species. The same applies to spiritual energy. Following its urgings leads to suffering and illumination by turns, allows one to take power or give it away, to serve or be served, to create or destroy, but over the long journey of *Homo sapiens* it has drawn us and continues to draw us forward into a future that is not ours to know, that nonetheless invites our conscious, moral participation.

In his essay "The Spirit of Earth," Teilhard de Chardin suggests that there is a passion moving through human evolution that will awaken "the dormant forces of human unity."[2] I will not pretend to understand fully (or agree with) all that he says in this essay, even though it is, compared to some of his writing, relatively straightforward. But it is hard not to be moved by his complete certainty that religion is a biological force operating within what he calls the "hominization" of life. The true purpose of religion, he says, "is to sustain and spur on the progress of life...the 'religious function' born of hominization and linked thereto is bound to grow continuously with man himself." He goes on, describing the "current which raises matter" as a tide within creation, the multiple that rises in a great attraction to be incorporated in the Divine or, in his terms, the "Already One":

> In the first phase—before Man—the attraction was vitally, but blindly, felt by the world. Since Man, it is awakened (at least partially), in reflective liberty which sustains religion. Religion is not an option or a strictly individual intuition, but represents the long unfolding, the collective experience of all mankind,

of the existence of God—God reflecting himself personally on the organized sum of thinking beings, to guarantee a sure result of creation, and to lay down exact laws for man's hesitant activities.[3]

But this is a mystic, and mystics always talk of union. What of the ministers and imams who draw boundaries with doctrine, foment division? There is a wide spectrum here delineated by the degree to which our dealings with the sacred are removed from creation. At its wild, mystical core, religious practice unifies and blends across all borders; at its most civilized, doctrinal extremities, it divides, sets categories, and hardens against invasion. Take any religion far enough from its native soil in the desert and you will arrive at dogmatic fundamentalism. We have good reason to be disenchanted with our religions—they are run by clusters of old men who haven't spent enough time in the desert sitting with the silence of stones. The saving grace is that there seems to be a natural pattern or rhythm at play, which now and then brings our dogmatized religions back in touch with the unifying core of mystical experience. The cycle begins when a scriptural, monotheistic religion leaves the desert behind and takes shelter in the citadels of social acceptance and privilege. Well-fed and protected, a faith eventually veers toward doctrine and ritual that is hostile to the otherness of creation—much of it entirely at odds with their own prophets' revelation. Having broken all bonds with the earth and its elemental, unifying teachings and dedicated themselves instead to heaven, their theologians contrive ways of justifying hatred, greed, and violence. Armed with new doctrines of just war and sacral violence, priests ordain the sin of princes and send young men off to do God's work in heathen territory. And that is where the articles of faith encounter the articles of creation and the forgotten force of nature in man's heart mounts a small but countervailing redemption.

Among the multitude sent out to slaughter or convert the unbelievers, there are always a small number who break rank. They turn their backs on the horrors they have seen at sword's length and head off into the desert where they undergo hardship and learn from all that is indigenous and wild. Once again with feet on the ground, discalced in God's creation, they discover the mystical way and its force of convergence. Those who return home become the leaven that allows truth to expand again within the old faith long gone stale.

Tradition has it that the Carmelites received Mary's scapular when she appeared to one of their English friars, Saint Simon Stock, who had once lived as a hermit on Mount Carmel. The story has the earmarks of other folklore from medieval times. Even the oak tree, that pre-Christian pillar between earth and sky, plays a role as it does in the legends of King Arthur. Stock's surname comes from popular belief that he lived in the hollow of an oak tree. One Carmelite account says that he drank nothing but water and subsisted on "herbs, roots and wild apples." Mortifying his flesh with "fasting and other severities, he nourished his soul with spiritual dainties in continual prayer."[4]

In the stories of Mary coming to Stock in a vision, it is July 16, 1251, and he is praying earnestly to Our Lady for aid. She suddenly appears "with a multitude of angels," holding the scapular of the order in her hands. She gives him the scapular for the Carmelites with a promise, saying, "This will be for you and for all Carmelites the privilege: that he who dies in this will not suffer eternal fire, that is, he who dies in this will be saved."

Carmelite historians have now discredited this story of the scapular's origins, suggesting that it may have been concocted in the fourteenth century as a way of preserving the order and increasing its popularity among the nobility. It seems that the Carmelites were struggling to survive and trying to outdo the Dominicans, who had their own legend of Mary bestowing holy garments upon them. At that time the orders were competing for the favor of the laity and of Rome, each claiming to be the order blessed by Mary's patronage. As for Simon Stock, there is evidence that his life story may have been conflated from two separate Carmelites alive during the thirteenth century. Perhaps most revealing of all, no documents mentioning Simon Stock's vision and no paintings of Mary showing the scapular are dated earlier than the period in which the order was fighting to survive. Yet, a story affects its own miracle. By the fifteenth century, the Carmelites were going strong and the scapular had become the undergarment of choice for pious kings and noblemen. Convinced that it would dispense with their sins and save them from hellfire, the likes of King Edward II and Henry, Duke of Lancaster, died wearing the scapular under their doublets.

In the library at Saint Peter's I found a document written by Father Chrysostom Hoffman, one of the Benedictines who came on that first scouting trip to the northern plains and stood on the top of Mount Carmel to scan the landscape. In it he writes about the work it took to build the shrine and he also refers to the scapular. According to Hoffman, most of the colonists who settled the fifty townships under the spiritual guidance of Saint Peter's Abbey were invested in their childhood with the scapular of Our Lady of Carmel. They had a German term for it, *Gnadenkleid*, which means "grace-garment," and during a ceremony of investiture they were told that they were being enrolled in the Carmelite family throughout the world and through history, reaching back through Carmelite mystics Teresa of Avila and John of the Cross to Elijah himself.

There is always an initial disappointment when a miracle is taken apart, laid bare on the dissecting table. Divine, magical origins carry an immediate appeal, but that appeal does not root deeply and it withers beneath the glare of reason. If the cosmos weren't made by God in seven days, then perhaps there is no God. As science spans one opening for mystery after another we are left with a diminished God of the Gaps. In a postmodern world, those who locate God in the gaps, who draw their faith from saints' miracles and their history from scripture face a difficult choice: either ignore the new evidence or stop believing altogether. But which is the more profound, faith-grounding magic—the creation of the cosmos in a week or its blossoming and unfurling over billions of years? A medieval monk's vision of Mary may stir the heart, but it cannot compare to the slow miracle of convergence among mystical traditions. If the spirit of Mary—the one who births a new unifying fire into the history of our religious striving—dwells with us yet, she is there in the cross-fertilization that a religion undergoes when a handful of its believers get lost in a foreign wilderness, when the flow of revelation and faith escapes arbitrary boundaries, and when the longing for spirit shows itself as a biological, womb-formed reality, governed by the same forces that operate in the sex lives of flowers and the evolution of species. Our religious tradition is the birdsong of *Homo sapiens*. It bears our racial memory in distinctive identities that evolve as dialect from place to place; it allows us to praise and celebrate the Creation but has its territorial side as well; and over time its long purpose is reproductive, a response to the desire to create more of this creation, and by engaging in that necessary reiteration it changes unbeknownst to its singers, grows and unfolds along with the rest of being.

Throughout the twelfth century and into the thirteenth, war-weary pilgrims and soldiers took refuge where they could throughout the Holy Land. The first Carmelites of official record were these disenchanted crusaders. They called themselves the "brothers and sisters of the Blessed Virgin Mary," and they lived a life of prayer and quiet in the spirit of the mountain's old prophet. There is archaeological evidence suggesting that they dwelt in caves in and around the Wadi ain'es Siah on Mount Carmel, a stream known to some as the Fountain of Elijah, where the prophet himself is said to have taken refuge from the predations of Jezebel.

In his description of the Carmelites, the earliest on record, Jacques de Vitry uses an apiary image: living "in little comb-like cells, those bees of the Lord laid up spiritual honey."[5] The written record says very little else of the lives of these early Carmelites. They were hermits who lived for a spell by Elijah's spring on Mount Carmel. They may have raised a small chapel, they dedicated themselves to imitation of Elijah and the Virgin Mary, and by the end of the thirteenth century they had dispersed throughout Europe. Where they received their fierce devotion to Elijah and Mary, who taught them what to eat and how to survive as an ascetic on a mountain, what influenced them, inspired them— none of this is answered or even asked in the writing about the early Carmelites. If you could fill those gaps in the story you'd have a few more of the invisible strands of meaning that connect points of light in the web of our spiritual ecology. But we can't, at least not without guesswork and surmising, and so a single point like the scapular, with its conflated and conflicted legacy, shines alone and strange in the darkness. There it hangs, suspended by Our Lady of Carmel above pagan lands around the world, a charm rubbed threadbare by the touch of a civilization at once terrified by and attracted to the wildness it destroys. Trying to gain a glimpse of the strands that might span those gaps in the story became an intermittent obsession for me, one stirred each time I came to stay at Saint Peter's. Propelling me along in my inquiry was the possibility that the missing truths might well align with moments when our hold upon religion slipped and the wind blew it here and there in unexpected, unacknowledged directions.

Something must have drawn the pilgrims and defeated soldiers to Mount Carmel. Something must have compelled them to stay. From the references in Jamblichus and Tacitus and from the archaeology, we know that people of undetermined religious affinity had been coming to the mountain in a succession of spiritual attendance since the days of Elijah. It seems fair to assume that when the refugees of the Crusades first came to drink at the prophet's spring, other spiritual workers were already hiving there on the holy mountain, distilling from the nectar of Carmel a mystic sweetness.

As surely as religious orthodoxy will raise ramparts to quarantine the faith against contamination, mysticism will find a way through the defenses. To one who leaves the world behind to look for God, wisdom has no denomination and holy ground no claimants. You could take one mystic from each of the three faiths that claim Abraham as progenitor, place them together for a chat about the correct path to union with God, and they would find plenty to agree upon. Mysticism flourishes in a medium of heterodoxy, even heresy.

In the twelfth century, when the Carmelite founders came to the holy mountain, conditions were more than favorable for an exchange of spiritual practice. Islam, the ascendant religion of the day, had an advanced and rich mystical tradition. Derived out of the deepest respect for the wisdom and prophets of its predecessors in Judaism and Christianity, Islam was in its early centuries relatively tolerant of its cohorts in monotheism. In its newness and its compelling call to turn back to the pure ways of Abraham—to peace and brotherhood under one God—the faith of Muhammad had a vitality that appealed to anyone fed up with the tribalism, corruption, and worldliness that had overtaken the established religions. Arabists say that to hear the poetry of the Qur'an in the original language is to be hypnotized, charmed by sweet music.

Like any religion, though, Islam is a faith of contradictions and conflicting verses. No better or worse than the scriptures held holy by Jews and Christians, the Qur'an sanctifies blood and vengeance on one page and peace and compassion on another. And for the same reason: Islam likewise sprang from the ancient monotheistic hostility toward the pagan. In fact, if anything, it is the most strident of the three in its railings against polytheism. Muhammad was born into an Arab religious tradition that served a pantheon of 360 gods with idols housed in a sanctuary in Mecca known as the Ka'ba. He came into his preaching as a prophet and founded his religion upon a vocation to cleanse the Arab world of its tribalism and idolatry.

It would be easy to slide here into the contemporary polemic in which detractors say the Muslim religion is fundamentalist and intolerant at its very footings, while its defenders point to verses in the Qur'an that entreat the faithful to live by peace and kindness. Instead, it might be better to step back a pace or two and consider Islam within the larger continuum of religious striving as it opened out upon the civilizations that have laid claim to Mount Carmel. Each time Abraham's desert tree of monotheism branched out into a new faith, the lead shoots blossomed on sap that carried a bitterness distilled from the scarred and blemished branches lower down. Moses, Elijah, and the old Hebrew prophets tried and failed to expunge the pagan urge from the House of Israel. Christendom, ignoring Christ's call for compassion and Saint Paul's assertions that there are "no more distinctions between Jew and Greek, slave and free, male and female," stepped up the antipagan campaign and applied it around the world with mixed results. Agricultural paganism, showing its own signs of corruption amid the feuding and human-sacrificing tribes of Europe, dissolved with apparent ease into the waters of baptism, but not without leaving a good trace of its earthiness, which can still be tasted in the sacramental streams of Christian practice.

The sixth-century Arab world into which Muhammad was born was, like much of Europe, still a largely pagan society and ripe for the entry of an indigenous strain of monotheism. There were always pockets of Judaism throughout the Middle East, but Jews, to their credit, were never keen evangelizers and many Arabs resented Jewish wealth and control of oasis land, finance, and trade. Christianity made a foray into the Hijaz region where Islam was later to rise, but between persecution, rabid infighting over doctrine, and the ongoing Greek-Persian conflicts of the time, it could not succeed in unifying Arabs under one God. All the more amazing, then, that within Muhammad's own lifetime, Islam achieved in the Arab world the task that took Christianity several centuries to accomplish in Europe—the rise to state religion and the whole-sale conversion of a civilization from pagan idolatry to Abrahamic monotheism. As in Christianized Europe, the transformation had its costs. Some of the Jews and pagans who resisted, persecuting Muhammad and his followers, were eventually killed, their wives and children sold off to slavery.

Forgetting their own history, Christians and Jews are appalled to hear that a man claiming to be a prophet should countenance such acts. As the sin that has scarred the evolution of religion from age to age, killing in the name of God is an evil that points toward the larger forces at play within, but certainly not unique to, religious striving. Enacted in the name of God or in the name of good, people have always killed for self-preservation, to save family, homeland, and tribe. Remember the Israelites atop Hakkarmel? That hobbling dance is deep within our natures, and civilization has not left the mountaintop yet. Religion plays the music as we shamble along, alternating between obeisance to the exhortations of God's prophets and the unrelenting call of our oldest desires. The teachings proscribe our sexual and aggressive expressions, showing us how to consciously resist or sublimate evolutionary forces within the human spirit, the very ones that carried our genes upward on the hominid family tree and that remain as the necessary fire of our spiritual advance. Insofar as a civilization (or an

individual) manages to transform these energies toward enactment
of the prophets' higher principles (love, sacrifice, peace), it will
progress in its attainment of consciousness and spirit. In a sense,
the laws of spirit in human nature revealed to us in the teachings of
Lao-tzu, Buddha, Abraham, Moses, Jesus, Muhammad, and others,
to the extent that we choose to follow them, become the biological
mechanisms by which human consciousness spirals toward God.
But we *are* human, we have wills, and therefore always there is the
failure and impatience, even among the prophets themselves. But
that, too, seems only to lay fertile ground for the next prophet to
come along, the one who sees again more clearly the mystic way
to unity between our natures and our spirits.

And so a prophet may try to force his people to mature, may
weigh the consequences of not acting to preserve the greater good
and decide that there is no escaping the sword. That isn't to say
that killing can sometimes be "holy" or wars "just." Whether it
is Elijah overseeing the slaying of Baalite priests or Muhammad
allowing one of his converted tribes to pass a sentence of execution on Medina's Jewish men, a prophet who pays such a price to
preserve the faith has fallen prey to one of the great weaknesses of
the human heart. Everything under heaven—species, ecologies,
children, civilization—is a work in progress, but most of us, including some prophets, become impatient with the long unfolding of
things and want to see results now. The growth toward unity under
one God and toward other as yet unseen offshoots of religious
ontogenesis cannot be rushed. This is a universe that takes pleasure
in its own slow ripening, that exacts a price whenever we force
a blossoming. I can trick hyacinths into blooming in my kitchen
prematurely, but the bulbs only blossom once and must then be
discarded while the ones quietly wintering in my garden bloom
year after year and multiply.

Still, the deeds of Muhammad, including the expulsion of the
Jews from the Hijaz, cannot be separated from the society from

which Islam sprang. This was the seventh-century Arab world—in many ways not that different from the Palestine where the warrior patriarchs of Judeo-Christian history spilled the blood of unbelievers centuries earlier. Life was punctuated by feuds, raids, and full-scale battles spawned by grudges and tribal enmity that carried over generation to generation. That Muhammad moved his people from tribalism to a religion of universal brotherhood in a matter of a few years is one of the marvels of Middle Eastern history. This could not have been achieved without some bloodshed, and there are those who argue that Muhammad took up the sword reluctantly to defend his followers and even then applied measures to minimize casualties. Alfred Guillaume, a British scholar who dedicated his life to the study of Islam, says that the battles between Mecca and Medina were typical of Arab-Arab conflict of the time. They were governed by a code of battlefield honor that prevented pursuit and slaughter once one side had the upper hand.[6]

The first time I looked into the Qur'an, I was surprised to find familiar characters and stories from the Bible. I was expecting something more exotic or strange, a broad departure from the old religions now set in opposition to Islam. Given his own upbringing in a pagan tribe, Muhammad either received his knowledge of the Hebrew scripture and Christian gospel directly from the angel Gabriel as tradition has it or, as most historians believe, he learned the stories directly from Jews and Christians living in the Hijaz. Either way, when he came forth as a prophet, Muhammad looked to the Jewish community for recognition and support. He hoped that, as fellow monotheists, they would affirm one who had been appointed to unite the tribes beneath the one true God. Receiving nothing but scorn from those he thought should welcome him, Muhammad took his place in line behind Moses,

Elijah, Jeremiah, Saint John the Baptist, and all the rest who called for a return to faith and were ridiculed. His own prophetic fire was stoked by the disjunction he saw between the less-than-holy lives of established Jewish and Christian leaders on the one hand and the unifying ideals expressed in their scriptures on the other. According to Guillaume, this was something of a turning point for Muhammad. He came to the conclusion that it would be up to him to foster unification among the children of Abraham, one way or another. Most in the Jewish and Christian communities, he believed, had broken faith with the God of Abraham and ignored the wisdom of their prophets from Elijah to Jesus.

After the battles were won, Muhammad walked into Mecca and cleansed the Ka'ba of the 360 idols. Polytheism would have no place in Islam. Yet he took measures to grant the remaining Jews and Christians safe quarter in the region. Where things go awry, in Qur'anic interpretation at least, is in a few of the sections, or suras, that have invited a broader definition of Allah's injunctions against unbelievers. Jihad, literally "to strive," was instituted by Allah's prophet not with co-monotheists in mind, but out of a conviction that it was his sacred duty to purge Arab society of polytheism. Nevertheless, Sura 9:29 and others have been used by extremists to justify attacks on Christians and Jews, lumping all non-Muslims into the category of *mushrik*, a term meaning "polytheists" but often widened to include those who remain outside the boundaries of faith in the one true God.

This, it seems, is where impatience with the pagan energy inbred in civilization has brought us. Now men weaned on hatred of the unbeliever—harboring grudges that refer back to the Crusades as though they were injustices experienced in their own childhoods, and to Muhammad's battle for Medina as though it had happened to their grandfathers—aim their mortars at ancient Buddhist monuments and blast the idols of the *mushrik*. Now, in an international tribalism driven by Western oil interests and decades of feuding over holy land once shared by three faiths, our long war against the pagan and the wild has turned at least for the moment against Christians and Jews, giving us a small taste of the fear the heathen has experienced at the terrible mercy of strangers who claim to know the will of God. The circle is coming round. For once we are the unbelievers, the *mushrik*, and the thought has us shaken to our roots. Television evangelists tell their flock that the attacks on New York and Washington in 2001 were a divine message. Eventually, they say, every Gomorrah has its day of terror. It is the will of God. On that presumption, the fundamentalists of Islam align with the fundamentalists of Christendom.

Long after I had returned home from Saint Peters and Mount Carmel, I was sitting in our living room going over some notes from the trip and thinking about the tensions separating the three faiths that still pay tribute to Elijah and his mountain. Maia, the youngest in our household, shuffled over in her housecoat and slippers and asked, "Dad, what are you writing about now?"

"I'm trying to write about the way people look for God."

She arched her eyebrows, lowered her chin. "Are you speaking for God?"

"I hope not," I said. "No one really knows God's thoughts."

A pause, and then, looking at the stuffed toy dog dangling from the crook of her arm, she launched into her homily. "I do. God wants us to not fight and punch, he wants us to care for each other, to love him, to love other people, and he wants us to love what we have and what we go to, and who we are…and our babies and pets."

Okay, so maybe we know a little of what God wants, in broad terms and while we still have some of our innocence. The trouble starts when someone claims to possess detailed knowledge of divine will and then acts upon it. A four-year-old sums up the Sermon on the Mount in fifty words, but that is not enough for grown-ups. We become impatient with the generalities of revelation and the paradox in all wisdom. We want details and clarity, and when these are lacking we make them up. And that is when the barricades rise and we find the enemy.

I kept following the story of the scapular and Mount Carmel because everywhere along the trail there were discoveries that testify to the survival of pagan energy in religion, despite all that has been done to tame it down and the delusions of those who believe they can destroy it. When Guillaume was writing in the 1950s, there were rural Arabs who still followed ancient ways not far from the Hijaz: a cult of wells and springs and faith in tree spirits. More important though, the wilder spirit in religious yearning lives on whenever and wherever people of different traditions open up to one another and delight in the complexity and diversity of spiritual abundance.

If you visit the Gothic cathedral in Seville, said to be the largest in Christendom, and walk away from the crowd of Americans gathered round the sepulchre containing Christopher Columbus's bones, you will eventually come to a chapel that holds the tomb of Seville's Christian monarch, Ferdinand III. A close look shows that it is inscribed in four languages: Arabic, Latin, Hebrew, and Spanish. That confluence of tongues comes from a Pentecostal moment in history when the Spirit blew into the upper room of Western civilization, creating an innocence within which the three strands of Abraham's weave could form a beautiful fabric for a short while. It was before the Crusades, a time when Islam was a refuge of civility and religious tolerance compared to Christendom. In Spain's Moorish Andalusia, Christian and Jewish communities thrived unmolested by their Muslim hosts and advanced to positions of high civic authority. From the eighth to the twelfth centuries, the interchange between the three Abrahamic faiths in Andalusia fostered a culture whose arts, philosophy, and science soared while the Christians of northern Europe struggled to hold on to the shards of civilization left over from the Roman Empire. Cordoba became known as the intellectual hub of Europe, "the Ornament of the World," as Maria Rosa Menocal refers to it, quoting a tenth-century Saxon writer in the title of her book on Andalusia.[7] Streets were well paved and lit, lined by mosques, churches, and synagogues, prosperous shops, lush gardens, and palaces. There were seventy libraries in the city, one containing 400,000 volumes while, according to Menocal, the best in the remainder of Europe held perhaps 400 manuscripts.

Imagine the street life of Andalusia: Christians, Jews, and Muslims, all speaking Arabic, rabbis arguing points of scripture with priests, the muezzin giving the morning call to prayer from the minaret, "Prayer is better than sleep…come to prayer, come to security." Certainly there would have been animosity, times of abrasion and bad blood. Andalusia was not paradise, and its people were not all virtuous and open-minded.[8] But they tolerated one another, coexisted in something that had the promise of a viable religious ecology. In a healthy ecosystem, stability is impossible without diversity. The whole is served by the complex interchange among its parts in a flow of energy that has little respect for boundaries and cannot be permanently contained as it cycles from one component to the next.

In their daily devotions, Muslim people recite verses that compare Allah to a mother. The Fatiha, the first sura of the Qur'an, names God "Al Rahmin," which is derived from the Arabic word for "womb" or "matrix." And when they bow to Mecca they orient themselves to the mihrab, a niche in the wall of the mosque that bears inscriptions from the Qur'an, most often the sayings of the prophet. Some of these sayings honor Mary or, as she is known in Islam, Mariam. Muhammad revered Mary as the purest of the pure, the most marvelous and holy of all women. There is a story, not in the Qur'an itself but in the narrative tradition of Islam, that shows Allah's prophet walking into the Ka'ba to rid it of the idols. He orders that all images and statues be destroyed save one—a fresco of Mary holding her child in arms.

Sura 19, Mariam, shows the angel Gabriel coming to Mary and saying, "I am the messenger of your Lord, to grant you a pure son." Service is a most honored attribute in Islam and Mary is considered to be the supreme model of selfless service. Some Qur'anic authorities describe Mary in ways that align well with Catholic doctrine, as an intervening force between God and those who seek God. In the twelfth verse of Sura 66, Allah says, "And Mary the daughter of 'Imran, who guarded her chastity; and We breathed into (her body) of Our spirit; and she testified to the truth of the words of her Lord and of His Revelations, and was one of the devout (servants)."[9]

Within Islam, its mystics, the Sufis, have been the most dedicated to Mary. One European orientalist has suggested that for the Sufis, Mary is "the symbol of the spirit that receives divine inspiration and thus becomes pregnant with the divine light."[10] She is the one pregnant with a divine inspiration that is born into the world and kindled in the heart of one who seeks God. Many of the Sufis expressed their mystical vision in verse and it is their poetry more than anything that has made inroads into the West. The Sufi poet we know as Rumi has become a fixture in contemporary pop culture. American celebrities from Deepak Chopra to Madonna now talk about Rumi on television, and every best seller on how to feed your soul or deepen your spirituality seems to contain at least one of the mystic's poems. If you didn't know any better you'd think he was a guru to California's rich and famous, perhaps living in a modest mansion up the coast from Malibu.

If Rumi's lyric wisdom has reached across the centuries to modern audiences, is it any less likely that Sufism would have crossed barriers of language, culture, and geography to reach the first Carmelites? After all, these men and women emerged from the caves of Mount Carmel during the golden age of the Sufi. At the time, Jalal'ud-Din Rumi was living in Persia, making a name for himself as a Sufi master, or Shaykh, and Sufi mystical orders were flourishing throughout the Middle East. The Sufis had established themselves as the desert ecstatics of the day, following ascetic and mystical practices that brought on visions of self-oblivion and feats of telepathy and translocation. Many of them had scant regard for the boundaries of orthodoxy and a few carried their devotion to lengths that ended in their martyrdom as heretics.[11]

Like the Christian Desert Fathers before them, the early Sufis shook themselves free of the city and its walled-in comforts. They took up lives of itinerant poverty in the dry country beyond Baghdad and Damascus. Muhammad himself was their model. Early in his ministry, as Christ had in his, Muhammad escaped into the desert to climb a mountain and sit in meditation. There he became one of the *nabi*, which is to say he was beside himself with the fervor of the prophets. Opening his spirit to the mercies of the Hijaz sky, Muhammad adopted the way of the Sha'ir, the poet prophets who spoke in the rhyming verses of devotion and mystic revelation. This oral tradition, with the verses of the great masters remembered and passed on from teacher to student, was to become the spiritual currency of the Sufi. Sufi men and women have carried this marriage of mysticism and poetry forward through the centuries, but its honeymoon seems to have been in the twelfth and thirteenth centuries.

Born in what is now Afghanistan, Rumi became a Sufi and studied under several Shaykhs, none more influential than Shams-ud-Din of Tabriz. Shams-ud-Din, though he is considered a saint of Islam, was one of those inclined to break with orthodoxy. In some of his verses he proclaimed, "I am the spirit which was breathed into Mary," and, "I am the soul which was the life of Jesus."[12]

This sort of adaptation of the Christian notion of incarnation is heard again and again within the poetic ecstasies of Islam's mystics in the twelfth to fourteenth centuries. Khawaja Muin-ud-Din

Chishti, the saint credited with bringing Islam to India, wrote, "Every day in the world the Mary of the time will give birth to a Jesus...Every moment the Holy Spirit breathes into Mu'in...So it is not I who says this, but in fact I am the second Jesus."[13]

My favorite piece of Sufi verse on the theme of Mary comes from a woman, Hajja Muhibba, who lived and wrote in the fourteenth century:

> There are as many paths to God as the
> Children of God have breaths, but
> Of all the paths to God the Way
> Of Mary is the sweetest and gentlest of all.[14]

With all of this inhaling and exhaling of Mary's spirit, there must have been some interchange between the Sufis of the Middle East and their Christian counterparts. It seems likely that some of these wandering poet ascetics of Islam would have made their way to Mount Carmel, the home of their ancestor, Elijah. There the early Carmelites and other devotees of Mary and Elijah surely would have fallen beneath the influence of these compelling poets who carried their own string of prayer beads and spoke so lovingly of Jesus' mother.

There is a Carmelite tradition that places Mary in spirit atop the Mountain of the Lord on that legendary night when Elijah called down fire from the heavens and purged Israel of its idolaters. Centuries before her life in Nazareth, when her womb would become the vessel of holy fire prefigured in Elijah's pyrotechnics, she manifested herself to the great prophet as the divine reply to his prayers for rain. Coming to Elijah in the form of that little cloud, "small as a man's hand, rising from the sea," Mary rained down her grace upon the drought-parched lands of Hakkarmel. This kind of folklore appeals not only because it threads a poetic line of narrative back from the New Testament into the Old, but because it charges

Mary with the wild purgative and restorative powers present in grassland or forest where cycles of drought, fire, and rain keep ecosystems healthy over hundreds of years. Divine love is the red of fire, but hope down here on earth is a green thing. The fierce green that follows fire and rain is one of the more commonplace miracles of this earth—though few people these days are privileged to see it.

The Sufi and Christian hermits of Hakkarmel, experiencing in certain seasons the divine grace of rain on a desert mountain, would have known what it was to walk into the green presence of Mary and Elijah. And the springs on the mountain where these holy men and women gathered were the living wells of that presence, places where it flowed unbidden and unimpeded, greening small clefts of hope within the dry face of a country scorched by generations of holy war.

Elijah's spring is still a place that moistens the roots of our religions in the benedictions that flow from nature, uniting a remnant among the horde that are now more than ever separated and sorted by the will to possess. On or about July 20 each year, Carmelite friars celebrate the feast day of Elijah on Mount Carmel. Joined by Jewish and Muslim counterparts, they make a pilgrimage to the site of Elijah's grotto, blessing themselves and one another in waters that have never discriminated in their timeless offer to quench the thirst of all who come with an open spirit.

One strain of the narrative tradition of Mount Carmel suggests that Elijah never died, that he waits like an underground well and springs forth into life when and where he is needed. The Elijah folklore has found its way into the esoteric side of Sufism in the person of a spiritual guide who reveals himself to the Sufi in dreams and visions, meeting them in their hour of need, saving them from the perils of travel, answering their questions, and inspiring them to carry on the mystic way. His name is Al-Khidr, sometimes Nabi Khader, but most often simply Khidr, which means "Green

One." In Muslim tradition he has been confounded with both Elijah and Saint George, whose myths originate in Syria. While this mysterious figure with many incarnations and reincarnations can be traced as least as far back as the pagan myths of Babylon, it was the wandering Sufi masters who made him their own. Peter Lamborn Wilson calls him "the very patron and personification of Sufi travel," and says that he embodies the Muslim hadith, or saying, "Three things of this world delight the heart: water, green things, and a beautiful face."[15]

Khidr's greenness places his spirit in the wilderness where the lost and troubled seem always to encounter him as the bearer of divine wisdom. The most famous Sufi who received the spiritual guidance of Khidr/Elijah is Ibn 'Arabi. Born into Spain's Andalusia in 1165 when the three great monotheistic religions were still living in open interchange and mutual respect, Ibn 'Arabi traveled widely throughout the Islamic world. His way of thinking about God, reality, and the spiritual trajectory of man has come to be seen as a point of departure of untold influence in modern spirituality well beyond Islam. Early in the twentieth century, Madrid priest and literary scholar Miguel Asín Palacios proved that the spiritual journeys narrated and annotated in Dante's *Vita Nuova* and *Divina Commedia* were directly influenced by the writings of Ibn 'Arabi. Asin and other critics have found structural similarities between *Vita Nuova* and Ibn 'Arabi's *Interpretation of Desires*, and between *Divina Commedia* and Ibn 'Arabi's *Alchemy of Happiness* that exceed all possibility of coincidence. Others have speculated, with less evidence for proof and greater possibility of coincidence, that Ibn 'Arabi's understanding of the spiritual journey may have contributed to the thinking of the two great Carmelite mystics of sixteenth-century Spain: Saint Teresa of Avila and Saint John of the Cross. By that century, the religious tolerance of Andalusia had been gutted by the Catholic Inquisitors in their rabid contempt for the unbaptized—in particular, Jews and "Saracens," as Muslim people were known. If a Catholic mystic living in Andalusia at the time had in any way come into contact with the thinking of a Sufi writer, she would have gone to pains to hide the fact. We will never know if Teresa's *Way of Perfection* and John of the Cross's *Dark Night of the Soul* and *Ascent of Mount Carmel* were at some level following ways, nights, and ascents taken four hundred years earlier by an Islamic country-man whose own mystical travels inspired him to write in detail of the *isra* or "night journey" and the *mi'raj* or "ascent."

I have found nothing that proves or in any way acknowledges an interchange between Sufi and Carmelite mysticism, nor any document that places Ibn 'Arabi on Mount Carmel. Yet, given his reputation for travel and claim to have been mentored by the great and immortal Khidr, I can't help thinking that he would have spent at least some time on Elijah's mountain. And, if he did, he might well have met the early Carmelite hermits there, perhaps spoken to them in Latin, or Spanish for that matter, for an Andalusian scholar would have known how to address a Christian. I imagine a figure such as Ibn 'Arabi, a Shaykh al-Akbar or "great master" as he is sometimes called, to be someone who speaks several languages and has lived in Europe. The Levantine winds carry him around the Mediterranean and eventually to the heights of Hakkarmel where he moves among the various hives of Christian, Jewish, and Sufi hermits, indiscriminately tasting and sharing the nectar that flows from the mystic's longing for union. With Khidr whispering in his ear he declares, "My heart is a temple for idols, a Ka'ba for pilgrims, the tablet of the Pentateuch and the Qur'an. Love alone is my religion."[16] He talks of Abraham, Moses, Elijah, Jesus, Mary, and Muhammad, reciting all the while the verses of the prophets and poets. And when the morning comes and the one they had named Muhyiddin ("Revivifier of Religion") has disappeared on the eastbound winds, the disciples of Mount Carmel find they can talk to one another a bit, about the ways of Elijah and Mary, and they live at least for a while in trust and community.

There is no reason to believe such a Pentecostal moment ever happened, of course, but I was able to find a reference suggesting that, at the very least, the denizens of medieval Mount Carmel may have swapped ideas on how to survive the heat of desert days and the cold of desert nights. Father Elias Friedman, who wrote the authoritative history of the hermits on Mount Carmel, said that the original mantle of the Carmelites was similar to the "carpeta worn by Sufi holy men who lived in the Mount Carmel region."[17] The name Sufi comes from *suf*, Arabic for "wool," referring to their habit of undyed wool. When the Carmelites suddenly appeared in England and Europe after emerging from the deserts of the Holy Land, they were wearing a distinctive barred poncho made of alternating bands of bleached and unbleached wool.

To followers of Elijah and Khidr, the bestowing of a garment is always significant. The tradition, in Hebrew scripture at least, begins with Elijah's investiture of his successor Elisha when the old prophet takes his own cloak and throws it over the back of his initiate. Muhammad, likewise, is said to have been given a tunic by wandering Christian monks during his early days in the desert of Hijaz while he was receiving Allah's revelations. The Sufi initiate, or *murid*, is given his sacred garment, the *khirqah*, during an initiation ceremony. Ibn 'Arabi claimed that Khidr himself invested him with the *khirqah*, as Elijah had Elisha in times past. Beyond proof or disproof, the striped poncho of the Carmelites allows us to imagine the circle of mystic and prophetic endowment coming round on the desert plateaus where it began.

We are a thousand years and a continent away from that moment when the mystics of one faith may have blessed the mystics of another. Yet, here on this prairie hilltop far from the home range of Khidr, there is this scrap of cloth that Mary holds between her fingers—the grace garment of the ones who settled Saint Peter's colony. It is easy enough to dismiss the scapular as superstitious and antiquated, something people once wore under their shirts to get a leg up on death and other diminishments. Those who have worn it, and the few who still do, say that it assures them of Mary's continuous prayers; that it is a silent way of saying to Mary that they venerate her and have confidence in her protection. They feel that by simply wearing the scapular, they express these beliefs every minute, praying without ceasing.

The scapular is much smaller than it was in early Carmelite times—two swatches of wool, each a few square inches, one in front, one in back, suspended over the shoulders by strings or strips of cloth—but it would still catch your eye in the locker room. We have strong reactions to this kind of piety. Part of us thinks it pathetic: *Who would ever wear such an item of overt Christian devotion?* It's more than a little off-putting. If you saw your friend take his shirt off and found him wearing a scapular, you'd think he'd quietly flipped his lid. It's weird and overpious, a foreign, antique gesture, something like bowing to a stranger with your hands pressed together.

Our discomfort may have something to do with our tendency to locate devout believers at certain coordinates along the spectrum of religious practice. We wonder how much further along that line we would have to slide before arriving at the folks who bind their children to their beds for not paying attention at church.

When you know better than to believe that your daily life depends on the favor of the Divine, when you are convinced that the magic has gone out of the world, when you have invested all of your belief in your own personal resources, in new idols of self-determination and individual achievement, it becomes easy to decide who is using religion as a crutch or a bludgeon. In a post-modern world, to wear something like a scapular is to admit that you are feeble of mind and spirit. Yet, if we recognize our spiritual longings, pursue them honestly, we come sooner or later to a moment of humility when we clothe ourselves in utter helplessness before the larger forces of Nature, before the mystery of the Divine. If we have any desire to dwell within a larger spiritual order, to worship anything beyond our own comfort, success, and achievement, such a basic admission is required. Which is why we see the poor and ignorant wearing scapulars and crucifixes. They have no illusions about saving themselves. You have to be rich and educated to afford the fantasy that you are in control, that you can make your own destiny and need not depend on any other saving grace.

Cree people have a term for this helplessness—*kitimākisiw*. All who have taken the spiritual path have come to this juncture—I am nothing, can do nothing without the grace of God, and here I am a weak and tremulous being, in need of protection and unworthy of the gifts that keep me alive and in the presence of love. It is the posture of self-oblivion of the Kabbalah, forehead down against the knees, the one that Muhammad saw the Nestorian Christian monks practice when they bowed toward Jerusalem at prayer time, the posture of Elijah praying for the divine grace of rain to fall upon the brittle pasture land of Hakkarmel.

# LEAVEN I

———————————————————•———————————————————

E very few minutes, yellow-rumped warblers pass above this
hilltop in twos and threes, tossing behind themselves their
characteristic *chip* calls. A meadowlark, feeling a resurgence of
summer longings, places a last song marker on the wind. The birds
are leaving: cranes, warblers, and meadowlarks, each kind on their
own pathway.

This morning I went for a walk at Saint Peter's to look for
migrant songbirds. I've made it a habit whenever I stay at the abbey
to rise early and walk along Wolverine Creek or down paths the
brothers have cut through the woods. There are always red-eyed
vireos and phoebes to keep an eye on and wild orchids to acknowledge at trailside. Afterward I scribble down some notes on the
species I see—birds, plants, and the few butterflies I am able to
identify with binoculars—but the abbey grounds are mapped in my
mind by the birds I have encountered on my walks: this is the swale
where the oriole was; this stand of poplar had a Cooper's hawk
eating a robin two summers ago; here is the place where I heard a
yellow-throated chat calling; this tree had a nest full of young red-
tailed hawks still covered by white natal down in July; the great
horned owls perch on this edge of the pines at dusk.

When I cross the lawn near the guest wing at Saint Peter's I
always think of the time two red crossbills flew by as I walked to the
chapel to attend Sunday Eucharist. They passed overhead and then
behind the bell tower as it rang out the call to Mass. This is a bird

of the northern forest but I wasn't altogether surprised to find it at Saint Peter's. The grounds include several acres of woodland containing white spruce, tamarack, and Scots pine, all planted by the brothers early in the last century. The large trees, all the same age, lack the successional ecology and structure found in a true forest, and the understory vegetation is a little strange, tending toward the alien, but the place behaves a little bit like an island of boreal life on the prairie. The mix of resident and summer bird species is proof enough to me that the Benedictines have managed to bring a sample of the north out onto the plains. I have found several northern forest species apparently breeding in the woods, including ruby-crowned kinglet, yellow-rumped warbler, red-breasted nuthatch, Swainson's thrush, and the two crossbills—white-winged and red.

The red crossbill is a Holarctic species, which means that it occurs in appropriate habitat across the entire northern region of the planet. Its breeding range follows the great boreal forest or taiga that wreathes the northern hemisphere. Seeing it here on the northern great plains, at a monastery devoted to a faith that has made its own wreath around the globe, brought an old story to mind. It is one that the Catholic peasants of Germany have told since medieval times, a story about the red crossbill coming to Christ's aid as he suffered on Golgotha. A version of the legend appears in a popular nineteenth-century German poem that the original Benedictines of Saint Peter's may well have known. Longfellow translated it from the original by the German-Jewish poet Julius Mosen, calling it "The Legend of the Crossbill":

> On the cross the dying Saviour
> Heavenward lifts his eyelids calm,
> Feels, but scarcely feels, a trembling
> In his pierced and bleeding palm.
> And by all the world forsaken,

Sees he how with zealous care
At the ruthless nail of iron
A little bird is striving there.

Stained with blood and never tiring,
With its beak it doth not cease,
From the cross it would free the Saviour,
Its Creator's Son release.

And the Saviour speaks in mildness:
"Blest be thou of all the good!
Bear, as token of this moment,
Marks of blood and holy rood!"

And that bird is called the crossbill;
Covered all with blood so clear,
In the groves of pine it singeth
Songs, like legends, strange to hear.

We often hear that the anthrocentric view that spins such tales has distorted our regard for nature and spawned the earth-eating monstrosity that is technological man. Being an anthro myself, though, I have trouble imagining, much less operating from or telling stories from, an ornithocentric world view. I am drawn to the old fables that suggest a sympathy between humanity and other creatures, including those that turn people into animals and animals into people, for the same reason children are drawn to them. They are stories about grace and they harken back to our racial origins, to the Esau spirit immersed in the sensuous, creaturely, and inde-terminate realm of wildness. Hunters, facing the mysteries of life, once warmed themselves by hearths that flickered with the narra-tive shadows of eagles, bears, lions, and deer. The mysteries we face now are not as different as we like to think, which may be why the thought of a magical encounter between a bird and the dying Christ can stir the embers of that oldest of religious feelings.

At mass this morning, as I stared sleepily up at the River of Life in the clerestory, I saw two pieces of red glass caught in the current and thought again of the crossbills. Then a voice talking about Elijah and Elisha entered my reverie. One of the brothers had risen and was giving the first reading. Remarkably, it was the story where the elder prophet Elijah tosses his cloak upon his prophetic heir, Elisha—the very piece of scripture that is often used in the Carmelite investiture ceremony, when people, lay and religious, are enrolled in the Confraternity of the Scapular.

Later I flipped through the Old Testament to the end of 1 Kings to figure out where the call of Elisha fits in to the overall narrative. Kings has some of the most fantastical, baffling, and bloodthirsty tales of the Hebrew scriptures, and Elijah, the wild man of Hakkarmel, features in many of them. The story of his passing on the prophetic mantle to Elisha comes soon after the contest of gods at El Marahka, when the Israelites submit to the power of Yahweh. The flood rains fall on the mountain of the Lord, flushing the slaughtered prophets of Baal out to the sea as the evil King Ahab flees in his chariot to Jezreel, Elijah running before him like one of the Arab marathoners of old who would cover fifty miles in a day, sleep the night, wake, and do it again.

Between the events on Mount Carmel and the account of Elisha's commission, the author of Kings has placed a poignant story that shows a defeated and despairing Elijah coming into the presence of Yahweh atop another sacred mountain. When Jezebel learns of Elijah's exploits on Mount Carmel, she vows to have him killed. Elijah lights out for the country, lamenting that his triumph has turned to ashes. The *New Jerusalem Bible* says that he "went on into the wilderness, a day's journey, and sitting under a furze bush wished he were dead. 'Yahweh,' he said, 'I have had enough. Take my life; I am no better than my ancestors'" (1 Kings 19:4–5).

Then Elijah falls asleep only to be woken by an angel who has delivered hot scones and a jar of water. After tasting the food and water he tries to lie down again, but the angel nudges him a second time. "'Get up and eat, or the journey will be too long for you.' So he got up and ate and drank, and strengthened by that food he walked for forty days and forty nights until he reached Horeb, the mountain of God" (1 Kings 19:7–8).

This is Sinai, *the* mountain of the Lord, where Moses saw God and where the covenant between Yahweh and Israel was first sealed. Elijah's journey to Sinai allows the author of Kings to bring his readers back in their imaginations to the first exile and the holy bond that carried them forth. Kings was written for people who were living in the aftermath of catastrophe—the Babylonian exile of the sixth century BCE. Early in that century, Nebuchadnezzar had stormed Jerusalem, reducing the holy city to rubble, burning the temple, and marching the citizens of Judea off to Babylon. The Israelites, exiled again and without their king, their temple, and their promised land, had only the Torah and their prophets to guide and console them. During the long decades of exile languishing by the rivers of Babylon, the Israelites began to wonder if the covenant of Moses had been a cosmic fraud, or if Yahweh had broken His promise to protect Israel. The writer of Kings, like the prophets of that era, knew that it was Israel who had forgotten and dishonored the covenant. Its kings had taken up with other gods, broken every law in Leviticus, and the people had followed their example eagerly. Yahweh, if anything, had extended his tolerance and favor long after Israel's faithlessness and sin had nullified the terms of the covenant. When the author set out to tell the history of Israel to her children lost in Babylon—for that is what the book of Kings is, a chronicle of a nation—he wanted both to chasten and give hope to his readers. If you could express in a paragraph the abiding subtext of Kings flowing beneath the prophecies fulfilled in the life of Israel and her monarchs, it might go something like this:

*Yahweh did not give up on the covenant; we did. A long path made by our own sin and betrayal has led us to this land of tears and longing. But there is hope nonetheless, for our God is a patient and forgiving god. If we can repent, learn from our errors, allow the blessings of our ancestors to encourage us, and rededicate ourselves to Yahweh, all will be well. This is not the time to walk away from faith in self-pity and despair; it is the time to take stock, dust off the ashes of exile and begin the Godward journey again.*

The angel urging Elijah to the mountain of God came in this same spirit of return and fidelity to the way of God. He makes the journey to the mountain, not because it is a fine place to escape from the prophecy business and its perils, but because it is the birthplace of the Hebrew faith, the last place anyone saw God and lived to tell the tale. Elijah climbs the mountain and spends the night in a cave. Again, the author has taken pains to place Elijah in Moses's footsteps, for it is the same "cleft in the rock" where Moses centuries before cowered in fear as Yahweh passed by. In Exodus, Yahweh shields Moses from the glory of His countenance and then finally allows the prophet a glimpse of His retreating presence. The theophany that follows Elijah's night in the cave is as stirring and lyrical as any in the Judeo-Christian tradition. It begins with the servant of Yahweh cringing in the crevice as Moses had long ago, half-expecting to have his wish beneath the furze tree fulfilled:

> Then he was told, "Go out and stand on the mountain before Yahweh." Then Yahweh himself went by. There came a mighty wind, so strong it tore the mountains and shattered the rocks before Yahweh. But Yahweh was not in the wind. After the wind came an earthquake. But Yahweh was not in the earthquake. After the earthquake came a fire. But Yahweh was not in the fire.

> And after the fire came the sound of a gentle breeze. And when Elijah heard this, he covered his face with his cloak and went out and stood at the entrance of the cave. (1 Kings 19:11–13)

With wind, earthquake, and fire as heralds, almost as bluffing fanfare to prove the contrast that follows, God comes as the softest of whispers in the prophet's ear. As always, there is the tension between the God of violent retribution and the God of compassion and tenderness. Not knowing which to expect, a prophet is bound to crouch and tremble. Hearing Yahweh's gentleness, Elijah begins moaning about his fate: I'm the only remaining prophet, I proved you are the one God, and they still want to kill me. Yahweh brushes off the complaint and tells Elijah to anoint two kings and then also to anoint Elisha as his successor in prophecy. Then, after predicting the downfall of all the warring nations, Yahweh promises to spare seven thousand righteous ones of Israel.

Elijah sets off with his marching orders and finds the young Elisha out plowing a field with a yoke of twelve oxen. Elijah throws his hair cloak over Elisha's shoulders, investing him with a new life as prophet. To show his breaking with the past of his life as the son of a prosperous landowner (twelve oxen was as much a sign of wealth then as an SUV is today), Elisha slaughters the oxen, breaks up the plow, lights it on fire, and roasts the beasts then and there. They celebrate with a feast and then walk off into their lives as prophets of the faithful remnant of Israel.

I am not sure what the priests and rabbis say about this sequence in Kings, from Elijah's attempt on Mount Carmel to win back the backsliding Israelites to his theophany at Horeb to the call of Elisha, but when I read it as one piece I can feel myself moving a step nearer to an appreciation for the way suffering and redemption, good and evil, play together within a field too vast for our comprehending. Behind all the prediction and fulfillment dramas, the exaggerated narratives of vengeance, the fantastical accounts of miracles and God making His ways known to man, there runs a tension of truths that settle into the heart as hope.

Near the end of 1 Kings 19, when Yahweh sends Elijah back to work with a prediction that the bloodshed will continue, I imagine the author again trying to console his people in Babylon with a voice that is realistic yet encouraging. Yahweh tells Elijah that, yes, there is going to be more death among the nations, the sword will continue to reign, but a few good people will be spared, a remnant to put things right and carry on. Franciscan writer Richard Rohr says it is always the small remnant—the leaven, the light, and the salt of gospel stories—that keeps us back from the brink. Or, as Teilhard would say, in the long run of the Creation's genesis, evil always leads down a blind alley, along a branch of evolution that sooner or later self-prunes. Within the time scale of the sun and the earth, the doings of humanity that are out of sync with God's ways will always fail. What survives is the gradually accruing results of love's energy and the building up of the earth by the people of God.

# LEAVEN II

A plume of dust boils up from a gravel road where someone is
hurrying to town. Karen, one arm outstretched to measure
finger widths from sun to horizon, announces that the earth has
come to a halt.

I point out to her the white steeples of three churches that have
emerged like buoys out of the fog now that the haze has dropped.
These country churches mark some of the early settlements on the
100,000 acres set aside for the colony of German-Catholic immigrants. From the beginning they have been served by one of the
Benedictines from Saint Peter's Abbey, a tradition that continues
in a few parishes today. Many of the chapels are well-maintained
and still hold regular Sunday services, which is surprising in a part
of the continent where most country churches serve no one but
pigeons, photographers, and city relatives looking for a landmark
at the turnoff to the farm.

At Saint Peter's I sometimes catch myself idealizing the lives of
the brothers. I see one of them walking with a hoe out toward the
gardens down the road overarched by elms, or watch the abbot in
jeans and ball cap drive by on a small tractor, and something not far
from envy creeps in. Maybe it is simple curiosity, a desire to know
more about those who kick off their shoes and retreat to a quieter
place. At the weeklong writers' and artists' retreats I've attended at
the abbey, where people from around the country gather to work
on their paintings, poems, and stories, few meals pass without at

least a comment or question about one monk or another. Someone is always wondering about the younger brothers, about their motivation, the *real* reason they joined the order. Theories emerge followed by rumors, placing the brothers into easy categories—the pious, the misfits, the escapists—that suit our mythologies of the religious life. That done, the next puzzle is how do they carry on, what secret compensations sustain them, what vices make up for all they have forsaken? If the celibate and ascetic are not pure, are even ridiculous or corruptible, then what cause have we to fight our own weaknesses and indulgences? We laugh at the coarse, appetitive monks of Chaucer or Kazantzakis because the irony soothes us with the knowledge that they are no better than the rest of us.

I have known Catholics who don't want to hear that ascetics are not all saints, who need to believe that there are holy men and women in monasteries leading chaste lives of unfailing prayer and devotion. Expectations of this kind might be even harder to live with than the idle gaze of skeptics, but none of it is fair to the individual ascetic. To some you are a morally superior being who must never falter or doubt, and to others you are a social failure hiding away in a cloister. Most monks and nuns, I would guess, are neither: just men and women who, like the rest of us, want to make the long ascent up the mountain, but prefer to do it in the company of others similarly inclined. No doubt people living in religious community regularly stumble into argument, lust, jealousy, bitterness, sloth, and from time to time *dysfunctional* might be the best word to describe the family they form. Even so, the religious collective survives over time, anchoring the larger community to a spiritual and cultural center.

In a civilization where even the smallest social units dissolve at the first sign of difficulty, a community of religious people sharing property and labor seems hopelessly utopian. Saint Peter's, the oldest Benedictine monastery in Canada, celebrated its one hundredth anniversary in 2003. Of course, held up to the longevity of monasteries in Germany, Italy, and France, the first century of a monastery is but a beginning. For this continent, though, any cooperative effort that outlives its members has done well. The history of the Great Plains is full of stories of colonists, farmers, and social reformers establishing intentional secular communities upon the highest of moral and civic ideals. Most did not survive to see a tenth anniversary. Meanwhile, the Amish, the Mennonites, and Christian religious orders have all been able to sustain themselves for generations, often thriving despite larger social and economic forces that militate against community.

More importantly, monastic orders, and the Benedictines in particular, have historically been able to exert an influence on the larger culture and religion outside the monastery walls. In a letter sent to the Vatican in the summer of 2001, Christine Vladimiroff, the prioress of the Benedictine sisters of Erie, responded to the church's order to prohibit one of her sisters from speaking at an international conference on women's ordination held in Dublin. The letter says that after holding a vote within the community she decided to send the nun in question, writer and theologian Joan Chittister, off to Dublin with the full blessing of the Benedictine sisters of Erie:

> My decision should in no way indicate a lack of communion with the church. I am trying to remain faithful to the role of the 1,500-year-old monastic tradition within the larger church. We trace our tradition to the early Desert Fathers and Mothers of the fourth century who lived on the margin of society in order to be a prayerful and questioning presence to both church and society.[1]

Apart from and within society at the same time, for fifteen centuries Benedictine monks and nuns have been fostering the simple communal values of the *Rule of Saint Benedict*, in effect leavening the world and the church with the expansive and humane vision of the gospel. From medieval times forward, Benedictine communities have been havens of civilization, scholarship, and egalitarianism surrounded by principalities where the mighty rule the ignorant.

People will often describe Benedictine communities as islands of hope, civility, and Christian peace, but when I visit Saint Peter's I have trouble seeing its edges. Islands are isolate, cut off from the main. Most of what I see at Saint Peter's testifies to its immersion in communities that ripple away from it in ever-widening circles: a local farmer pulls in next to the kitchen delivery door and unloads forty freshly slaughtered chickens from his half-ton truck; a priest at a church thirty-five miles to the south announces that everyone is invited to come and dig themselves a sack or two of potatoes from the abbey gardens; a woman pins her children's laundry on the line beside a small hermitage in the bush where the brothers are allowing her to take refuge for a few weeks; local farmers who can no longer trust their own water supply stop by to draw the purified water of Saint Peter's from a tap on the side of the carpentry shop; townspeople gather on the lawns on the Feast of Saint Benedict to eat barbecued buffalo burgers, celebrating not only the first Benedictine, but one of the most recent ones too, a young man who chose the day to profess his sacred vows before a gathering of the monks, a few friends, and relatives; Buddhists from the cities come to stay for residential retreats; *The Prairie Messenger*, the weekly newspaper produced at the abbey, prints letters from Mexico, England, and the United States, remarking on and sometimes complaining about the paper's progressive theology, its trenchant and Christ-centered analysis of politics in Brazil or the American "war on terrorism"; and each May, when the phoebes and warblers have returned and farmers are gearing up to seed their crops all around Saint Peter's, the abbot holds a ceremony to bless water from the spring runoff and seeds to be planted.

In such ways as these, a religious community becomes more heart than island, circulating its life within the farms and towns that surround it, all the while sustaining and in turn drawing sustenance from the spiritual, cultural, and political spheres of the world beyond.

If you were to place a pin on a map of the northern Great Plains for every small-town, locally owned industry, there would be a thin scattering here and there showing no particular pattern, except for the distorting effects of rail lines and highways and a small cluster of pinheads you would see in the towns surrounding Saint Peter's at Muenster. These would mark many of the Catholic communities that sprang up after the Benedictines arrived and are still dominated by the descendants of those original colonists. Throughout the area once within the abbacy of Saint Peter's, there are burgeoning industries in towns of less than a thousand people: seed and tillage equipment manufactured in Saint Brieux, semitrailers and grain haulers in Anaheim, wind-powered pumps and aerators in Englefield, filtration systems in Watson, grain augers and small utility trailers in Drake, tarpaulins and covers in Saint Gregor, and industrial hydraulics and candles right in Muenster itself.

Humboldt, the only town of any size in the region, lies a few miles west of Saint Peter's, between the abbey and Mount Carmel. Small but steadily growing at 5,100 people, Humboldt has several industries of its own and is often held up as a model of regional economic development. Bruno, the little town named for the venturing Benedictine who brought the colonists to the region, doesn't have a manufacturing business of its own, but it is the home of the Sage Hill Business Development Co-operative, an agency that offers financing, counseling, and business-plan advice to new enterprises in the region. The story has been repeated again and again: an inventive farmer tinkers away in his barn until he has made a better grain hopper or windmill. He builds a couple of them, sells them to neighbors, then hires their sons to help him make a few more. Soon he is running a small factory on the edge of town, short-circuiting the prevailing system where money spent on machinery supports economies of scale in eastern cities. The years pass by, with the hair salon, the café, and the co-op store in town thriving while others down the highway have gone out of business.

Much of this economic well-being can be attributed to wealth that comes from a German immigrant work ethic applied to fertile land over several generations, but I know too that some of the people who started these local industries attended high school at the abbey and planted trees or worked the gardens there when they were teenagers. The relative strength and communitarian ethic of this district—while others on equally rich soil dissolve within the global deluge of industrialized agriculture—is inextricably bound up with the legacy of the Benedictine brothers of Saint Peter's. During the abbey's first decades, when prairie farmers were still feeding themselves and their neighbors, and cropping methods were still being adapted to the northern soils and climate, Saint Peter's hosted annual field days where farmers from the colony and beyond would gather to learn about the latest in agriculture. Meanwhile, each church within Saint Peter's abbacy was served by a Benedictine priest and formed the core of community life, creating a cohesion that bound household to household and parish to parish. This interdependence has sheltered the townships of Saint Peter's Colony from some of the depredations that fall to a farm economy when it places itself at the mercy of distant markets.

While some of the industries that help keep these communities alive depend on conventional, chemical-intensive agribusiness, lately the region around Saint Peter's has become known for alternatives in agriculture as well. While at the abbey, I heard references to a little place a few miles to the north called Marysburg, where several families have switched to organic farming. Today Marysburg is a community hall, a couple of homes, and a baseball diamond spread out along a single street dominated by a twin-spired church far too large for the community it serves. Nevertheless, the surrounding area has its own chapter of the Organic Crop Improvement Association and a marketing organization that is one of Canada's largest suppliers of raw ingredient organic produce.

Once the crops are in the ground, summer in Marysburg is for baseball. Their teams have for decades sustained a tradition of trouncing their counterparts from much larger towns and cities. The little I have heard about the ball-playing Catholic farmers of Marysburg comes from talk around the abbey and accounts in local histories. Ball field or wheat field, Marysburg people have a tradition of working together against any force that might keep them down. The center of their communal survival, though, has always been the place they gather on Sunday mornings, the sanctuary that their forebears rebuilt and rededicated to Mary shortly after its predecessor was taken up into the prairie skies. It was a wild assumption leaving behind the grace lessons of destruction and renewal against which rural people shape their lives.

The first large church in town was an ambitious edifice with an eighty-foot steeple and a four-hundred-pound bell named "Maria Immaculata." Late one afternoon in the summer of 1919, though, the skies to the west turned dark and sent a tornado through the village. The grand church disappeared in a few moments, leaving nothing but a bell and a churchyard strewn with splinters. The settlers picked up Maria Immaculata and built another church around her—a bigger one with two spires and entirely made of brick. They named it Assumption Church, referring to Mary's assumption into heaven.

The Assumption is an ancient Catholic belief that can be traced back to the apostles. It claims that Mary's tomb was found empty soon after her death, and that, like Elijah, she was taken bodily to heaven. It's the kind of article of faith that has enraged protestants and led to some Catholic shoulder-shrugging. Still, believers point to the negative proof that no town or church in Christendom has ever claimed to possess Mary's remains, despite an early and long-standing practice of preserving the bones of saints. Belief in the Assumption eventually became Church doctrine, supporting its counterpart, the Immaculate Conception, which argues that God intervened when Mary herself was conceived to create an immaculate (that is, without the stain of original sin) vessel within which Christ might be formed into flesh and blood. The Assumption follows the logic that if the Mother of God was made immaculate she would also be made incorruptible. Catholics on the fanatical Marian fringe take the thought a step beyond doctrine and choose to believe that Mary never died.

On a hot July Saturday afternoon in Marysburg, after the ball game is over and the boys from Muenster have climbed into their half-tons and driven home to console themselves with a pilsner, one of the local women will walk over to the church to make sure things are in place for Mass the next morning. She does her round in the sanctuary, checking on the supply of hosts, refolding linen, and then, before leaving, she rests a moment on a pew near one of the side chapels. There, coolness and solitude come together, filling an interior so unlike the sun-glazed fields on the other side of the walls. Soft violet ribbons of light ripple over figures of kneeling angels that flank the altar. She doesn't think of Mary or the Assumption, or whether Mary is immaculate, dead, both, or neither. She is looking at the paintings and statuettes she dusted last week when a few of the women got together to clean the church, and she is happy to have something solid and beautiful to care for, to hold with pride when everything else in life, no matter how much care or work she invests, seems to slip away like breath into evening air.

# LEAVEN III

A car parked at the bottom of the hill a moment ago and now we are watching two people walk the shortcut up to the stone chapel at the base of the grassy slope Our Lady surveys. It is a couple in their early thirties. The man is pointing here and there as he talks. After walking to where we are at the foot of the shrine, he says hello and tells us with some enthusiasm that he was confirmed here as a boy.

"We used to come to the pilgrimages in July. Been a long time... Have you seen the old cathedral in Muenster, the one covered with all the pictures of saints? We were just there. I'd forgotten how beautiful it is. That guy sure was some artist."

Karen and I had been there too, earlier in the afternoon. Even more lavish than the church at Marysburg, Saint Peter's Cathedral in Muenster is known across the prairies for its elaborate murals covering the interior walls. Karen hadn't seen it before, so we made the one-mile walk from the abbey through the town of Muenster and across the highway to the west side of the Wolverine where the monastery was first built in the early decades of the twentieth century. The cathedral and a couple of small outbuildings are all that remain of the Benedictine's first stand on the banks of the Wolverine. How strange it would have looked, this square behemoth rising summer by summer at the hands of the German colonists. By 1910 it was finished, a massive white structure thrusting upward from the fescue plains, sixty feet higher than anything else from one horizon to the other, without so much as a poplar tree to join its vertical intrusion to the Wolverine tableland.

Today, there are poplar bluffs, and along the building's sides rows of large spruce trees, but Saint Peter's Cathedral still strikes the eye as a strange vertical imposition. Like our grain elevators, it is one of the stubborn upright gestures we've made to change a landscape that is even more stubborn in its preference for the recumbent. Against every flattening force the prairie has mustered over a century, it stands yet, a plumb-straight monument to a faith that, in its better moments, has found ways to bear the transforming tension held in the coincidence of such opposites. A cathedral is a cross with an interior that articulates the intersection of opposing values. Even as the windows remind the faithful of the world outside, as the nave and pews place everyone shoulder to shoulder, and as the flat altar and kneelers suggest a side-to-side encounter with one another on this earthly plane, still, the dominant movement in a building like Saint Peter's is upward. Vaulted ceiling, towers, choir loft, and pillars all rise from footings anchored in tradition that is always under the horizon of the present. The lines in a cathedral of this era draw our attention aloft, from the ground of all that is past to the transcendent elsewhere above the plain of human longing.

I felt that rise earlier this afternoon the moment my thumb pressed the door latch at Saint Peter's, sending a metallic *click* up into the arching sanctuary at the far end of the church and back again. As the door pulled free of the jamb, my eye caught a movement in one of the pews near the center of the nave. It was an elderly woman, her white head stirring at the sound of someone entering the silence of the church. There was a clatter as she fumbled for her cane and quickly unfolded her knees to stand. We watched her make her way to the aisle and then toward us in steps almost lively enough to mask an arthritic wobble in her gait. She was a small, frail creature, elfin and haloed by the afternoon light spilling in from the stained glass.

Her nametag read Marie. I began to apologize for disturbing her, but she smiled and broke in, "Have you come to see our beautiful cathedral?"

I said we had and, with a nod, she turned on her heel, pointed at the ceiling with her cane, and launched into a polished presentation, which she delivered at a breathless pace. Our first stop was to peer up at a painting of a lamb.

"Take note of the artist's genius in showing the lamb of God trapped in a thorn bush as our precious Lord and Savior looks on—just look at the compassion in his face. Isn't that amazing?"

From there we made our way swiftly up the aisle, viewing overhead frescoes of each of the apostles.

"If you look closely you will see that each of them is holding the instrument of his martyrdom..." In a detailed and lurid monologue that would not be out of place at a wax museum, she went through each of the apostles, giving their traditional names, the heathen nation they evangelized, their earthly trials and grisly exits. "This one traveled all the way to Egypt, that one was martyred with a long knife. They say he had his throat slit. That one holding the saw was cut in half.

"Notice the eyes, how they seem to follow you as you move... and here we see Mary's death and assumption into heaven. Did you know the story of Mary's death? She lived in a house with only three walls—who knows why, maybe penance—but when she died and they placed her in a tomb, her body disappeared in a matter of days, never to be seen again."

When we arrived at the sanctuary, Marie paused to tell us about her own history. She grew up in Muenster and then moved away as a young woman. "Sixty-five years away, but now I'm back," she said, and then returned to her narrative, directing our attention to the host of saints surrounding the image of the risen Christ. There were dozens of men and women, apparently positioned by rank: the inner circle of Abraham, Moses, a few key apostles, and then, beyond them, a community of the most beloved saints including Benedict and his twin sister, Saint Scholastica. In a church like this one, in which religious artwork utterly dominates the space, you almost feel entombed in the history of the faith, as though you'd fallen down into catacombs, lit a match and found a visual record of the myths of every saint and martyr lacquered to the walls. As we toured the cathedral with Marie, though, hearing the stories of each painting—"Saint Paul has the face of the abbot at the time, Bruno Doerfler"—what seemed most remarkable about the artwork was its very persistence in exile well above ground and so distant from the soil that yielded these stories and this way of keeping them.

At the abbey I had read a brief biography of the artist. It came to mind as Marie mentioned his name: "Imhoff, or Count Imhoff, as some called him, was born and trained in Germany. He came here because he loved the wilderness. He was a great hunter."

Bertholdt Imhoff, son of a Catholic gamekeeper, was born in a Rhineland castle in 1868. Although he felt more at home in the woods than in any salon or studio, his talent with a brush marked him for a career as an illustrator. After studying at art schools in Halle and Düsseldorf, he set out for the Americas, settling first in Pennsylvania, where he established himself as a muralist, decorating the interiors of churches and public buildings throughout New England. After marriage and several children, he returned to the Rhineland in the 1890s to set up business. The valleys and forests of his childhood, however, were disappearing rapidly into the throat of industry and so he decided to return to Pennsylvania. By 1914, Imhoff could see that the New England states were headed the same way. On the strength of an advertisement promoting virgin land available on the northwestern plains, he packed up his family and joined a band of settlers bound for the frontier country along the North Saskatchewan River.

It must have been the right soil for Imhoff's dream of subsistence in the hinterland, for he stayed the rest of his days on a patch of prairie and parkland near the town of Saint Walburg. He had little interest in the details of livestock and plowshare, left that to his oldest sons, but continued to paint, decorating the churches of immigrant Catholics all over the Northern Great Plains with images of angels, prophets, and saints. Among the devout of this region he has taken on the mantle of a saint himself. There are stories claiming that during the Great Depression he routinely refused to take any payment for the churches he painted.

The eighty-one images lining the walls of Saint Peter's Cathedral took him a year to complete and were a gift to his friend, Abbot Bruno. They are technically sound and fall faithfully into line with the accepted lineage of Western European Christian art from Giotto onward. Nearly a century before Imhoff's time, though, another German religious artist who also loved the wild dared to take a step off that line and received the expected whipping. In 1808 a young Caspar David Friedrich unveiled his now famous *The Cross in the Mountains* painting, showing Christ on a cross high atop a mountain crag, surrounded by fir trees and a moody sky. I remember twenty-some years ago seeing a slide of the painting in art history class and thinking, *What's the big deal? Why would a cross on a wild mountaintop cause such a kerfuffle in the art salons of Europe?* Not long after, Friedrich's name came up in a seminar on Romanticism and I began to understand.

We still bask in the afterglow of the age that captivated the Western imagination, starved as it was for an antidote to the stark determinism of the eighteenth century. When Friedrich painted *The Cross in the Mountains*, the rules for religious painting had scarcely been tested. To suggest that the sublime in nature and the divine in religion might consort in the wild corners of our world was to volunteer for banishment to the fringe with the likes of that lunatic engraver, Blake. The German art establishment excoriated Friedrich for much of his career, charging him with sacrilege and pantheist (read pagan) sensibilities. Though he continued to paint his haunting, melancholic images engulfing man's longings within unruly skies and seascapes, decrepit churchyards, and ruined cathedrals, he never recovered from the rejection and died a pauper in Dresden, sad and alone in 1840.

By the time young Imhoff was wielding his brush in the fresh chapels of a heathen world, Friedrich's work had been rediscovered by a post-Enlightenment civilization hankering for its romantic blend of religion and nature. I've looked in vain at the backgrounds behind the saints and martyrs that adorn the walls of Saint Peter's, hoping for a hint that this German painter may have felt the pull of the romantic landscape tradition launched by his countryman a century earlier. As he filled in the outlines of yet another image of Saint Thomas, this artist who hunted wild fowl, deer, and moose for three weeks every fall and who fled civilization to find a wilder place to work must have dreamed of the balsam-scented paths, the elk whistle rising from thick-wooded valleys. If he never showed it in his murals, perhaps his desire to serve modestly within the bounds of Catholic mural tradition prevailed over any influence of the secular imagination. But I wonder also if it simply never came to mind because, on the northern prairie of the early twentieth century, nature was so all-encompassing, so utterly dominant that the mere presence of a church within that sky-and-grass realm expressed to the artist all that can ever be said of the juxtaposition of Christian faith and the sublime in creation. Perhaps each little chapel Imhoff adorned was his cross in the wilderness, and there was romance enough in enclosing the stories of God's servants on earth within a landscape that a few years earlier had been the sovereign domain of the buffalo.

As we toured Saint Peter's looking at paintings made with oils, canvas, and mythologies shipped in from Europe, I thought about this tension between the indoor religious drama on the one hand and the overarching outdoor realm of wildness that drew the artist and his civilization here from a world where nature had been reduced to a residue circumscribed by the lines of an ode or the frame of the picturesque. Even more distracting was a polarity in my own regard for the Christian enterprise in the New World. Away from a place like Saint Peter's and from people like Marie, it is easy to embrace the anticolonial critique and condemn every assertion of European values within this already sufficient landscape. I am assured of my opinions until I walk down the nave and find a holy woman whose life has covered the short spell during which imported narratives *seemed* to overtake indigenous ones.

After sixty-five years away from her beloved cathedral, she has returned to die in one of the last places where the myth of the chapel in the wilderness can still be remembered. Amid paintings made by a Christian hunter in love with pagan places, she lifts her prayers. Who can fault her devotion to the myth, her love of tradition, her simple piety? Whenever I meet someone who says he has the solution to the conflict between the indigenous on the one hand and the introduced on the other, I turn and head in the other direction as fast as I can. Any prophet too impatient to bear the tension contained in the paradoxical mysteries of our passage through time is a false prophet. An old woman at prayer alone in a church is engaged in that primitive gesture of helplessness, that admission that we *don't* have the answers or the power to resolve all that jostles our lives, sets us at odds with one another. And all that she ponders, every power she relinquishes runs to the sacred inter-section of the opposing values modeled by the cruciform building in which she makes her prayers. When Marie enters her beautiful cathedral, something within her but beyond her knowing senses that she is entering the cross that holds together a tension reflected in the very warp and weft of creation, in a cosmos that is both chaotic and ordered, bad and good, broken and whole, nurturing and threatening all at once.[1]

During our tour with Marie from image to image, her reverence for the Christian story and her admiration for the creative powers that built and decorated the church was always tempered by an awareness of more destructive forces afoot. Looking up to the ceiling, this time to the heights above the choir loft, she pointed again with her cane.

"See that water damage up there. There's been a leak for years that no one can fix, though they've tried and tried…It's not easy to keep an old church like this going. There was a time when they'd pretty well given up on her, decided they'd just save the sanctuary with its dome and move it across the highway to the abbey. They brought building movers in all the way from Minnesota and they tried to lift her but she wouldn't budge. Foundation's just too solid."

Marie's eyes glistened with fervor as she told us of another time when the cathedral held her ground. The day the cyclone came, touched down right in front of the church steps and then blew around both sides, taking out most of the spruce trees. But the building didn't shift a hair off plumb.

After Marie concluded our tour, I wandered up to the sanctuary toward the lectern that serves as pulpit. There was a sheet of paper there, likely from the Sunday Mass held a few hours earlier. The heading read "EARTHCARE CONNECTION— INTENTIONS FOR SEPTEMBER 16." First on the list was "May the spirit help all people see the value in healthy drinking water and healthy food. We pray to the Lord."

The appropriate response ran through my head, automatically, "Lord hear our prayer." Words again, but, given a chance, prayer can reach for an older, wilder power that will survive and even bring tornadoes no matter what happens to our crumbling cathedrals, can address not merely the God we carried here in our haversacks, books, and murals, but the God who is also of this holy land, dwelling here and now in this ground. A sense of urgency and powerlessness runs beneath such an intentional prayer in rural communities, where the quality of water and the means of food production are increasingly at odds. Crisis and vulnerability tend to make us better Christians, better pray-*ers*, returning us to the early People of the Way, that motley band of peasants, slaves, and displaced people who had no churches, privileged no space over another, for all was sacred under heaven. In their New Jerusalem, property was held in common and no temples were required, for the stones themselves shouted the good news they celebrated in the Eucharist. On such altars they placed nothing more extraordinary than their story as resurrection people. They were in effect a new kind of pagan, marginalized by the city and its established powers, until Emperor Constantine converted for his own reasons, declared amnesty for all Christians, and let them into the Roman polis. Once the cross showed up on the banners of conquerors, it was not long before the faith became a church and moved inside the same old walls raised by the sons of Jacob against the desert wild, the dangerous other, and the ritually impure.

Nonetheless, great forces were unleashed in that budding of human civilization. Forces of equal magnitude mingle now in the shadows of all the crosses we have fixed upon the New World's hillsides, and in their reiteration as quadrangled property line and roadway, church, town, and farmstead. God only knows what will come of this new round of wrestling between hunter and shepherd, shaman and priest.

Karen and I left the cathedral, our minds awhirl with the names of saints. Outside, we walked past rows of spruce trees running east to west. Most were mature, perhaps eighty to ninety years old, but in their midst was a gap where several young trees marked the path of the tornado. I thought of Marie, still inside. She'd be settling back into her pew again, waiting for the next visitors, contemplating the sorrowful mysteries of her Lord shown in the paintings and sculptures, preparing for her own entry into mystery and quieting the struggle within her heart by looking at the images that as a child moved her to a faith worth coming home to six decades later.

# A NEW SMALL-RENTED LEASE

*Woe to those who add house to house*
*And join field to field*
*Until everywhere belongs to them*
*And they are the sole inhabitants of the land.*

—Isaiah 5:8

"If you could, wouldn't you like to come to a place like this when it's time to die?" I ask Karen, thinking of Marie. "Remember that line from Eliot? He's praying to a hilltop shrine like this one, talks about sons and husbands setting forth and never returning—fishermen lost where the sound of the sea bells no longer reach them. Here it's farmers instead of fishermen: 'Lady, whose shrine stands on the promontory, / Pray for all those who are [on farms], those / Whose business has to do with [earth].'"

Eliot's *Four Quartets* was just a title of a long poem I had never taken the time to read until I learned that it was a favorite of one of the monks at Saint Peter's—one whose life is an angelus ringing out above the waves of this cropland sea. His daily prayers, now more than ever in his old age, hold up for consecration the lives of the people who continue to farm the land contained within Saint Peter's fifty townships. Father James has lived alone in the bush south of the abbey for thirty years. We met on my very first visit to the abbey, introduced by a mutual friend, Nolan, who drove me there on a day trip. As we sat and drank tea in his hermitage

245

in the woods, I asked if he'd mind my coming by for another visit sometime. He smiled and said that would be fine, but as we left I wondered about intruding on his silence. What else does a forest-dwelling monk have to claim, if not his solitude?

The prayers of intention left on the cathedral's pulpit were an encouraging sign, but not everyone in the area is in love with the idea of organic farming. Places like Marysburg and Muenster have all the expected tensions between conventional and chemical-free producers. Nonetheless, some of the local zeal for alternative agriculture and rural renewal seems to be gaining a foothold at the abbey itself. The Benedictine brothers have always been quick to adopt the latest farm methods and equipment for use on their 1,800 acres of cultivated land. As farming became more mechanized and dependent on synthetic fertilizers and chemical solutions to weeds and pests, the farmer monks were swept along in the change. They now find themselves riding monster tractors, spraying pedigreed crops, and employing the very technologies that have been emptying the countryside around the abbey, sending the casualties of industrialized agriculture off to distant urban centers. Today, though, there is talk at Saint Peter's of going back to chemical-free, low-input agriculture. Some of the brothers are trying to make the transition to organic methods and dreaming of once again leading the local farm community by example.

On the second floor of the college at Saint Peter's there is a room that houses the Center for Rural Studies and Enrichment (CRSE). In recent years, the CRSE has made a name for itself by producing some of the best research on sustainable rural communities to come out of the Great Plains. The day I stopped for a visit I was greeted by Noreen Strueby, a Marysburg woman who works at the center. We talked briefly about a prairie watershed study the center has launched, and Noreen handed me reports from other studies on a wide range of subjects: the unrecognized labor of farm women and children; family violence in rural areas; the gross discrepancies between farm-gate and retail prices; and the effects of poverty on aboriginal and nonaboriginal children living in the country.

Noreen grew up in the Muenster area, moved away to the city for a while, and then returned several years ago with her husband to take up farming and raise four children in Marysburg. She and her neighbors live many of the realities that are charted and graphed in the reports of the CRSE: farm input costs increase by 22 percent to 56 percent in fifteen years while prices for some farm products rise a few percentage points and others actually decline; 23 percent of household income on "family farms" actually comes from farming; the store price of a box of cereal rises $2.44 in twenty-two years while the farm-gate price of the grain to make the cereal increases $.03 over the same period.

Looking through the shelves of books in her office, I found titles from the likes of Wendell Berry, Wes Jackson, Brewster Kneen, and the other modern prophets of agricultural reform. As I prepared to leave with a collection of CRSE reports, I asked Noreen if she and the people in the movement think faith has a role to play in rural renewal. She told me about something called the Marysburg Project, a demonstration farm sponsored by the abbey and two other local religious orders. A fellow named Duane Guinau runs it through Earthcare, the organization responsible for the prayer intentions I found on the pulpit.

Then Mahakashyapa asked the Buddha, "World-Honored One, some monks declare themselves to be forest-dwelling monks.

World-Honored One, how should a monk act to be called a forest-dwelling monk?"

The Buddha replied to Kashyapa, "A forest-dwelling monk must delight in a secluded forest and live in it...A monk should think of eight things if he wishes to live in a secluded place." What are the eight?

> To renounce the body;
> to renounce life;
> to relinquish material possessions;
> to leave all beloved places;
> to die on a mountain like a deer;
> to perform the deeds of a forest dweller when in a secluded place;
> to live by the Dharma; and
> not to abide in afflictions.[1]

I was covered in road dust by the time the trucker dropped me off at the side of the highway the first time I came to stay at the abbey. After unpacking my things and showering, I walked out past the gardens and cemetery to the hermitage woods. I had come to Saint Peter's in large part to see Father James and I knew that if I procrastinated at all I'd lose my nerve. I could have had one of the brothers pass a note to Father James requesting a meeting time, but Nolan had told me just to knock on his door and make the arrangements in person, so off I went.

I plunged down a likely looking trail and had not gone far when I saw the white siding of a cottage flickering within the gloom. As I drew near, a child's voice rang out and I saw a young but tired-looking mother hanging laundry on an improvised clothesline. Later I was told that she and her children had been evicted from their home in a town nearby. The Benedictines were giving her a place to stay as long as she needed it.

I passed the cottage and turned down a fork in the trail, following it into the heart of the thicket. The trees closed in on either side and I began to recognize on the forest floor some of the signs I'd noticed on my visit with Nolan. The caragana, an invasive Eurasian species, had been thinned. Spruce and tamarack saplings reached up through the understory. The mature poplars were well spaced and healthy, and moss-covered deadfall lay in neat rows on the ground like ancient gravesites. The farther down the path I moved the more I could feel the presence of one who had been long performing "the deeds of a forest dweller," opening the canopy to bathe seedlings in light and lowering dead trees down to the soil.

I slowed my pace as I remembered how badly I'd started off with Father James when Nolan introduced us. I had tried to say something about his tending of the forest but it came out awkwardly. He gave me an assessing glance and answered, with a hint of consternation, that he didn't like to see a tree hung up in the branches in a limbo between life and death, and that the dead should be returned to a place where they can undergo new life.

The trail seemed longer than the one in my memory, but just as I was about to backtrack I caught another glint of white paint through the latticework of aspen leaves. The cottage took me by surprise that first time and it has done the same on every visit since. I walk through aspen and caragana wondering if I have made a wrong turn and then there it is on the other side of some branches, like an elephant munching silently in the shade of acacia boughs.

I stepped onto the doorstep made of glacial boulders. There was a single dove feather in each corner of a small screen window on the door, and beneath that a sign saying Maranatha, Aramaic for "Come, O Lord." Around the side of the building I could see a small bird feeder and, where the sun was breaking through from the edge of the woods, a patch of summer annuals the size of a tabletop, including some sweet peas climbing a trellis of chicken wire staked into the ground. There was a bench made of a plank resting on top of two pin cherry stumps.

I mustered my courage and tapped on the doorjamb lightly. Some movement within and then the door drew open a ways, until I could see Father James's face in the interior shadow: lined brow, wire-rimmed glasses, sharp nose, a circumspect mouth surrounded by a neatly clipped beard of gray.

"Yes?"

I apologized for coming unannounced and then muttered something about meeting him with Nolan a few weeks earlier.

"Would it be okay if I came sometime during the week for a talk?"

"How long will you need?"

"Oh, not long, just an hour or so." I wanted to reassure him that I wouldn't be popping by for daily chats.

We agreed on a time and then, after a pause, I pointed to his flowers and remarked on the color in the sweet peas.

"The gophers are getting to them," he said, "too many of them and I can't keep them away from anything. It's those striped ones. I'm going to have to deal with them." Then a glance to see how I'd react to the idea of a gopher-killing monk. Perhaps I had expected Saint Francis or Thoreau.

We moved onto the caragana problem—"It's a fight but you can't beat them"—and how he has begun to leave more dead poplars standing for chickadees to nest in.

As he talked he gestured gently with a hand and I noticed for the first time the size of his forearms. He is not a big man, perhaps five foot eight and spare fleshed, but his arms are thickly roped with muscle and his hands are surprisingly large.

I could tell I was keeping him from something so I said good-bye and walked back through the woods to the abbey. *James.* Jesus had a brother James, but the name goes back to those other brothers, Rebekah's archetypal twins wrestling in the womb. *James* is a form of *Jacob*, the dweller in tents, the one who gripped the heel of his older and wilder brother.

"The harvest is rich, but the laborers are few." Agricultural reformers are people who live that gospel truth every day. They labor on, surrounded by social dysfunction and hostile forces in communities they care deeply for, and with each incremental shift, with every conversion, they seed a little more hope. In this part of the world they are as rare as long-billed curlews, but, on the midsummer day I jumped into the passenger seat of Duane Guina's half-ton, I knew I had stumbled across two of the best.

"Hope you don't mind someone tagging along with us," Duane said as we set out from the abbey. By a turn of good fortune that no longer surprises Duane, he had received a call the night before from one of the nation's strongest voices of change in agricultural and food-distribution systems. Brewster Kneen, author of books with titles like *Farmageddon*, *From Land to Mouth*, and *Invisible Giant* (a book about Cargill), was in the neighborhood to participate in a debate on GMO (genetically modified organism) food. Later in the morning I'd have a chance to hear the two of them talk about Earthcare and a land-trust project Duane has been working on. But first we had the short drive from Muenster to the Earthcare office in Humboldt.

As the sunlight from a clear July morning filled the truck cab, Duane, one hand on the gearshift and the other on the wheel, began talking about how he came to be the director of a sustainable agriculture program. His talk had the imagery and enthusiasm of a teacher who believes in his message and who comes to the task out of compassion rather than anger, and belief rather than despair.

"The way I see it, what we call good and evil are just two sides of one coin. Most things give and take away at the same time. When the government axed the Crow Rate [a rail transport subsidy for prairie grain] it caused some loss and pain, but it is bringing some long-term good as well because—let's face it—it was a distortion, a subsidy that artificially maintained a system that is economically and ecologically unsustainable. So, while a lot of people are nostalgic and sentimental about the good old days, the changes have been good because they are forcing us to refocus on regional, sustainable approaches to agriculture and rural economy.

"I think the connection to the land is innate. When I was growing up we had a small dairy farm, just four quarters [640 acres] near Radison. I farmed for five years before deciding to go to university and get an agricultural economics degree. Then I started with Farm Credit [a federal agency that lends money to farmers and others in the industry]. I worked there for several years, on the other side of the desk. It was right when the farm crisis hit in the 1980s. There was a moratorium on debt foreclosures and I was mediating settlements, watching good people losing their farms through no fault of their own. I started asking myself, *How can this be happening to something as basic as our food-supply systems?* Something was wrong and it had to change. But there I was, living in the city, earning a good salary on the backs of farmers, while good farmers were going under. I started to wonder what was expected of me—what the Creator expected of me.

"Back then Saint Peter's had its own abbacy—the only entirely rural diocese in the province. When things got bad for farmers, three of the religious orders in the abbacy—the Benedictines at Saint Peter's, the Ursuline sisters at Bruno, and the Elizabethan sisters at Humboldt—got together to see what they could do about encouraging alternative, sustainable agriculture. I'd already decided I had to make a change in my own life when I heard about this and about other religious and interfaith organizations that were starting up small projects. The Catholic Church had a Rural Life Ministry and they were in the early stages of setting up a land-trust project. A pretty challenging idea in terms of how the farm culture regards property and ownership, but wonderful in a Biblical and communitarian sense. With all this going on we started up the Marysburg Project—a demonstration farm modeling sustainable livestock practices, organic gardening, bees for alfalfa pollination, grassland restoration, and solar power. To get it off the ground I received funding from Saint Peter's Abbey and the Ursulines and Elizabethans. It was as if the spirit was moving in a number of different directions all at once, flowing like water. Everything came together in ways that no longer surprise me. That was 1997, and it was good finally to be doing something positive instead of just talking about the problems we saw.

"About that time the guy who was running the Catholic Rural Life Ministry was starting to burn out. Paul Brassard had spent years rushing from one local farm crisis to the next, and it had taken its toll on him and his family. The ministry had been preoccupied with trying to mop up the mess caused by things like the loss of the Crow Rate subsidy, but it was an impossible job. As far as I was concerned, that train had already left the station. It was time to start laying some new track. So we started to develop some new terms to renew the ministry and give it a new focus, using Paul's land-trust idea and other positive alternatives. That was when Paul was diagnosed with cancer.

"A few months later he was gone. That hit the movement hard. There were a lot of people who depended on his ministry. Then I started up Earthcare, a new name and a new organization to focus on the interdependence of rural and urban people. We made it an entirely ecumenical organization, with financial support and board members from all the major churches. It's gone really well, with Marysburg and our Genesis Land Trust. My only regret is that Paul never lived to see his land-trust idea up and running."

> And when they make a long blast on the ram's horn,
> Then all the people shall shout with a great shout

And the walls of the city will fall down flat. (Joshua 6:5)

As Duane and I were talking at the Earthcare office in Humboldt, a building that they share with the Catholic diocese, Brewster Kneen arrived. He had come out from the city for the afternoon to meet Duane and to visit an organic farmer in the district who has been trying to persuade the federal government to ban GMO wheat. Organic wheat growers, almost wholly dependent on European markets, are worried that GMO wheat grown by their neighbors might cross-pollinate with their wheat, rendering it contaminated and unmarketable by European standards. GMO wheat could destroy the burgeoning organic wheat growers movement in a single breeze.

Kneen publishes a newsletter on agriculture and food systems from his farm in British Columbia's interior. He calls it *The Ram's Horn*, after the passage from Joshua, which he prints on the first page of every issue. He travels widely, talking and listening to people who are finding more wholesome ways to grow and distribute food, people who are more than ever now raising voices in that great shout. For Kneen, the groundswell of public concern over GMO food and genetic engineering in general is as good a sign as any that the walls of the city are beginning to tremble.

When Kneen talks about GMOs, genetic diversity, and what he calls "proximity food systems," there is no mistaking his fervor and the faith from whence it springs. With a full head of wavy white hair, a face square from brow to jaw, and eyes that hold you to your chair, this man could start up his own religion and people would flock to his side. Monsanto would say that he has done just that, but instead he has chosen to revive a venerable tradition within the religion he was born to. Every generation needs its Jeremiahs, the ones who are not afraid to tell us that much of what we do in private and public life, in our households and in the marketplace, is an abomination and that we must undergo a change of heart. I was not surprised to discover later that Kneen is a former cleric and that some still regard him as a theologian.

Distorted monotheism may have accompanied us on this journey of colonization, filling us with the audacity required to stake our claims, even inside the nucleus of a living cell, but it is truly religious people faithful to the original covenants that seem to be leading the way toward transformation and renewal in our land-to-mouth bargains with the Creation. You see it on a local scale with people like Duane and his prairie network of rural reformers, but it is even more noticeable on the national and international stage, where Brewster Kneen is joined by the likes of Wendell Berry, who from a hill farm in Kentucky cries out in beautifully crafted essays and poetry, and by Wes Jackson, a plant geneticist who writes and speaks of ecologically sound prairie farming when he is not patiently coaxing domestic and wild grasses toward a food-producing blend of native and alien he calls "perennial poly-culture." These men speak from strong, some would say strident, positions, grounded in faith, favoring always the local over the global, the ecological over the industrial. They never hesitate to point to the forces in academia, in government, in business, and in human nature that are driving farmers away from a right livelihood in a vocation they hold to be sacred and fundamental to a civiliza-tion's moral character. Like any Old Testament prophet they shine the light of righteousness upon corruption, call into question laws and lawmakers, vex the powerful and privileged. They strive not so much to comfort the afflicted as to afflict the comfortable. We, the Israelites, are a recalcitrant lot, and change rises always from the faithfulness of a small remnant who heed the voice of Yahweh speaking through his prophets.

The federal government, says Kneen, has painted itself into a corner on the question of GMOs and genetic engineering. By declaring that all decisions regarding agriculture must be 100 percent science-based and nothing else, they've not left any room for cultural, social, or even economic values. So, if their scientists tell them that GMO wheat works, is more efficient and productive, they have to approve it. The multinational patent owners will see that they do, even if it is bad economics and even if the nonorganic market for wheat might be hurt.

We talked about the need for proximity food systems—community gardens, farmers markets, community kitchens, and the like—ways of linking local growers to local eaters. We talked about people finding new ways or rediscovering old ways of getting good food to market and on the table. And we talked about our civilization's addictive tendencies, how easily we become dependent on chemicals in our compulsive desire to keep the unclean at bay. Our bodies, rivers, and soils are tainted by the residue of our chemical addictions: the drugs, pesticides, and poisons we use in the name of health and comfort. There is an encompassing logic at work here, Kneen says, that the chemical manufacturers have always understood and to which the public is just now beginning to awaken.

In the middle of all this I asked Kneen what keeps him going in the face of such overwhelming powers.

"It's visiting people like Duane here across the country," he replied. "That and faith."

"Religious faith?"

"Traditional religious language fails us here. Think of a seed bank. People who want to preserve seeds sometimes put them in a seed bank but seeds are best preserved in situ. If you want to preserve a variety of some plant, you need to grow it in the actual environment—because the real world environment doesn't stand still. So there has to be intergenerational succession. In our religions we preserve the words and are faithful to the language but are we faithful to the people using the language in the here and now?

"We tend to think of preserving things we value by storing them somewhere in a bank or a zoo—whether it is endangered species or scriptural values—but for something to live it has to be cultured, grown in the soil and ecology of our time. That is how we keep something vital, by taking seed from one viable generation and then planting it again and again in each generation's soil."

He stopped short of calling the church a zoo, but in retrospect now I wonder if this was Kneen's way of saying that he made the transition from cleric to activist so that he would be freer to keep the word alive in the soil of this generation. The seed, the word. Some of the language may falter from generation to generation, but two thousand years ago, crowds gathered on the shore of the Sea of Galilee received this same message from one who stood in a fisherman's dory anchored in the shallows.

Later, when Duane talked about how well the Genesis Land Trust was doing, Brewster's eyes welled up with emotion. He was thinking of Paul Brassard.

"I remember talking with Paul about a land trust and it seemed to be bogging down in problems, seemed like it would never get off the ground. Now he's gone and the land trust is thriving."

I've seen others react this way to the memory of Brassard, and somewhere in their esteem is the mystery held within another parable from that Galilee generation, the one about the single grain of wheat that falls to the ground, dies, and yields a rich harvest.

From the *Rule of Saint Benedict*:

> The second kind are the Anchorites or Hermits:
> those who,
> no longer in the first fervor of their reformation,
> but after long probation in a monastery,
> having learned by the help of many brethren
> how to fight against the devil,
> go out well armed from the ranks of the community

to the solitary combat of the desert.

How to tell a Buddhist forest-dwelling monk from his Christian counterpart? The Christian forest-dwelling monk admits he kills gophers.

When a monk withdraws to the eremitic life, as Father James did many years ago, he places himself on the margin of a margin, yet, paradoxically, in his contemplative practice he becomes a heart within a heart, the anchor's anchorite. Just as the Benedictines provide the spiritual harbor in which the larger community surrounding Saint Peter's is moored, the abbey in turn is anchored by the prayers of one who has gone out well armed to the solitary combat of the desert.

For many years, Father James taught English literature at the abbey college, introducing prairie kids to the poetry of Eliot, Donne, and Herbert. From 1962 to 1972 he was the editor in charge of *The Prairie Messenger*, bringing the message of the social gospel to an agrarian community of Catholics and a larger readership scattered across the country. That more active phase of his life, teaching and proclaiming, has given way to a time of listening and prayer, though he continues as book-review editor for the paper, sometimes reviewing three or four books himself each week.

"Do you know the first word in the *Rule of Saint Benedict*?"

I had come for my first talk and James was pouring tea. I admitted I hadn't read the *Rule*.

"*Obsculta*—'listen.' That is how the prologue begins. 'Listen carefully,' it says, 'and incline the ear of your heart.'"

We had been talking for an hour or more and it was almost time for me to leave. Listening takes effort; gawking comes naturally. I was distracted by the feeling of being surrounded by books and words, books on shelves, books in piles upon his desk, books stacked in corners, and words on small plaques on his walls: "Fear knocked at the door; faith opened it. There was nothing there." Here is a man who lives within the word. "Make the word your home," Jesus said, "you will learn the truth and that truth will make you free" (John 8:31–32).

Listening should be easier, I told myself, in such a silent place. The only things in the hermitage that might make a sound now and then are a clock, a gas stove, a radio, and an ancient computer. When I arrived at 3:30 sharp, though, my mind was awhirl with things I wanted to talk about, questions I felt I had to ask. Instead we ended up talking about prayer.

When we sit to meditate, he said, we must realize that it is not ourselves praying. It is the Spirit who is the pray-*er*, and through the act of prayer we open ourselves up to a relationship with the person of Christ. I told James that I don't feel that when I meditate, never have, and that it has always been hard for me even to conceive, much less relate to, Christ as a person. But we have to, he said. It *is* a personal relationship, not in that glib way of some who claim to have Jesus in their pockets, but in experiencing, touching, and sensing the *person* of Christ in all of creation. Faith is a struggle for us in a postmodern world, James said, because we have lost touch with the divine personhood. Later he told me that he is often excited to hear or read about the latest forays of science. The more physics, astronomy, or evolutionary biology give us glimpses into the heart of matter, the more we see that particularity, distinctiveness, is stamped on every particle. If there is personality in creatures— singularity in locus and character—then it makes sense that the Creator, the source of personhood, is the divine person.

There is a logic here that I can follow with my mind, and by its exertion I can sometimes speak the name Jesus out loud without a flinch of unease. But faith belongs to the heart not to equations of argument, and in the end something like personhood and relationship must be felt and listened to rather than possessed, seen, or understood. That heart sense for the Divine in this world, despite the hours I spend looking at wild birds, plants, landscapes, has always eluded me.

We finished our talk so that James could keep his afternoon appointment with the wind and rain. At set times each day he goes out to a little box mounted near the south side of the hermitage and takes readings of wind velocity, precipitation, and barometric pressure, which he relays to a government office. As we stood outside next to his door, he said that one thing that gives him hope is that all cultures, all religious traditions, seem to be arriving at the same conclusion about the importance of awareness—what the Buddhists call mindfulness and Saint Benedict called listening.

After Brewster left, Duane and I drove out to look at the Marysburg Project. We continued talking about land trusts as he showed me the solar-powered electric fencing and the restored pastures they are using in a grazing rotation at the model farm. I was surprised to see the northern wheatgrass, a native species, thriving in seeded rows flanked by the usual volunteers: quack grass, wild oats, Canada thistle. We walked over to the edge of the fence—a single band of electrified tape supported on lengths of rebar pushed into the ground to serve as posts. Duane opened a section up to let the cattle into an ungrazed stretch of pasture.

"People are kind of like livestock. Once one is through the gate, the rest tend to follow. Farmers are watching our land trust from a distance, seeing how it turns out. Everyone agrees we have to do a better job of keeping people on the land. Not everyone agrees that land trusts are a good way of doing that. Our trust is intergenerational, in a nontraditional sense. We work with seniors and retired farmers who don't have heirs to take over their land and who are willing to forgo income from it. They come to us because they see what is happening and they want to help create an alternative. Once we have a piece of land we match it up with young people who otherwise might never get an opportunity to farm. We look for beginning farmers, people eighteen to thirty-five years of age with demonstrated ability, skills, background. People who couldn't afford land otherwise. We lease it to them at a rent below market value. Once you take on values other than market ones—ecological, social, cultural—you begin to see the benefits of keeping more people on the land and that it is worth leasing it at a lower price."

We moved to a field of organic seed alfalfa nearby as Duane described the workshops on alternative agriculture that the tenants attend as part of their obligation to the land trust. Scattered across the field there were hut-sized hives for leafcutter bees. Alfalfa, an important forage crop for cattle, is a legume and not a grass so it needs to be pollinated by insects. Seed growers introduce colonies of the leafcutter bee to improve pollination and yield. The name comes from the bees' habit of cutting tiny disks of leaf and arranging them as dividers between eggs in the long cylindrical brood cells they build.

Duane plucked an alfalfa flower and held it up to the sunlight. With the point of his pen he touched the flower's keel, simulating the action of a bee and sending the stamens and pistil upward in a barely visible puff of pollen. I took the pen and tried it myself a few times. It's nearly enough to make you blush, that trip of mechanism, the sudden thrust of reproductive organs in an explosion of eros and then the slowing down as they press into a slot in the upper petal. Next, Duane pulled off some alfalfa leaves and showed them to me. Sure enough, on many leaflets there were neatly incised holes, as though a compulsive ticket puncher had wandered through the pasture just ahead of us.

The hives themselves are marked in bold and distinctive patterns so that the bees will readily recognize their home colonies.

We stepped inside one to watch the bees at work stacking their leaf disks into the cigarette-sized brood cells. The hive, four or five feet wide, was thrumming with thousands of small bees flying in and out, ignoring our intrusion. Duane pointed to a new arrival toting a green dot of alfalfa leaf beneath its thorax. I followed it as it flew down to the stack of brood cells, hovered while awaiting its turn, and then entered the hole to contribute another layer of leaf. That done, it turned and headed to the pasture again.

We walked back to the truck, talking about the possibility of such elegant bargains between the land's giving and a farm's taking. The wild and the domestic teeter on this exchange, in the way we choose to feed our bodies, just as the mystic and the dogmatic hinge upon our attempts to feed the spirit's longings. And, in the end, the balance we strike for one is the balance we strike for the other, and the only weight that matters in farm or "desart wild," around the dinner table or before the altar, is our perspective and practice on the question of ownership.

The morning after my talk with James I was in my abbey guest room, trying to meditate. Trying is all I ever do. Buddhists call it a practice. I've been practicing daily for fifteen years and have little to show for it other than a desire to do it again the next morning. I had just sat down on the floor, let the silence settle into me, and then fastened my breathing to a word—using "abba" in honor of something James had said the day before. A few breaths and heartbeats later there came a sharp rap at my door.

Surprised that anyone would knock on my door in the quiet of an abbey morning, I opened it and found Father James standing there with a beret on his head and a light jacket over his black habit.

"Didn't wake you, did I?"

I invited him in and he began telling me that I mustn't merely seek peace and pleasant reverie in my meditation; that it must be a way of knowing Jesus in the heart. To do that, he said, you have to enter the mystery of the word. Instead of meditating for a full forty-five minutes, cut it back to thirty and first spend some time poring over a short piece of scripture, reading it not to think about it but to allow the word to touch the heart.

As I recovered from the surprise of having him there in body talking to me about prayer at the moment I had sat down to meditate, he handed me some material he wanted me to read, including an essay on a story in Luke that he said is very mysterious.

"Are you familiar with the Road to Emmaus?"

I laughed and showed him the handwritten draft of a story on my desk, titled, "Back to Emmaus."

"Jung would've called that synchronicity. We used to call it Divine Providence. These days we don't say it comes from above; we say it comes from within—but that's all right too."

I thanked him and he invited me to stop by for another visit later in the week. Then he told me I'd better get down to breakfast.

"It smelled awfully good when I walked by, but I had mine at five."

That was the beginning of James furnishing me with things to read. In our regular correspondence he mails me photocopies of articles that he finds in his daily reading. When I stay at Saint Peter's I will often find a slim sheaf of papers slipped under my door or placed upon my desk. Always with a note attached in his handwriting—"Thought of you when I read this" or "You might find this helpful." Signed always with "bd," for "bush dweller," a moniker some of the brothers have given James. The papers may include a couple of sonnets by George Herbert, a magazine essay on the cosmic Christ, a prayer by Teilhard, an interview with an expert on the fourteenth-century mystic Meister Eckhart, or an entry from Butler's *Lives of the Saints*. I read them eagerly but carefully because I have come to expect fresh insights from the voices he sends my way. Often the teachings they offer illuminate or anticipate questions I am struggling to resolve. When they don't, and synchronicity or providence is somewhere ahead of me, I set the papers aside, read them a month or a year later, and then, if the time is right, the poem or essay opens a doorway and I feel a welcome breeze come in from the bush.

A land trust is a Christian idea impregnated by a pagan spirit. Something pagan wants to trespass on our property and return us to the commons where the milch cow grazes without anyone laying claim to the grass. As always, nature provides models for a more graceful fidelity to place and for the necessary succession from individual to individual, generation to generation. In mid-March I was walking home from downtown and my eyes went up instinctively to the top of city hall where peregrine falcons have nested for many years now.

It was far too early for their arrival but spring was finally here after one of the coldest winters on record for this part of the plains. We'd had six months without a single twenty-four-hour span of above-zero temperatures, but in recent days the Arctic low centered over Hudson's Bay nudged off to the northeast, and warm air from the south rushed into the vacuum it left behind. Overnight the snowdrifts began to melt and rivulets ran down the city streets. As I walked home I looked at the puddles, each holding a mirror up to the heavens, showing patches of sky and the lacework of elm branches.

At city hall I looked up—too early for him to be back, I knew—but there he was, on the eyrie, waiting. The male, or tercel, comes back first to the nest site and waits for his mate to join him for the summer. How odd that he would come back so early. He might have to wait two or three weeks for her. That was when I remembered. She wouldn't be returning at all. After fourteen successful seasons on that ledge, she died last year, the day after a late snowstorm, one last volley from winter near the end of May. She'd already laid her clutch and had done her best to protect them from the cold, but the next day she went missing. Her body was never located, but desertion wasn't even considered a possibility. Her fidelity to the nest site and to her young had never faltered in the past. She was old and the storm had taken her.

For every one of those fourteen summers I'd watched her hold court above the rooftops of the city, choosing as she sometimes did from two or more competing males. On my walks to work each morning I'd crane my neck to see her and her mate in courtship flight, or the two of them mating on a radio tower in a brief flurry of wings and tail, a sudden coupling that happens over and over for several days until the clutch is complete. Many mornings I came across scraps of what they had been eating. On the sidewalk sixteen stories below a favored plucking station I'd find the saffron shanks of a yellowlegs sandpiper or the head of a sapsucker. Exotic fare to vary the usual diet of rock pigeons, these were the morsels the tercel would bring to her to seal their bond to one another and to the nest site.

Then, in August, sitting in the park at the annual folk festival and listening with two thousand others to Buffy Sainte-Marie or Fred Eaglesmith, I'd see the lanky silhouettes of the young birds taking their first awkward forays across the tops of banks and offices empty for the weekend and warm with the colors of sunset.

And what did he, the tercel, her third or fourth mate, hold within his memory as he waited on the eyrie, perhaps hoping that another female would find him and his nest site worthy? When I returned the next morning to check on him he was still at his post watching the skies to the south and east. From the top of city hall, even human eyes can see a hundred square miles of landscape well beyond the edges of town. With his binocular vision, he'd be able to spot a falcon passing by at a great distance.

He was there the rest of that second day, but when I looked the next morning he was gone. What was it, if not fidelity, that brought him back even after losing the one who had carried his renewal within her, had taken his genetic material and made it, with her own, into a new generation? The faith of a wild falcon is like our own when we show that we are capable of acting with good intent even when we have no guaranteed outcome. Parents do it all the time, farmers too. Our children may die before reaching adulthood, the fields may wither in drought, but we enact the rituals of fidelity that bind us to one another and to the localities of regeneration.

The tercel came early, waited in remembrance and respect, and then flew off to look for another place to belong, letting this one go. This is the correct movement of belonging: we belong to places, places do not belong to us. We are capable of possession that yields to succession. Our species, too, has known and can learn again the limits of entitlement and where it flows from one usufruct lease to the next in transitions that preserve, even honor, the material of this good earth.

Rebekah's twins parted ways over issues of possession and succession. Our myths of unchecked entitlement have divided the hunter's view from the farmer's. The wildness within the idea of a land trust frightens the descendants of Jacob because we have founded civilizations on the covenant-breaking misapprehension that God gave us title to the earth. Entitling ourselves as individuals, families, tribes, and nations, we've distorted scriptural tradition, rewritten mythologies, and created laws and theology to justify our heedless expropriations. Everything in our increasingly dysfunctional and dangerous agriculture, everything that makes rural renewal seem impossible flows from this misbegotten lien we registered soon after we became People of the Book. To change now to a more communal notion of tenure, recognizing that all land belongs to the Creator and we at best are leaseholders indebted to the Creation, to our ancestors, and to our descendants would seem so utterly alien and inimical to our current practice as to be the remotest of utopian fantasies. That it has been done before by others much like ourselves in mind and body, and has indeed been the norm for most of our sojourn on this planet, seems to count for little. Property rights are one of the few verities in the modern world that most people hold sacred and well above any obligation to God, earth, or community. Land trusts, precisely because they run counter to private ownership, allow us to recharge our primitive, pagan belief in the sanctity of land, water, and air by siphoning off some of that inflated regard for the individual right to use land as one sees fit.

We do not own our changes, are not entitled to complete understanding of where we may evolve or even from whence we came. We may never know every link in the chain, the precise timing of increments from Peking man to Darwin, from archaeopteryx to oriole, but here we are just the same, wielding coarse instruments of science and religion to plumb bottomless depths and then mark our progress against the cosmic riddle. To admit that we do not know and do not own something is a pagan gesture, an idea from the margins where weeds bide their time, while to claim knowledge and ownership—for instance to say we know this genome and own the patent on that microorganism—is to act from the civilized center of fear and loathing where we fiercely guard our domestic order, our farms, our households, and our religions from the dark mysteries at the edge of the garden.

As Wendell Berry says, "The forest is always waiting to overrun the fields." In his landmark book on culture and agriculture, *The Unsettling of America*, there is a core essay entitled "The Body and the Earth." It is a powerful treatise on wildness, agriculture, and sexuality, and among its many fine passages is this favorite:

> Domestic order is obviously threatened by the margins of wilderness that surround it. Marriage may be destroyed by instinctive sexuality; the husband may choose to remain with Kalypso or the wife may run away with godlike Paris. And the forest is always waiting to overrun the fields. These are real possibilities. They must be considered, respected, even feared.[2]

However, Berry continues, this does not mean we can afford to destroy that margin of wilderness or protect ourselves in any final or absolute way. A culture or religion that succeeds in raising such protective barriers effectively cuts itself off from the sacred. Forbid your prophets from entering the desert and, Berry argues, you "lose the possibility of renewal":

> And the most dangerous tendency in modern society, now rapidly emerging as a scientific-industrial ambition, is the tendency towards encapsulation of human order—the severance, once and for all, of the umbilical cord fastening us to the wilderness or the creation. The threat is not only in the totalitarian desire for absolute control. It lies in the willingness to ignore the essential paradox: the natural forces that so threaten us are the same forces that preserve and renew us.
>
> An enduring agriculture must never cease to consider and respect and preserve wildness. The farm can exist only within the wilderness of mystery and natural force. And if the farm is to last and remain in health, the wilderness must survive within the farm.[3]

When I come to Maranatha, James and I talk about everything under the sun: the disappointment of the latest G8 Summit, the pope's unwillingness to budge on the ordination of women, the divine revelations of the Hubble Space Telescope, the luminous web of Indra's Net, Derrida and deconstructionist thinking, the confounding mysteries of Teilhard's Christogenesis. On all of these subjects and many others I am at a distinct disadvantage, as I was when James and I first talked about Eliot's *Four Quartets*. I recall his saying that it is one of the most important pieces of writing from the last century, and that it bears new fruit no matter how many times you read it. I got a copy of the poem and started to read it in the contemplative way James had told me to read scripture. In recent years I have read its stanzas hundreds of times and now the text is part of me, so that when I read "Figlia del tuo figlio/ Queen of Heaven," instead of thinking of Dante and Eliot's fisher folk I am transported in spirit to Mount Carmel and the image of Our Lady. And when James closes a letter with "Fare forward," the next line comes without thought, "Lady, whose shrine stands on the promontory…"

I have tried to understand what it is in James that appeals to me. His interest in ideas and poetry is the merest part of it, and though I have felt something like absolution after telling him of my failures and vanities, I do not regard him as a confessor. I look to him for spiritual direction and imagine myself participating in that long tradition of laymen seeking the counsel of ones who have chosen a life of prayer and silence, like the citizens of Kiev heading out to see Saint Theodosius in eleventh-century Russia. But this is one thousand years and half a world away. What is the meaning of a desert mystic in this time and place? Given our distrust of religious fervor, and our fear of the world beyond the borders of the city, what does it mean to find one who has turned away from posses- siveness and let himself be possessed by God's silence in a place apart? Perhaps even now, a monk praying alone in the woods is keeping the leaven alive by staying body, mind, and spirit in contact with the unrefined elements of God's presence in creation. If that contact eludes the rest of us, starving the wildness within ourselves, it is not necessarily our location that is to blame so much as our claims upon the material of creation.

By the *Rule of Saint Benedict*, a monk is to claim nothing as exclusively his own. If he needs something, a new pair of sandals or a book, he must ask the abbot for permission to buy it. James lives the life of a religious squatter: here for now, using this modest lease with no delusions of entitlement. Shortly after we first met he handed me a copy of four poems by George Herbert. One of them, entitled "Redemption," made little sense to me then, but I read it now and see James's life on his "small-rented lease":

> Having been tenant long to a rich lord,
>> Not thriving I resolved to be bold,
>> And make a suit unto him, to afford
> A new small-rented lease, and cancel the old.
>
> In heaven at his manor I him sought;
>> They told me there that he was lately gone
>> About some land, which he had dearly bought
> Long since on earth, to take possession.
>
> I straight returned, and knowing his great birth,
>> Sought him accordingly in great resorts;
>> In cities, theatres, gardens, parks, and courts;
> At length I heard a ragged noise and mirth
>> Of thieves and murderers; there I him espied,
> Who straight, Your suit is granted, said, and died.

The thought that religious communities in the region helped Duane Guina start his land trust is some cause for hope. Here on the Northern Great Plains, as throughout Christendom, the church has always been there swabbing the moral grease upon the wheels of colonization and the accumulation of property, ordaining, at least implicitly if not explicitly, the rights of state and individuals to appropriate parcels of the Creation. Popes once drew lines on maps of the New World to apportion the spoils of exploration to kings and queens of Western Europe. In early sixteenth-century Hispaniola and Cuba, Spanish priests amassed great wealth on their private plantations where the labor was provided by African and Indian slaves. Catholic missionaries helped translate at treaty talks across the northern part of this continent, and when the Indians insisted that the land was not theirs to own, the Crown took them at their word. To the church and the Crown, this was unclaimed land full of unclaimed souls, all free for the taking. *Here*, the tempter said, *make these stones into loaves of bread*, and we did. We picked up those stones, made them into loaves and schools and missions so that the unclaimed could be brought inside the barricades.

Jesus' answer to the same proposition—"Man does not live by bread alone, but by every word that proceeds from the mouth of God"—is an attempt, retold in parables throughout much of the Gospel, to disabuse us of our notions of entitlement. One of the more pagan stories Jesus tells in his public ministry is the parable of the vine keeper who hires workers to pick grapes. It is part of the larger Kingdom of God discourse that shows Jesus cleansing the temple, renouncing wealth and property, advising the rich to give up all they own, and telling stories about tenants, laborers, and vineyard keepers.

In Judea at the time of Christ there was among the learned and privileged citizenry a great deal of emphasis on title and status, as there is in any culture that has a class structure based on land tenure. Nursing a distortion of the covenantal promises of Yahweh that persists yet in modern Christianity, the pharisees and scribes taught that wealth was a reward for virtue, and that virtue therefore entitles one to certain privileges. Imagine their consternation as they listened to Jesus' reply to the rich young man's question, expressed typically enough in terms of virtue and the possessions it may bring: "Master, what good deed must I do to possess eternal life?" (Matthew 19:16).

Jesus rebuffs him, saying, "Why do you ask me about what is good? There is one alone who is good. But if you wish to enter into life, keep the commandments." The young man, after having Jesus list the commandments he has in mind, says, "I have kept all these. What more must I do?"

The advice Jesus gives in answer to this question has been taken to heart by few Christians in the two thousand years since this dialogue was first written down. When it is enacted, though, as in the case of Saint Francis of Assisi or Bartoleme de las Casas, the world gains a prism through which the light of the kingdom shines for a time.

"Go," says Jesus, "and sell what you own and give the money to the poor and you will have treasure in heaven; then, come follow me" (Matthew 19:21). At that, the young man walks away, down at heart, for he had a great many possessions. Jesus then turns to his disciples and makes the point clearer just in case anyone might be looking for a loophole: "I tell you solemnly, it will be hard for a rich man to enter the kingdom of heaven. Yes, I tell you again, it is easier for a camel to pass through the eye of a needle than for a rich man to enter the kingdom of heaven."

Peter, as usual worried about his own skin, pipes up and asks, "What about us?" Jesus assures the disciples that they have done the right thing in renouncing property and family ties to follow him. Then he repeats one of his favorite phrases, "Many who are first will be last, and the last, first" (Matthew 19:30).

Everything Jesus says in this dialogue turns the reigning wisdom of the day on its head: wealth and property are not rewards for virtue, they are encumbrances that one must shed to follow God's way and find the kingdom. By all that you claim as entitlement, by every measure of status, privilege, or property that you cling to, you are held outside the reign of God. As if that is not enough to enrage the people of Judea, he goes on to tell a parable that strikes at the very heart of an agricultural people's notion of entitlement.

It begins, "Now, the kingdom of heaven is like a landowner going out at daybreak to hire workers for his vineyard." The story shows the landowner hiring the first workers and agreeing beforehand to pay them one denarius for their day's labor. Later in the morning, however, as well as in the middle of the day and near its end, he hires more workers. When evening comes, he has his bailiff gather the workers, paying them their wages starting with the latecomers and finishing with those who started in early morning. All receive the same wage, a single denarius. The ones who worked all day in the heat kick up a fuss, incredulous that they are receiving the same wage as people who arrived late and only worked for an hour or two.

To an agricultural civilization, or an industrial one, this is one of the strangest tales in the Gospel and we have trouble making out what its moral might be. Biblical commentaries say that Jesus was using this parable to tell the Jewish people that their coming into the covenant earlier than non-Jews didn't grant them a primary position in the kingdom. That interpretation has the hollow ring of other Christian efforts to set their Jewish forbears straight. There must be something else being said here that speaks to an agricultural-, property-, and entitlement-obsessed nation, given that it follows hard upon a lengthy dialogue admonishing the rich and urging the relinquishment of property and privilege.

The outcome of the story disturbs us today no less than it must have disturbed the hardworking citizens of Judea. The god we have in mind rewards the virtuous, and the good things of this life come to those who work hard to attain them. Yes, we know that God loves the poor, but people get what they deserve. Now we are supposed to believe that clean-living, industrious people are entitled to no more than the guy with his hand out on the street corner? News like that is hardly good. It hits us like a mackerel in the face, or a sudden assault from a stranger.

Many years ago I read a Flannery O'Connor short story in which the main character undergoes such an affront to her smug Christian rectitude. In "Revelation," the good Mrs. Turpin is sitting in a doctor's waiting room sizing up the other patients and making polite conversation with another woman. That woman's daughter, a graceless teenager named Mary Grace, reads a book on human development while her mother and Mrs. Turpin chat. Mrs. Turpin's prattle and interior monologue become ever more overweening as she sorts through the categories of people in her rural community. She and her husband, Claud (Claud Turpin, Clod Turnip), own a house and some property where they raise pigs whose feet never have to touch the ground. As landowners and farmers well-versed in modern hygienic agriscience, they are a notch or two above other white folks who only own a house. Black people might own more land than she and Claud, but being black they are down the ladder some, though obviously above Negroes who do not own land. Her filing system stalls out, however, over the subtleties of white folks who have good breeding but no land or money and people who have lots of money and property but behave badly. Can these people really be superior to someone like her who only has a small piece of land but volunteers her time at the church?

Eventually, her cup of self-congratulation bubbles over the rim and she exclaims, "If it's one thing I am, it's grateful. When I think who all I could have been besides myself and what all I got, I just feel like shouting, 'Thank you, Jesus, for making everything the way it is! It could have been different! Oh thank you, Jesus, thank you!'"

Mary Grace decides she's heard enough from the old battle-ax and pitches her book at Mrs. Turpin, hitting her in the face. Then she lunges across the room and begins throttling her right there on the floor of the doctor's waiting room. After someone pulls the girl off she falls back onto the floor in a fit, her eyes rolling in her head. Here is where one revelation comes. Mrs. Turpin leans over Mary Grace and asks, "What have you got to say to me?" An odd thing to ask someone in a fit, but she is hoping for an apology and just too opaque to see the state the girl is in. At another level, O'Connor is referring to pagan religious tradition in which epileptics were often thought to be oracles who might well impart important spiritual messages. Some of the prophets, the *nabi* who were in more ways than one beside themselves in ecstatic vision, may well have been epileptic. And so the revelation of the story's title comes through a rough form of grace at the hands of a girl named after the one we say was full of grace.

In answer to Mrs. Turpin's question, Mary Grace yells, "Go back to hell where you came from, you old wart hog!" It is a disturbing message from God and Mrs. Turpin struggles for the remainder of the narrative to make sense of it. In the final scene she has her own epiphany in which she sees her virtue and all other human values burned away in a parade of souls mounting to heaven. All manner of people are in the column rising upward and bringing up the rear she sees "[a] tribe whom she recognized at once as those who [were] like herself and Claud." All accepted into the kingdom under God's grace, but in an order opposite to the one we follow in life.

Mrs. Turpin in O'Connor's "Revelation" and the early-bird vineyard workers in Matthew's gospel are disturbed because they operate within civilizations that are founded upon claiming and exploiting resources as individuals. If Jesus had come among the

Kalahari Bushmen, the tribes of these northern plains, or any other people who lived entirely by the hunt, and told them that parable of the vineyard keeper and his laborers, he would have received nods of recognition from his audience. Yes, this is the world the Creator has made. The Creator gives what the Creator gives. No one can claim special entitlement or extra wages.

Exactly opposed to the gospel value of the first shall be last and the last first is the economist's declaration that land trusts hurt the economy because they dampen the profit motive and reduce productivity. Pharmaceutical companies and plant breeders have made the same argument over questions of patent. If the law will not protect our title to this new drug or that plant, they say, then what motive is there for research and development? Even our best intentions, though, are often infected by the same dominant ethic. Farm cooperatives and secular communes are torn apart by squabbles over who is doing the work and who is getting most of the profit. And now we see Indian bands—people who still hold their land communally and who short generations ago prospered or starved together according to the gifts of the Creator—deeply divided over who gets the jobs in the band office or the new split-level homes built with money from Indian Affairs.

The ways of man Jesus inveighed against now cover the planet, and it is harder than ever to see beyond them to the possibility of another kingdom. Even so, the truths of those old kingdom parables still apply. When I read them now, I hear a distant but clear voice offering two avenues for anyone who chooses to experience something of that other reign beyond the ways of man. The first, explicitly stated in the parables about wealth and entitlement, tells us that we can spread the seeds of the kingdom and watch it grow by giving up our possessions and possessiveness, by loosing our grip on the things and people we have been treating as our own. The second way is indicated in the very metaphors of seed and growth that Jesus used in talking of the kingdom. The Kingdom of God is contained in a mustard seed, that small seed that grows into a tree "so that the birds of the air come and shelter in its branches" (Matthew 13:32). Seed is the vessel of God's ways of wildness: fecund, magnifying, diversifying, self-organizing but interdependent, vulnerable in the short term to the appropriating grasp but over the long term of many generations triumphal in its surprising leaps of adaptation and renewal.

Perhaps these are the ways of God that come to the mystic in the desert when stones show themselves to be not bread for our taking, but grandfathers whispering to anyone who will listen: *Be grateful as the hunters you have descended from. Today there is sun, a rabbit in the pot, medicine in the hills, a river in the valley.*

The day I visited the Center for Rural Studies and Enrichment, Noreen mentioned a farmer living in the Arm River area: "Peter Farden. You should look him up if you can. He talks about spirituality and rebuilding farm communities. He's even got the new minister of Rural Revitalization talking that way."

I'd heard Farden's reputation as a tractor-seat visionary before, once from a biologist and another time from a friend in the city who had worked with Paul Brassard on the Rural Life Ministry. It was mid-August when I finally made my way out to his farm an hour-and-a-half drive southwest of Saint Peter's. The Arm River, like Wolverine Creek, flows from the periphery of the same sprawling watershed down to the Calling River, all of it collecting the scant prairie runoff that ultimately rolls east and then north into Hudson Bay.

A conventional farmer who turned out to be anything but, Peter Farden showed me around his land, introduced me to his neighbors, and told me stories for two days straight. Conventional because he uses pesticides and artificial fertilizers on his land, antibiotics on his cattle, Farden nonetheless has one of the most distinctive and unconventional voices you will come across in this corner of the northern plains. First thing we did after I arrived was to head out for his pasture in the Arm River Valley.

"This is the Camp of Plenty," he said. After a rollicking truck ride and a hike through the pasture, we were looking at some stones in the blue grama and June grass, the remains of a winter camp, according to a visiting archaeologist. We had already looked at a fish weir ("They told me it's the best one around"), a buffalo jump, and a burial site on the side of a draw. Next it was a spiral-shaped medicine wheel: "A medicine wheel is a reference library of traditional information."

As we drove from site to site, Peter talked about the farm economy and its effects on his community, his passion for regional history, his theories of rural renewal and the role of religion, his love for Paul Brassard, and three or four other subjects—all tumbling together in a maelstrom of images, facts, ideas, and stories that stream out of him like swallows from under a bridge.

"I function orally. I'm dyslexic, not much of a reader but I get along well on an oral plane. I didn't do well in school because they didn't know what to do with guys like me back then…We are living in a society that is making the transition from a factory economy to a patent economy. About four hundred years ago we left the agricultural economy behind. That economy was based on food. It was the most important element of trade. Then things urbanized, industrialized, and we started bringing the product to people living in cities. That was the beginning of the factory economy and specialization. It lasted up until the last decade or two, when the new patent economy took over. Now all life-forms are things you can say you own, and the same people who control the seeds control the hydrocarbons—Monsanto, Cargill, Hoechst. They call the shots and the rest of us still think we're living in the old factory economy. Farmers still have the old farm-gate mentality—

I produce the product, ship it off, and wait for the check. The rest of it—methods of growing, marketing, or distributing—is someone else's specialty.

"I've got three sons. Best farmers you can imagine, but there's no place for them on the land. They all had to leave and find jobs elsewhere. One of them works for Monsanto—imagine how that feels…Resources are being concentrated in small areas, cities mostly, and we can't afford the concentration of waste it causes. And as a farmer I can't afford the economies of scale, the technology it demands. When you're working in a primary industry like this where the resource is exploited at or below the cost of production, a $100,000 tractor is a liability…

"Even if a farmer's got 50 percent equity you're still in the bank every other day saying 'Sir' or 'Ma'am' and everyone's living in holy terror of the interest rates. Everything's fine until three days later you're going under just with the interest rates changing. It can happen that quick. I'm in a totally ineluctable position as a farmer. The change is monthly and the more we understand the angrier we get. The whole agricultural system is running on equity and depreciation. Your equity drops from 93 percent to 85 percent and so you dig out some mothball money and put it into the operation. This is happening a lot, so in a sense we're now running on money that has been accumulated over the last forty years, from the 1950s or 1960s. Young people just starting up go down the tubes and take their parents' equity with them. Lot of retired people in town living hand to mouth. The ones whose kids left the farm early, went into town, and got jobs are doing okay. They sold their farm, they're comfortable. Their counterparts who maybe had one of the kids start farming, they're broke. Leads to an awful lot of family discord and intergenerational abuse, senior abuse. It's happening because, with the cheap food attitude out there, we are exploiting the land at or below the cost of production. But no one wants to leave the land, let it go. The farm is sacred, your great-grandfather homesteaded it, and it's hard for people to let it go even if it's tearing the family apart."

(Later that night, talking with Peter's friends from an inter-church group, I would hear a bit of the gallows humor that helps bleed off the tensions of watching your community in crisis. A town nearby held a fundraiser one spring by selling tickets on an old tractor placed on the ice of a dugout. There was a stuffed figure of a farmer sitting behind the wheel and the sign advertising the gambit read When Will the Farmer Go Under?)

"When I was a kid we used to celebrate a rain in the middle of harvest. Now people are stressed out because the rain coming means real physical damage. There didn't used to be any difference then between number one and number two wheat, but now the margins are so narrow. Whether you get number one protein now makes all the difference. A two-inch rain at the wrong time takes three or four pounds of protein off a bushel of your product...Any resiliency we have comes from the spiritual base, in the eyes of a newborn calf, the sunrise, the smell of the soil. The community can be in a shambles, but twice a year there's an emotional recharging. Spring and fall, the whole community focuses on what has to be done, despite everything else. Any other time the equipment dealer in town will tell you it's cash on the line for the part you need but at planting and harvest time it changes. You send your wife down to get the part and he just hands it over on credit. The community can be absolutely disintegrating as a functioning family, but at seeding and harvest we become a real community of healthy families for a short while. Husbands and wives quit fighting over the books, meals get out to the field, the work gets done. *That* is why people keep farming. These things don't carry any weight, but it's real.

"If there is a solution it is in community and connecting people back to the land. We've been so isolated from one another. People who are in trouble are paranoid that their neighbors might be waiting to capitalize on their misery, take over their land. So no one was talking but we're all more or less in the same boat. Eventually we formed a farm and town self-help movement. We started getting together so we wouldn't be going to our creditors absolutely green. We started talking, brought some things out into the open. Neighbors found out a little about one another's finances, the deals one another got at the bank, so they were prepared next time with a stronger bargaining position. Caught the banks by surprise. That took care of suicides and people leaving in the night...

"If we're going to come up with ecological solutions, we're going to have to place a higher value on food. In the 1920s my grandfather could trade a bushel of wheat for a pair of coveralls. Right now it would take me twenty or thirty bushels to buy that same pair of coveralls...

"In the current cost-price squeeze there is only one place left to squeeze and that's the price of land...the day could come when Cargill comes to me and says, 'We'll take over all of your debt and make you a deal. You grow what we want you to grow, we get the produce, and we give you a salary.' That isn't that far off. They're already surveying farmers to see where the line is, to find out at what point most of us would turn things over to them in some kind of agreement where we'd use their technology and they guarantee the farmer an annual income...

"I visited one company's research-and-development library in the city. Those guys have it all figured out. They know what color of toilet paper you're going to be using two years from now. According to their corporate vision, the future of this land is two hundred sections of crop per farm, the farmer a figurehead with a salary, and beneath him there'll be an agrologist, an accountant, a foreman, and an itinerant group of workers who do the work. The major arteries in the country would still be serviced with gas, light, and telephone, and off of those trunks there would be eight-mile branches that are still serviced, but beyond that no services, nothing. There would still be the odd half-section to one-section farm subsidized of course with off-farm income, but to the agribusiness companies they're just deadbeats, something you have to work around. When I saw that library I realized then and there what we are up against."

More stories, about the big landowner who plowed up the scrap of native grass where the last burrowing owls in the region nested, about the community coming together long enough to seed a widow's land a few days after her husband's death, about establishing a "talking circle" to work on building trust and spiritual connections between people, about projects to develop local tourism, and about the times he has waited at the roadside in town like a highwayman, waylaying tourists when they slow down near the grain elevators, offering to show them around, taking them through an elevator then out to the Arm River Valley for some history and archaeology, and when they offer to pay him he refuses. "No, thanks, I was just doing some market research."

Back at the farm I sat beside a koi pond he built in the yard, its rock ledges made with stones the same dimensions as the tipi ring boulders we had looked at earlier. The yard is an oasis cloistered away from the dust and weeds just beyond its hedgerows. Warbler migration was underway. As I watched, a common yellowthroat came into view and a northern waterthrush, bobbing as it walked toward the water. Then a Canada warbler and three Wilson's warblers. I watched the birds through my binoculars, aware of a desire to feed something in myself with their bright lives and trying all the while to be better than that, more worthy, to see instead each in its own elegance and mystery, the waterthrush's pale yellow underparts streaked with burnt umber, the near silent fly-catching of the Canada warbler, sallying out from a limb with a soft flutter and the snick of a beak closing.

The small movements of these birds, invisible except in stillness, brought to mind some of the stories Peter had confided to me during our day together, stories of personal encounters with powers in the land that farm people will sometimes mention in private. Even then, as he related experiences of the heart and spirit, Peter deferred always to the aspirations and interests of the community around him. The dissolution of grain-farming culture has broken Peter open, made him intensely aware of the tenuous ties between his family farm and those that surround him and, at the same time, vulnerable to the derision and ridicule of doubters in his midst. Like most farmers, he saves his ire for the chemical companies but he stays with the mainstream, high-input agriculture because that is the norm among his neighbors and family.

"You know what I'd really like to do? I'd like to go around on an old John Deere R two-lunger on eighty acres of land. Most of us would rather be doing that. A little while ago I was out plowing a thin strip of native grass next to a field. I stopped for a minute and got under the cultivator to put a bolt back in when I smelled this really nice smell, familiar but I couldn't put a name to it. Then it came to me. It was the smell of organic matter. When I was a kid the whole farm smelled like that. But it doesn't smell that way anymore."

No, most days, it smells like Roundup or 2,4-D. Nostalgia for the virtuous farm of yesterday is always compelling, but there is little to be gained in wishing for the return of a time when the scent of fresh-plowed prairie was in the air. Those were the days when our grandfathers, with every pass of the breaking plow, were releasing into the atmosphere the store of nitrogen sequestered in twelve-thousand-year-old grassland ecosystems. The irony is that, while nostalgia and the twice-a-year experience of an almost functioning community keep a farmer like Peter Farden on the land, with each passing season the scale and methods he applies as a modern farmer take him ever further from the experiences he carries in his memories. And he feels there is damn little he can do about it without leaving family and community behind. Go organic is easy enough to say, but to do it in his region he would be choosing isolation, placing himself above his neighbors who have seen him dedicate two decades toward building community within the mainstream of modern grain production.

While we were talking about organic farming, Peter's brother came into the yard and began loading up the herbicide sprayer, a machine that looks like an airplane with abbreviated wings and outsized wheels. Foam dripped from the marker spout and onto the gravel path with audible splats.

"If I became a strictly organic grain farmer, I'd be setting myself apart from my neighbors, leaving them behind, deciding to go it alone. My relationships with neighbors are all I have, my only real asset. The organic farmers I see have isolated themselves and they sometimes can't even share information with one another. They have to protect their own market niche because they don't have the same marketing system there is for conventional agriculture. No, I can do more good by staying with the community. We all want to reduce our dependence on sprays. The guy who is looked up to in the community these days is the one who has figured out how to get high yields with a minimum of fertilizer and chemicals."

As I listened to him explaining why he stays with conventional farming, it occurred to me that he is underestimating his own role as a leader. I remembered something he had said earlier in the day, repeating an image I'd heard also from Duane Guina: "People are a lot like cows—not to slight cows or people, mind you. They ball up and resist going through the open gate, and then one goes and right away the whole herd starts to flow. That's how values and ethics change, and the ethic of doing with less and living ecologically will happen the same way."

> The land shall not be sold forever: for
> The land is mine; for you are
> strangers and sojourners with me.
> (Leviticus 25:23)

I'd like to believe that we will come through the gate on our own, following someone's lead, but it seems likelier that we will continue to resist until something forces us through. Flannery O'Connor felt that the generation she wrote for was so inured to the truth that the only way to bring it to their attention was to take each reader by the scruff of his neck and hold it before his eyes. In a letter to a friend, O'Connor explained the shocking violence in her stories by writing that "the kingdom of heaven has to be taken by violence or not at all."[4]

When I first read this it struck me as such a peculiar statement, as being so utterly opposed to the conventional understanding of how the kingdom is attained or established, that no matter how I looked at it I could neither reconcile it with Christian belief nor with O'Connor's moral universe. I knew she didn't mean that the desperate characters in her narratives bash their way into the kingdom with violence, but I could not imagine what she did mean. Remembering that Father James used to teach O'Connor to his students, I wrote him a short letter asking what he thought of the statement. His reply suggested that O'Connor may have been thinking of some of the layers of meaning that underlay the passage in Matthew where Jesus makes the enigmatic statement, "up to the present time, the kingdom of heaven has been subjected to violence, and the violent are taking it by storm" (Matthew 11:12).

"The violent bear it away," another translation of that last phrase, is in fact the title of one of O'Connor's novels. The Jerome Biblical Commentary goes over various possible meanings of the statement, interpreting the violence as either the violence of humanity inimical to establishing the kingdom or the self-violence of renunciation required by those who would follow the way of the kingdom. The commentary's editors conclude, however, with this: "No proposed interpretation is entirely satisfactory."[5] Reading this along with James's letter, I began to wonder if O'Connor was perhaps attempting to hold together the two sides of violence as it is revealed in the individual and within life in general. In humankind there is the destructive violence of man grabbing and often destroying what is not his to possess weighed against the creative violence of self-sacrifice and purification. In nature a similar duality of destroyer/creator drives the cycles of succession and renewal. You could say that violence is the crux of wildness where death and rebirth cross paths. Look far enough down the list of synonyms for violence and you will find *wildness* at the end, after *disorder, fury, power, rampage, savagery*, and *storm*. The association is not undeserved, nor is it merely an artifact of our cultural fear of wildness. The universe we live within is still expanding outward from a moment of cosmic violence, and its scattered debris has evolved, at least in this corner, into haberdashery and hummingbirds—all in the presence of inter-mittent cataclysms separated by long spells of relative peace. Life is violent with some regularity and somehow the kingdom is borne forward on that wild, destructive, and creative force.

There is one place in the New Testament where Jesus acts in a physically forceful manner. It is the clearing of the temple, when he knocks over tables and swings a whipcord to drive money changers and livestock salesmen from the complex of courts and buildings that made up the temple in Jerusalem. The merchants would have been in the courtyard and not the temple proper. Nonetheless, they were permitted in the temple complex because their trade expe-dited the steady stream of ritual sacrifice being offered upon the temple altars. In Palestine of that era all sorts of money was in circu-lation, but only the Tyrian half-shekel was accepted in the temple and Roman coinage was forbidden by the Jewish religious hier-archy. Money changers, therefore, were necessary to help newly arrived pilgrims prepare to make their offerings. Animals suitable for sacrifice under the law were sold by livestock salesmen to save travelers the effort of transporting their own from home. While wealthier Jews might have purchased sheep or even cattle to offer in their oblations, the common rabble settled for doves.

The practice of ritual sacrifice as laid out in Leviticus had become a streamlined religious procedure, distorted by the abuse and greed that inevitably sneak in whenever we increase the scale of our worship and hand it over to a privileged priesthood. It was this abuse of the law and not the law itself that enraged Jesus, bringing him to a rare moment of violence. He cleared the temple not merely to get rid of some small-time pigeon hawkers but to demonstrate that there is a force in creation that one fine day will bring down those who place themselves above others, who entitle themselves in the name of God, claim more than their due, and use the law for their own ends.

Depending on which gospel you use for a chronology, this may have been one of Jesus' first acts upon entering the Holy City. Up to that time he had seldom made reference to the religious hierarchy of the day. After the cleansing, however, much of his ministry in Jerusalem was aimed at those who claim title, wealth, and privilege, particularly religious leaders. Soon after leaving the temple he tears a strip off the scribes and pharisees, who "clean the outside of cup and dish and leave the inside full of extortion and intemperance... [who] pay your tithe of mint and dill and cumin and have neglected weightier matters of the Law—justice, mercy, good faith...straining out gnats and swallowing camels...who shut up the kingdom of heaven in men's faces, neither going in yourselves, nor allowing others to go in who want to" (Matthew 23:13–25).

The Gospel of John, always aberrant, emphasizes Jesus' purging of the temple by placing it up front, immediately following the wedding at Cana, by adding the detail of the whipcord, and by alluding to the words of Psalm 69, "Zeal for your house will devour me" (John 2:17). This psalm of David shows a servant of God fasting and mortifying himself, in a sense undergoing that self-purifying violence by which one might take the kingdom of heaven. But the other kind of creative violence is implied here as well, to the degree that the "Father's house" is not merely the temple but the whole of creation which in turn longs for the kingdom of heaven.

There is such a zeal within each of us and it is the religious congener of the forces of creative destruction within nature that purges
an ecosystem in need of succession and renewal. A mystic is one
who lets that wildness cleanse the temple of his being, ridding it of
all that claims privilege or exalts the self above the other. The zeal
that cries "abba" within Father James's heart is the same power that
levels mountains, floods valleys, lights a fire on Hakkarmel or on
the high plains of this continent. It is the whipcord of the Cosmic
Christ passing through the places we claim to own, making them
fit sanctuaries for new life. It covered this land with glaciers once,
melted them away in torrents and will do it all again before too
long. It brought Father James to the silence of Maranatha thirty
years ago and it will carry him out one fine day. Perhaps I come to
see James for the same reasons I come to the river: to pay respects
to the force that storms the gates of heaven, to see a house that is
not a marketplace. Christ got here first and kicked the tables over.
There are no high priests here, no salesmen. Only one who claims
nothing, buys nothing, sells nothing. All that was devoured in him
some time ago by the son's zeal for the father.

# INTO THE PRESENCE OF GOD

———————————————•———————————————

## 1. DESCEND

*Now let us to the blind world there beneath descend.*

—Dante's *Hell*, Canto IV

The circle of farmland we see from Mount Carmel is now darkening at its far edges. To the east, in the shadow of the hill, the
middle ground has turned dingy, the foliage drained of its shimmer,
the roadside willows covered with dust. All of it weary, worn, and
used, hanging on until the darkness wipes it clean again. Eastward,
at a brighter hour, the colonists looked out over this plain not
knowing what might wait in its shadows.

Like other prairie people, my imagination is easily seduced by
written accounts of first settlers looking out from vantage points
like this one. The story follows a familiar pattern: there they stand,
hands shading eyes, facing the dawn of their tomorrows, dreaming
of the prosperous farms and villages that will civilize the wild lands
they now survey. One hundred autumns ago, when the German
Catholic land scouts first crossed these hills, their leader was a
Benedictine priest who thought, and wrote, like a geographer.
Father Bruno Doerfler, his mind on salinity, soil structure, and
water, stood on a hill like this one and scanned the terrain that was
to become their Catholic colony centered on an abbey. Bruno's

reminiscence of the expedition, written down decades later, bears
the explorer's enthusiasm for newfound land as he describes the
plain, lake, and valley of the Wolverine:

> When finally we arrived at the summit of the slope, we were
> greeted by a gently rolling plain, studded with beautiful groves
> and chrystal [sic] lakes. The soil on this plain was of the very
> choicest, for it was a deep black humus, covered with a heavy
> growth of peavine vegetation, an evident sign that it was entirely
> free of alkali. Several miles ahead we observed a prominent hill
> rising from the plain. For this hill we headed. At its foot we
> found a long, narrow lake containing good drinking water. An
> abandoned ranch stood on the wooded bank of the lake, and a
> fine spring burst forth in a wide deep ravine which ran in a north-
> westerly direction.[1]

It was the fall of 1902. By then, the Cree, Nakota, and
Saulteaux people of the Northern Great Plains were already on
reserves far from Wolverine Creek and Mount Carmel. Many of
the great leaders of the time had died in the previous fifteen years:
*acāhkosa k-ōtakohpit* (Star Blanket), *mistahi-maskwa* (Big Bear),
and *pīhtokahānapiwiyin* (Poundmaker). *Payipwāt* and *mistawāsis*
remained. Gabriel Dumont was an old man, four years away from
his grave at Batoche. His mixed-blood people were still recover-
ing from the battles there and the execution of their leader sev-
enteen years earlier. The Métis, however, were still clustered in
small settlements along the banks of the South Saskatchewan River,
at places not far from Carmel—places like Saint Laurent and the
settlement at Fish Creek where Hattie McKay once lived.

The Benedictines came upon Saint Laurent as they made their
way east across the unpeopled plains toward the river. Father
Bruno writes that they were "surprised to see what appeared a fine
village on the opposite bank, with a good-sized Catholic church

and a commodious residence for the pastor. Mr. Ens [a guide] explained that this was the half-breed settlement of St. Laurent at Fish Creek."[2]

He described the village in some detail, its single street of wooden houses verging the riverbank, how each family's farm ran back from the settlement in a long narrow strip: "Thus they secure the advantages of village life without the drawbacks of having their farms away from their dwellings." By the time of Bruno's visit, that arrangement—village and farm flanked by prairie river on one side and prairie wilderness on the other—had been sustaining people on the plains for almost one hundred years. The family farm economy that replaced it, with individual households isolated on sectioned holdings far from rivers, has not lasted as long and has given way now to something more industrial, though its grid pattern, well suited to industry, still dominates the landscape when you look out from heights like this one.

Bruno's scouting party had several encounters with the "half-breed" people of the plains. Eating bannock at the wayside, the priest who would eventually become abbot of Saint Peter's grew to admire the Métis. And he saw that the newly arrived settlers were already showing their disdain for the mixed-blood people. "There is no doubt," he wrote, "that many of the 'breeds' are more truly gentlemen than those that look down upon them."[3]

It was their welcoming nature that moved him. Here were a people who still had no official recognition of their long-standing claims to land they had used for decades. Meanwhile, new settlers were arriving week after week to claim the surveyed parcels granted by distant magistrates. Rejected and ignored by all signatories of the treaties that had swept the land away from beneath their feet, the Métis faced bigotry from the Englishmen in government, from the new immigrant settlers, and sometimes from Indians who had taken up life on reserves. Yet they shared food with Bruno and his colonists, opened their homes, and told them where they could find good drinking water as they continued east. To Bruno they must have seemed a prairie embodiment of the hospitality that forms the core of the Benedictine way. His written account suggests that he would have recommended setting up the colony and abbey in their midst, on the plains immediately east of Fish Creek, but most of the land in that region had already been taken up by settlers.

After staking their claim instead upon the Wolverine, Bruno and his scouting party went home to Minnesota for the winter. The following spring Bruno returned with the prior and five other Benedictines to build their abbey in the wilderness. They pitched tents on the side of the creek and gathered prairie grass to fill their straw-tick mattresses. It was May 21, 1903, the Feast of the Ascension. The Benedictine brothers and fathers must have considered all they were letting ascend on that day, not the least being the relative comfort of their lives in the abbeys they had left behind. There was a descent underway as well on those plains but it, like most, was not on a hilltop in the light of midday, though glimmers of its truth came to them even in those early days. Once, a hungry Cree man came into their kitchen tent, sat on the floor, and placed his knife at his feet to show that he was friendly. The cook, Brother Adolf, offered him a cup of milk fresh from their cow, which earlier that same day had slurped up all the holy water from the limestone basin positioned at the door to the tent chapel. That was the nearest the Benedictines of Saint Peter's came to baptizing the original people of their new home.

Not that it would have made a difference. Christian baptism only seemed to hasten the decline of the indigenous, and even so there is always and ever the going down before the rising up, and a long time of overlap between the two, descent and ascent, as now, disguised as one another in all our dreams and futile questions, in the cold arrival not long past of missionaries on these plains. Some few of these, always too few, bore the mercy, pity, peace, and love that should mark a Christian. A late one was our child mystic of

Wicklewood who, seeing the brown-skinned wanderers in his first parish in the New World, asked to be posted to a reserve mission, to the dismay of his superiors who reserved those unwanted placements to exile the perverse or the merely incompetent and who had better things in mind for their recruit from England. The missions are all but gone, insufficient apologies and cash settlements stand in for justice, and what dreams and questions remain are still about entitlement, the passages where we are suspended in that limbo between the falling and the rising.

One, who has a star for a blanket, born to a lineage of chieftains, to blood leadership, his grandfather the son of the great *acāhkosa k-ōtakohpit*, whose father in turn was *wāpi-mostosis*, who with reluctance but deferring to the yet-to-be-born pressed the pipe to his forehead and heart and placed its stem upon the queen's paper—he who was to become the fourth-generation son of old White Calf to sit as chief has been haunted all his days by visions of his great-grandfathers' ignominious fate at the hands of Christians. Their first reserve, across the valley from where *kā-kišīwē* and his people settled, was taken from White Calf when he stayed on the land made alien and followed the hunt, hoping the buffalo would return, not wanting to consign his people to an earth-grubbing existence upon the quadrangled apportionments allowed by the Indian Department. He died without taking up reserve land but his successor, the eldest son, Star Blanket, was forced to move the band to some land unclaimed in the File Hills. Not long after came the unrest among the Métis and the Cree led by Poundmaker and Big Bear. Star Blanket had always been a friend to the Métis, whom he knew as *āpihtawikosisān* (the "half-a-son" people). This, together with his reputation as a critic of the territorial government, worried the police, who had heard also of the riders coming in from the northwest almost daily with messages from the discontent nations. Not wanting to chance Star Blanket joining up with the others already talking of rebellion, the police took him from his reserve and put him in jail until the Métis and the Cree had been defeated and brought into court for treason.

Such stories, told to him by his father's father, the son of that first Star Blanket, who was in turn the son of old White Calf, entered his heart on nights his grandfather, maker of sun dances, would talk as he prepared his medicines. Hearing them in his own language by lamp and firelight, this youngest Star Blanket even as a boy tasted that bitter decoction of pride and shame, resignation and outrage that is the legacy of the colonized. And, as a man, after undergoing the Christian indoctrination that substituted for the education that his grandfathers thought they had assented to by the terms of the Pipe and Crown, it was all the more galling to discover in church archives an account of his great-grandfather, whose name he carries, being thrown back into his lodge with his wives, admonished as "four little devils sitting around a drum."

But we, the ones who have reaped the rewards of land our ancestors wrested from aboriginal title, are haunted too by visions, ancestral memories, angels or spirits who come to us at night by the riverside after we send our progeny on ahead.

*In a dream I am standing just outside the front door of our home in the city and my vision reaches far into the country. I am holding binoculars and I can see hills, the valley where our land is, our neighbor's barn, and then our cabin on the meadow. I watch as someone—not one of us—comes out the cabin door. A girl, ten or twelve years of age, black-haired, of mingled blood. Then a man walks out of the cabin and joins her. I feel that I must talk to the man and in that feeling am transported there and he asks me if I want to sell the land. Not sell, I say, but we would lease it out. The man shows his disappointment and so I add that we'd let him stay for nothing if he could hay the top meadow.*

*"Which meadow?" he asks and so I walk him down the road allowance toward the meadow, and on the way he tells me he remembers the road and he lights up with enthusiasm, talking about his memories. We walk on a long way, with wildflowers on either side of the road, until we come to*

*another man, older and with braids emerging from under a ball cap. He is*
*sitting on a culvert next to a railway track and he looks like he's been there*
*for some time. The two men greet one another and strike up a conversation*
*about the old days. Wanting to join their talk I ask if there were squatters*
*living here once. They ignore the idle question and then I tell them that*
*our property had been claimed by Métis people, but they chose to let their*
*title lapse when the battles broke out in 1885, believing perhaps that such*
*documents would soon be superfluous.*

*"What was the name?" the old man asks.*

*"I can't remember," I say, "but I have it written down somewhere.*
*I'll go get it."*

*"No, don't go get your papers. I want you to remember yourself."*

*After a pause, I remember the name and speak it aloud, "Alexander*
*Fisher."*

Call him Virgil Two-fathers, this one who insists always on
remembrance. More than one, yet not quite the sum of the many
who have learned to ignore the questions that accuse in the asking,
degrade in the answering we cannot bear anyway: why did you
spend the winter in jail; why did your cousin kill that old priest;
why did your uncle embezzle from the band office; why does your
twelve-year-old boy have diabetes; why did your sister kill herself
last month; why did I see your brother breathing into a plastic bag
in the alley behind the Wellness Store; why are you standing on
the corner giving passersby a note that says, "I am a deaf man. Two
dollars please"; and why am I always wondering if you are telling
the truth, what the strange smell is when we talk?

The last time Virgil came to me I was in the ditch south of the
valley, looking through my binoculars again, trying to find a Baird's
sparrow. I heard someone humming or singing softly to himself on
the other side of the road. It was him, in orange coveralls, carrying
a single grocery bag in each hand. In one he carried a few empties,
in the other, branches of mint, some bearberries, wild bergamot.
He showed me the medicines as I walked alongside. It was to be a

day for talking of the old times, at first in that voice of grandfathers he sometimes uses, not looking anywhere, speaking of events in a timeless always and even now, not merely happening today but some even tomorrow, as though I and my race had disappeared or never come at all.

"People die in their lodges. There is a skull on that hill where one crawled up in a fever to feel the cooling wind. We die this way: some of fever, others of hunger. Waiting for buffalo, eating coyote. It isn't the new tools or prayers that kill—it is sickness and starvation. Death has made a circle in which the Pipe sits down with the Crown. Dying again in the breaking of those promises, but we are still here and we know what we are doing in this place."

Then he stopped, turned to face me, and shifted to his storytelling voice: "'Hell,' they told us. 'You'll be in hell!' I heard that first day from the nuns. They were right. We were ready for hell by the time we left. I was lucky though—my parents hid me 'til I was ten. Then the Indian agent came to our door with the RCMP. Told my dad he'd go to jail if he didn't let go of me. So they put me in that car and they drove away to that school. I walked through the doors of that building and hope went out of me like wind when you get punched in the stomach. Wouldn't let us talk in our language. I felt like I couldn't get enough air, like something was stopping my breath. Such a dark place, and it was cold, eh, at night. All those strange people in long black dresses. When you were trying to sleep you could hear homesick kids, little ones, crying all the time. It was a smelly, dirty place. We didn't get hardly any meat to eat. Kids were always getting TB or something. The cold was enough to make you sick. There was a little coffin once for a girl who died.

"I was frightened at first. They cut my hair off, told me I had to speak English. One priest told me the ceremonies of my grandfathers were the work of the devil. Said my ancestors were all in limbo because they'd never been baptized. I didn't believe it—I was in limbo. My ancestors were at home with my people.

"Until I got to that dark place I'd always thought that going to church and going to ceremonies were all part of one thing. But not there. Even though I knew better, after a while I started to feel ashamed of my name, of my language. Everything felt bad. The first winter I was there I used to look west out the windows to watch for sleighs coming down the lake trail. I thought my parents would come to get me, but they never did. The next spring I was outside playing and it was a warm day, really nice, so I started walking west. I made it past where I couldn't see the school anymore behind me and I just kept walking. Walked all day and night, following the old sleigh trails. I fell through ice and got my feet wet a couple times. Made it home the next morning. Thirty-some miles. A few days later the Indian agent showed up to take me back.

"Never got molested or nothing. Well, they hit me with a hockey stick once on the hand, for writing bad. Broke something and couldn't write much after that. No, they weren't all like that. One of them was kind to me. And I got to learn some things. We got used to it I guess, learned how to get by. But they shouldn't have taken us from our parents and grandparents.

"I left when I was fifteen, tired of weeding their gardens, shoveling out their barns, praying their prayers. Some schools make you ready for a job. Those schools made us ready to be victims. My cousin was molested at that school up on Gordon Reserve—it was a bad one. A few years ago she left her babies alone so she could go out drinking. One of them walked outside and froze to death. She drinks every day, lost somewhere in the city. No one's seen her in a while. Her little brother was taken from their mother as a baby. She was a drunk too. That boy was raised by white people but he hanged himself when he was sixteen. Three of the boys I went to that school with died before they were thirty: one in a knife fight, one was hit by a car when he was walking home to the reserve, and one was found frozen a mile or two from the city, no shoes or jacket, just another drunk Indian. That one, he had a daughter and my mother took her in, tried to keep her on the right path but she went to the city when she was fourteen. Police found her body in the ditch. She'd been dragged behind a car for half a mile. Some John did it to her. They never found the guy. My brother had two boys, but their mother wouldn't stop drinking when she was pregnant. They were born looking funny. Small heads and you couldn't get them to listen or to understand anything. Couldn't learn when you told them. They're in the city now too, living on chocolate bars, watching TV all day, and sniffing away the money they get from Social Services.

"I've worked all over the West—slaughtering cattle, laying pipeline, digging potatoes, building dams—but I got tired of doing their work, came back to the reserve, the only place that feels right now. Been helping an elder, learning some of the medicines. Did my second Sun Dance last summer. I take my grand-nieces around on the powwow circuit these days. We go to every one of them, except the one in Lebret—I know it wasn't as bad as some of them other schools[4] but I get that feeling in my chest when I go there. I don't want to go back to that place. I heard they tore the old school down, but I still can't go."

You don't have to be a residential-school survivor to shrink from the ghosts in a town like Lebret. I camped there one night during a two-day paddle down the lakes with Robert Stacey, an art historian from Ontario whose grandfather, C. W. Jefferys, was here painting watercolors in those early years of repression and hunger. But first we made a visit across the lake, Mission Lake, to look for the remains of the old oblate scholasticate where, from 1927 to 1965, the order ran a seminary to fill the demand for more priests to serve in residential schools and remote missions. Valley people still talk[5] of the mid-August evenings when they would see two or three freighter canoes loaded with oblate priests and seminarians paddling their way downstream. They were celebrating the Feast of the Assumption of the Blessed Virgin with a trip past Lebret, through the channel and down the next lake, singing hymns in French all the way.

The seminary was torn down years ago. We found nothing more than a few chunks of slab foundation here and there in the tall grass now surrounded by cabins built by weekenders from the city. As dusk neared, we paddled across the lake to Lebret, drew our canoe up on shore, and pitched our tent beneath cottonwood trees in the churchyard cemetery. On the headstones we found the Métis names of the first families to settle in this region—Amyotte, Welsh, LaRoque, Racette, Fisher, Grant, Pelletier, Poitras, Delorme, Desjarlais—some dating back to the 1880s. Above the veranda door of the empty rectory, a once grand edifice, there was an inscription in Latin, *Evangelizare pauperibus misit me.* "He has sent me to evangelize the poor."

In the early twentieth century, the fellow in charge of evangelizing the local paupers at Lebret was Father Joseph Hugonard. He and the other oblates set off into the Great Lone Land with honorable intentions, hoping they might be able to help aboriginal people make the shift from their old life ways to the new ones thrust upon them by white settlement. As with any group of men, most were self-serving and weak, and a few were almost compassionate and virtuous enough to countervail the effects of the inevitable reprobates, the rare but not rare enough ones who devour innocence. In times when almost no one in religious or secular power had a care for the plight of the continent's first peoples, the oblates were sharing lives of poverty among them, learning to speak Cree, Déné, and Ojibwa. Coming from a church that has always treated any other faith as inimical to the one true way, that in the preceding centuries had done little to stay the hand of armies and mobs killing in its name Jews, Muslims, Protestants, and nonbelievers of

every variety, some oblates have shown unusual openness to indigenous cultural and religious practice. In spite of their evangelizing
mission and the standard theology of demonizing the pagan, many
members of the order have seen the good in Native religious traditions. In recent decades, some of the fathers who live in aboriginal communities have begun to encourage indigenous spirituality,
even blend it with Christian practice.

All of which is apologetics, of course, for the evil that happens
when religious people allow themselves, even unwittingly, to
become tools of colonization. Father Hugonard at Lebret was
caught between his apostolate as an oblate on the one hand and
the demands of the Indian commissioner on the other. Both priests
and bureaucrats wanted to bring Indians into the burgeoning settler
culture; both agreed that the key was a good Christian education,
which, for men of that day who had themselves been educated in
boarding schools, meant the children must be taken away from
their parents. If there was a difference of opinion between the colonial government and the missionaries it was perhaps over details of
how the transition was to be achieved and on what schedule. The
government wanted Indians brought into line as quickly and as
cheaply as possible. Letters between Hugonard and the Indian commissioner show the oblates demanding more funding to improve
living conditions at the school and the agency responding with
pressure to squeeze more garden and industrial production out of
the children. In these same letters, however, Hugonard reveals the
fear of the pagan that ran through missionaries of that era, oblates
included. In one instance, he suggests the commissioner begin
jailing Indians caught participating in traditional ceremonies and
says that he sees many who are too busy "dancing like demented
individuals and indulging in all kinds of debauchery" to ever be
successful as farmers.[6]

Some have said that the school at Lebret had little of the abuse
that occurred at some other schools, and there are graduates alive

who claim their years there were the best of their lives. Nonetheless, in 1991 the oblates made an official apology to the people they had set out to serve, in a statement read before a crowd of twenty thousand aboriginal pilgrims at Lac Sainte-Anne. They now recognize that all of their schools have hurt aboriginal people, not only through the violation of innocence—the mental abuse, fondling, rape, and beatings that carried headlines—but also in the simple act of taking children from their parents and in leading whole generations away from the wisdom and integrity of their own culture. Those who say the sexual and physical abuse has been exaggerated, that there were few genuine cases, and that by and large the system was sound are counting as nothing the forced removal, confinement, and cultural annihilation that went on for decades in every residential school, and their real, though unintended, contribution to the program of assimilation, treaty abrogation, and disempowerment that the first peoples of the plains have undergone in the past 130 years. The suffering compressed into that span of time was the same all civilizations have experienced in their exile from the original immersion in wildness, but where most come to agriculture, monotheism, and writing gradually over thousands of years, our residential schools forced these drastic conversions upon indigenous peoples in a child's passage from innocence to experience.

Facing every temptation of the desert in the wilderness of the New World, Christians have failed the gospel time after time. Prairie theologian Erik Reichers categorizes the human disposition to sin according to the three brushes with evil experienced by Christ in his forty days. Food, fame, and fortune, Reichers says, are the temptations that get us in trouble and they correspond to inherent weaknesses in the heart that make us vulnerable: our ego, our ignorance, and our impatience.[7] The model applies well to the Christian enterprise in the Americas. Following every appetite represented by that trio of food, fame, and fortune, we arrive on the shores of land as yet untaken, charged with the ego that assures us we can possess that which, in our ignorance, we regard as unused and unsanctified, even waste, and, instead of letting it gradually reveal its gifts, we take it impatiently in hand, and force it to produce on our terms, by our schedule. As for the people who have lived here in a humility grounded in knowledge and respect for the plenitude that is received and not taken, our ego would not permit sharing it according to that alien ethos, which we deemed inferior and savage, and we could not wait for them to make their journey at their own pace, so afraid we were that it might take us all to a different destination.

Impatience, taking shortcuts, putting a flame to the chrysalis, is always damning. Residential schools, and the church's complicity in them, took us all down into the dead zone where impatience leads. We wanted the birthright and the blessings of this land and we wanted them now, so we put our hunting brothers through the crucible of learning the plow, the alphabet, and the cross. Jacob has long been wrestling on that riverbank, and the wounds are not healing well. Cover them, dress them any way we like, our children find them out anyway. For two mornings in a row, my youngest daughter woke to ask her mother, in her first words of the day, "Are there people who eat Indians?" We asked her if she'd heard something that worried her.

"No," she answered, "I dreamed about people who kill Indians." She could have heard us discussing the latest allegations of police abusing aboriginal people, stories of shoeless men tossed from police cruisers far from the city limits on cold winter nights. A small child may not understand what she sees and hears among adults, but will sense when something is broken, divided, not whole between us. At Halloween she watches strange-looking Indian men, victims of fetal alcohol syndrome, drifting silently down the street from door to door, gathering candy in grocery bags; then hears the grown-ups complain, feels their fear and revulsion. In the iron cold of January, on the drive to playschool, her mom is flagged down by two ill-dressed children shivering on the street. They ask the time and the little boy says to his older sister, "See, I told you we were late. We missed our bus and we can't remember how to get to our school. Do you know how?" And her mom smiles and asks if she can be their bus today and when they get in the van, she stares at them wondering why they are not like her. At home she is afraid of the man who comes to the door for bottles, especially when he winks at her, smiling with broken teeth above the black thread of fresh stitches showing on his chin, or when he comes in for tea and a visit, plays the guitar and sings strange old songs in a whispery voice. She hides behind her father's leg, watching everything, reading the tension, tracking the energy that moves toward the other but can never close that gap.

To get to know aboriginal people, as friends, at work, or in the community, is to feel the throb of that ancestral wound. An artist friend of mine, Deborah, was happy when she got a position teaching English in a high-school diploma program run by and for aboriginal people. She was excited to be teaching English, and she was also excited about having a chance to get to know more First Nations people, and to learn from them. She looked forward to discovering with them—in their own literature (granted, in translation)—a way of celebrating and sharing stories from their traditions and from their experiences as urban Indian people.

A few months into the job I saw her again and the enthusiasm had been overtaken by worry. After we talked for a while I realized that she had come face-to-face with her own misperceptions about what Indian people should be or should not be and was struggling to find a way to see and accept them as they are. It is in such moments that the enormous gap between our cultures must be contemplated and accepted for what it is. As admirable as it may be to attempt to span the divide from one's own culture to another, we can never completely step into the shoes of the other. There will always be a gap.

Deborah told me that she'd had some good days as a teacher at the college, days filled with learning, respect, and laughter, when she could feel that she was making a difference, helping in a small way. But there seemed to be no way of escaping the reality of standing before them as a white teacher in a roomful of students who have every reason to mistrust, even despise, white people and their system of learning.

"I have people in my class who shout 'Assimilation!' at me regularly. They say the language itself is a tool of assimilation. Last week they called me a 'plastic shaman' so that's over with." She said she had expected there would be a gulf between her and the students but she had been naive enough to think she might be able to do something to span it. Then, by way of explaining the insults tossed across that distance from both sides, she told me of the times she has gone out in public with a group of her students. They enter a candy shop and the storekeeper screams at a young Indian woman for taking a sample from a bowl marked Try One; or at an office supply store, where the clerks tail them up and down each aisle.

"If you'd have asked me before I got this job whether I thought this town had a problem with racism, I'd have said, 'Well, maybe a bit, but not really.' Now I know different."

She knew that before long someone of aboriginal descent would replace her, and she knew too that that was as it should be. When it happened she would miss some things about the job, but then she'd have more time to work on her sculpture. Everything in her studio these days, she said, seems to be a bridge of one kind or another. Some of them hang in the air in two pieces that head toward one another but don't quite meet.

The day Robert Stacey and I camped at Lebret we made it over to the hotel bar for a pilsner, and as soon as we had sat down we were joined by the only other customer in the place, a garrulous old guy, farm bred, the kind who will talk your leg off once he has three beers aboard.

"Gerry," he said, thrusting forth a surprisingly soft palm. Scandinavian blue eyes, a yellowing mustache, and blond hair on its way to gray and spurting out from beneath a ball cap that promoted a gutter company. "Used to live around here. For fifteen years or so…So, how's the fishing?" he asked, taking his lower lip in a bit farther than a sober "f" requires.

Canoeing, not fishing, Robert replied.

"Canoeing? Jeez, by gawr, you know, that's somethin' I always said I wannad ta do—love it, love it, love it!" From there he launched into a rambling story about his family and the farm where he grew up ten miles down the valley. By the time our bottles were empty, he was telling us he'd come that close to being born a rich land baron.

"My granddad coulda bought this whole damn lake for five hunerd dollars. Govmint offered it to 'im, but he said, 'What do I want with that piece of sand? Can't grow anything in it. I'm a farmer!' By jeez, if he'da been smarter I'd—well, I wouldn't be here talkin' to you, I'll tell you that!"

We left Gerry and went back to our cemetery campsite to warm up a can of pioneer stew for supper. In the half-light I went for a walk over to the ruins of the residential school, which the local band council had put under the wrecking ball a few years back. A shadow against a low pile of bricks looked like someone sitting in the rubble and I thought again of Virgil walking the ditch. How he had touched me with a hand wet from dew on the plants he'd been gathering and told me not to feel guilty, that he does not blame me or anyone else. He said it took him twenty-five years to figure out that he was clinging to his rights as a victim the same way white people cling to their rights to do what they like with the land they say they own.

"We got used to being victims. Started just after the treaties when land was taken from starving people forced to stay on the reserves. Eating poisoned coyotes to stay alive. Holding a ceremony to pray and getting thrown in jail for it. Some had nothing left to give their children, just that victim way of living and now we have to throw that away too. You can't stay in that old blanket—it'll rot you alive, and the little bit of power it gives you is a lie. It steals your spirit so we trade it in for some anger, which is better than giving up. Some of us find a way to forgive. It's not easy, but we do it."

There was a tipi in one of the yards along the main street as I walked back to the cemetery, and on the hilltop overlooking the little town a crucifix outlined in blue electric light—the final station of the cross, a tragic flourish, beautiful and ridiculous as the civilization it has never quite contained in its tension of opposites. At the lakeshore I heard children's voices, laughter rising and cast out upon the waters of the bay ringed by modest cottages. There was no wind, nothing to stir the hinged and heart-shaped leaves of the cottonwoods overhead, nothing to cover the words of cottagers half a mile away or the chug-chugging of an outboard motor waiting to be revved. I sat on a bench bearing a plaque that read "Bide a while with me" in a dedication to the memory of longtime Lebret residents, and I watched the little brown bats, out now from their belfry roosts, swooping from tree to tree. There were alarm notes from an agitated robin. Fish leaping just offshore. Orange blobs of mercury vapor lighting up the farthest cabins. Avocets calling out in distant flight.

# 2. RISE

*For examples of a whole and indigenous American society, functioning in full meaning and good health within the ecology of this continent, we will have to look back to the cultures of the Indians. That we failed to learn from them how to live in this land is a stupidity—a racial stupidity—that will corrode the heart of our society until the day comes, if it ever does, when we turn back to learn from them.*

—Wendell Berry, *The Hidden Wound*

Noel Star Blanket, great-great-grandson of old White Calf, has the aristocratic bearing of a chief but it shines through a modesty that disarms and lets you into his life on equal terms. The day we met, I sensed in his manner something of the way he had come, the gains, the setbacks, and the renewals he had undergone. Later, as we got to know one another better, he would tell me, "I look back today on my life and I do not have much material wealth. There was a time when I did, and for all kinds of reasons I don't have that anymore. I count my blessings: I have relatively good health. I have a house on my reserve, a vehicle that gets me around, allows me to do my work, gets me out to ceremonies. I am challenged in the work I do. I exercise; I take care of my spiritual side, pray every morning, go to my elders, to the sweat lodge, ceremonies, feasts. I have a son who makes me proud. This is what keeps me going these days."

As a boy, the youngest son of the third Chief Star Blanket, Noel would often read for his father, whose eyesight was failing from long years reading by lamplight. And in his ears, his father's famous words, "You must learn the wit and cunning of the white man, learn what the treaties say." From the age of eight, Noel was reading the treaties, the Indian Act, and position papers from Indian organizations across the country. He would accompany his father whenever he traveled to meet with other chiefs. It was the 1950s and his father was helping organize an independent body of chiefs to present an alternative to the more quiescent element in Indian leadership that had control of the new provincial federation. Noel told me that his father always resisted the efforts of Indian Affairs to remake his people in the image of the colonizers.

"My father rebelled against that and became known as a rabble-rouser because of his defiance. Indian organizational activities were being put down by the government in those days and there was no money, so when we went to a community for a meeting, the people fed everyone, took up a collection for gas money for travelers. The leader of the host community was always the chairman. I remember those as the best times of my life. I listened to those great orators, great leaders, spent time in those communities. I got my steeping, my education from those men and those communities.

"So I learned at a very young age about politics, about treaties, about the Indian Act, and about the Department of Indian Affairs. After residential school I went east for a while. I worked for the National Film Board and the Canadian Indian Youth Council. We did not have our own administration, we did not have an office, we did not have electricity, we did not have phones—we had next to nothing. Then I became a chief at twenty-four. It was 1971. The first thing I did was set about trying to get electricity and phones in my community. I started reading up on grant programs that were available. We got most of our people working at that time, using what they called LIP programs, Local Initiative Projects, Federal Labor Intensive Programs, Local Employment Action Programs, whatever. We used to have acronyms for them all—we called them FLIP, LIP, and LEAP. We also had some money that had been put aside over the many years in the treasury of the government of Canada from land leased on our reserve by white farmers. The money was held in trust by the department. So we took that money and we bought some cattle, and we built shelters and fences and feeders and you name it. We had all the women working too, doing things that they wanted to do. They did quilting for old people, cleaned homes, fixed up yards, painted. They did whatever they could. We had all our people working. Those were the glory days of Star Blanket."

From there, Noel's star kept rising. Soon he was chair of the local council of chiefs. After that he was elected vice-chief of the provincial federation of Indian nations. And then, in 1975, at the age of twenty-nine, he found himself heading the National Indian Brotherhood, elected by acclamation to lead the organization that was soon to become the Assembly of First Nations, which we now know as the body that brought aboriginal rights and treaty rights into the political mainstream.

"At that time in Ottawa, there were many young Indian professional people around my age, late twenties, early thirties, people with law degrees. So I gathered up a few of those men and women and put them to work for me, and we put together many policies and many developmental programs. We cut a big swath in those days. We dressed up in three-piece suits, handled ourselves very professionally. We challenged government policies, and we put our own forward. We were young whippersnappers and we were giving them what for.

"That was about the time we began talking about Indian self-government. And the government of Canada would not even deign to use the word. I remember meetings with Prime Minister Clark and telling him, 'Say the word, just say it, just utter it, Indian self-government,' but he wouldn't."

The peak of Noel's political career may have been the day he led a delegation to the gates of Buckingham Palace, asking to speak with the Queen. They were turned away, but Noel knew that they had done what was right, what his grandfathers would have wanted him to do. Preparing for that trip, he had gone for the first time in many years to consult with the elders and they affirmed that his trip to England had their blessings and those of the ancestors, and they told Noel how to conduct himself and what he must sacrifice in his own life to be effective. In the early dawn when the elders blessed Noel and his delegation, raising the pipe and saying, "By this stem we remember what our grandfathers negotiated for us," Noel thought of his own grandfather and of his father. Something awakened in him then, a call back to the old ways that he would not fully heed until it came again in the voice of pain and betrayal.

After his four years as chief of the National Indian Brotherhood, Noel continued working as a contractor for the organization, now known as the Assembly of First Nations, as well as for private companies, both Indian- and white-run, and for various Indian bands and tribal councils. Several corporations retained him as an associate who could help them find contracts in aboriginal communities. For this kind of work he received a finder's fee as well as per diems if and when the company required his services on a job. One day when Noel was at the assembly's offices, an anonymous phone call came in directing the staff to a manila envelope that would be left in a garbage bin in a certain alley. Around this time First Nations leaders were embroiled in a dispute with the federal government over the question of income tax on income earned off-reserve. Although all income earned off-reserve is now taxable even for status Indians, in those days First Nations people were just beginning to earn enough income away from reserves to gain the attention of the government. The matter had yet to be settled, but the treaties had rendered aboriginal people exempt from taxation. Noel and others like him had always claimed this tax immunity and refused to pay income tax, filing official notices of objection on the advice of their lawyers and accountants. The mysterious manila envelope, however, contained a Revenue Department position paper outlining plans to make examples out of key First Nations corporations, bands, tribal councils, and individuals. No names were listed. Noel was not worried because he was being advised by one of the best corporate lawyers in Ottawa and was himself an associate of an accounting firm that included a chartered accountant who worked for the auditor general and had a very high security clearance. In his mind, his affairs were all in order; the tax man would have to look elsewhere for examples.

Not long after that, the Revenue Department sent out their special investigations unit, accusing Noel and others of tax evasion and slapping writs on their homes. Then Noel learned that he and several other First Nations leaders were being investigated by the RCMP for other alleged wrongdoings. A change in federal government to the Progressive Conservatives had brought a new chill to the relations between First Nations leaders and the political power in Ottawa. The Liberal government under Indian Affairs ministers John Munro and Warren Allmand had advanced the cause of aboriginal people steadily throughout the 1970s and early 1980s, but when Brian Mulroney became prime minister in the fall of 1984 in a general rebirth of right-wing politics sweeping across much of the Western world, that advancement came to an abrupt halt. Outspoken First Nations leaders in Ottawa suddenly became a threat to the government, a source of "extra-parliamentary opposition," as RCMP investigators referred to them. Something would have to be done to cut their legs out from under them.

By 1989, Mulroney's government had charged former Liberal Indian Affairs minister John Munro and several prominent First Nations leaders, including Noel, with seventy-seven counts of fraud, corruption, breach of trust, and tax evasion. Noel was accused of corruption for his finder's fees, but the only cases they cited involved contacts with First Nations–run firms and organizations. Companies run by white people and for which he provided exactly the same services—such as the accounting firm linked to the auditor general—were noticeably absent from the investigation. The Crown took more than eleven months to present its case, calling several hundred witnesses and referring to investigation documents totaling hundreds of thousands of pages. The records of five prime ministers were subpoenaed during the trial. Early in the process, Noel's lawyer succeeded in having him severed from the trial under a motion of nonsuit. When the Crown finally rested, the judge threw the case out of court, not even bothering to hear the defense. Noel will never forget the judge's words that day: "The Crown has presented what they call their evidence, but in my opinion in a case like this, theory is one thing and evidence is everything, and the Crown has none."

All charges were dropped but by then the accused, including Noel, were bankrupt and had lost homes, jobs, reputations, and relationships.[8] Faced with the growing threat of aboriginal self-determination and their rightful demand for a fair share of the wealth of the nation, the Conservative government had struck a decapitating blow.

It was the same old plan, just new tricks: keep the Indians weak, don't let them get their hands on too much power or resources. The good news is that over the long run the plan is failing. Despite all that has been done in the name of God, government, and civilization to foist our spiritual bankruptcy upon the ones this land knows as its exact people long nurtured by its generosity, despite each renewed effort to keep them in a disenfranchised adolescence, despite every program of assimilation, the deliberate exertions of law and public policy to erase their ways of being human, despite hatred, disease, extortion, corruption, impoverishment, larceny, and every other violence of body and soul, the people remain. They resist, heels fast to the soil into which the lives of their ancestors bled once in death and bleed even now into the lives of all who remain here, native and new; they stand yet, holding the pipe, the circle, the tobacco to their hearts, yes, inclined a little toward a past glory that is partly nostalgic veneer but necessary nonetheless as the reservoir of blessings from which they now call one another to rise from bitterness and shame to new life.

And the others—the enactors of law, surveyors of title, beneficiaries of grand schemes of land alienation whose grandfathers
ran the transits, passed out the scrip, put the reserve children in
cars and drove them off to the darkness of brick schools—meet
the bitterness of the victim race with an equally inoperative guilt.
The open wounds we gave one another now bear the possibility of
forming new flesh, one race's trust grafted upon the skin of the other,
repentance mending where forgiveness allows, scars not fading but
worthy of old shame—the marks of a perdition undeserved.

An old muskrat coat, my wife's and before that her grandmother's,
now in shreds and showing thin strips of the original skins stretched
and tanned sixty years past by a Métis trapper, sat upon our garage-
sale table for half a June day before a shy Indian girl looked it over,
showing her boyfriend something as she spoke in whispers.

"One dollar and it's yours," I said. She smiled, the boyfriend
paid, and I asked what they would use such a ragged coat for.

"She will sew pieces from it onto her dancing costume," the
man replied. Later that day I saw a poster for a professional wrestling
event to be held at the Eagledome in Lebret. One of the villains
listed on the bill was characterized as a residential school principal
and another one was made out to be the local Indian agent.

How strange this world we've made with the remains of our
first failed accommodations: an old coat, sewn from pelts prepared
by aboriginal trappers and sold to become a farm wife's pride as
she sat in Sunday Mass, is now turned back into skins and dangling
from the skirt of a dancer swirling in her moccasins to the drums of
a dust-borne powwow; while in another arena, the crowd jeers in
popcorn-tossing catharsis at the memory of their childhood spent
in cold dorms and laundry rooms now strutting on the boards.

☙

On the edge of Fort Qu'Appelle, once the stockade of traders in
fur and flesh, then the garrison of a police force sent out to the
plains to hold it back from the predations of the young republic
to the south and make it safe for rangemen and plowboys, and
these days half resort town, half reserve town, where sandal-shod
cottagers studiously ignore their aboriginal counterparts with
better tans who drive in from where treaty land is named for
the ones who made their Xs—Piapot, Pasqua, Muscowpetung,
Kawacatoose, Okanese—there is a place made sacred by that confluence of the Pipe and the Crown, now maligned and forgotten
by its primary beneficiaries. The land had been forgotten too by
almost everyone, though it was the place the bands in the early
years could come each fall, just after the time of molting and
ripening, to receive their annual gifts and to renew their faith in
the sacred partnership to which their leaders had committed the
generations in perpetuity. Those first annual gatherings on that
thirteen hundred acres, with large tipi villages upon the alluvial
bottomland between the lakes that are a slowing and a widening
of a river's movement east across the plains, were cause of concern
to the nervous citizens of town and farm whose bedsheets were
tangled by night thoughts of Sitting Bull and his restless starvlings
fresh from routing Custer at Little Bighorn. Columnists and magistrates called for a change. They wanted the Indians to stay on
their reserves, and by 1894, only twenty years after the signing
of that treaty, the fourth one made between the colonial government and the First Nations of the land, they had their wish.
A pass system was in place, keeping Indian people on reserve
land that was already diminishing under pressure from settlers
who wanted it for farming. The annuities—five dollars for each
member, twenty-five for the chief—were paid thereafter on each

reserve in a brief and unceremonial visit from the Indian agent. The Treaty Four signing grounds, promised as the site where treaty business would forever after be handled between the races now sharing the land, fell into disuse by the time the babies born the summer the treaty was signed had come to adulthood. The Indian Department handed the land over to the Department of the Interior to dispose of as they would any other parcel.

In the 1970s, Cree historian Blair Stonechild, who had heard elders speak of a treaty ground near Fort Qu'Appelle, started digging for old maps. When he found a survey map of the area drawn in 1882, clearly showing the acres set aside, he had all the proof the Treaty Four nations would need to make a claim. In the middle of negotiations with the government, researchers discovered burial sites on the land in question, adding weight to their case. In 1995, one year and a century since the land was expropriated, the Treaty Four nations and the federal government reached an agreement.

With the settlement of $6 million, the thirty-four member nations of Treaty Four have been able not only to buy back most of the original thirteen hundred acres, but to build a governance center, including a massive, tipi-shaped legislative assembly, office space, a keeping house, and archives. The tipi rises up from the lakeshore now, visible all the way from Lebret against the sage green folds of the valley where eagles pass in season and pelicans lift in single-file squadrons, one after another, to cross from lake to lake above the dowdy bungalows of residential-school survivors, the gardens and verandas of wealthier residents, and the hot-tubbed, vinyl-sided resort homes of city people looking to retreat to summer memories of a time when the valley was surveyed and safe and settled and altogether untroubled by the vexing claims of Indians.

But there was much else to be reclaimed, brought back to rightful hands, and not all of it was land. Those who learned that land can be swindled from hungry people found that the same techniques will work for family treasures, the tools and clothing of ancestors, and even their sacred ceremonial objects, everything from headdresses to medicine bundles and pipes—much of it confiscated, traded, and sold into the possession of the race who made possession sacred above all else. Just beyond the memories of the old people lay the days of the house-to-house searches by Indian agents, many of whom would take sacred objects and sell them off to private collectors and museums. Missionaries, convinced they were freeing a people from heathen superstition, provided the moral justification for the gathering up of what was, to a priest, the accoutrement of idolatry and, to a curator, the artifacts of a bygone culture.

Of course not all of the sacred items that ended up in the hands of nonaboriginal people were stolen. Over their century of evangelizing the people of the Qu'Appelle Valley, the oblate missionaries gathered a small but significant collection of sacred items given freely to them by Indian elders. The oblates received these pipes, rattles, and medicine bags as gifts that symbolized the good relations they had established between themselves and the first peoples of the region. The elders offered the gifts in that same spirit, knowing that just as the oblates had shared the articles of their faith, they had given the most sacred of their own.

A gift is made and received. Two faiths, one alien, the other indigenous, share a momentary exchange of trust, a gesture of spiritual reciprocity across the distinctions of belief and practice. Not what we think of as a typical encounter between priests and elders, but probably more common than recent versions of history would have us believe. Whatever we may think of relations between the church and aboriginal people, such moments of grace will not be denied and find their own ways of bearing fruit over time.

In November 1996, the spirits that whispered blessings upon those early gifts spoke again—this time loudly enough to be heard in the offices of the Roman Catholic archdiocese for this region. That was the day, long decades after the oblates closed their scholasticate on Mission Lake, that three First Nations people met with the archbishop in charge of the Lebret parish, where the collection has been stored in recent years. One of the three, an aboriginal RCMP constable, explained that he wanted the church to hand over the pipes and other artifacts that it was holding at Lebret. He spoke at length and with great agitation in his voice and manner, describing how he had been unable to sleep at night, because his ancestors were coming to him in his dreams asking him to restore the pipes to their proper place.

Archbishop Peter Mallon, who had not been aware of the collection, listened respectfully to the appeal and then promised he would look into the matter. The story of how Mallon oversaw the safe transfer of those sacred objects in the face of some resistance has now, years later, taken on the narrative luster of local myth. The version I heard first, from a man who attended meetings at the Lebret parish, tells of conflict and a dramatic intervention. The parish caretaker who kept the collection in the church under lock and key did not want to give up any of the artifacts, arguing that they belonged to the parish and if given back to the Indians could easily be lost or destroyed. Mallon, the legend goes, listened to the protests and then asked politely for the keys. When he was refused, he walked out of the building to his car. Moments later he was back in the room with a large set of bolt-cutters. He cut the lock, flung open the door to the room, and said to the people who had come for the artifacts, "There. They're yours. Take them."

A good yarn, but Archbishop Mallon was quick to set the record straight when I asked him how the objects were returned. He laughed at the bolt-cutters flourish, said he was much less theatrical than that. Although I could see he was suitably proud to have been given a small chance to repair relations between First Nations and the archdiocese, he gave all the credit to Blair Stonechild and the others representing the Treaty Four nations. Before I left, he showed me his handwritten notes from the meetings between himself, the parish, and the Treaty Four nations. Nothing in the notes indicated strong resistance from the parish, but the archbishop admitted that he did have to exercise the authority of his office to ensure that the Lebret people would cooperate. In the end, it became a fine working out of the idea of gift as community endowment that characterizes traditional gift giving in Cree culture. When someone receives a gift, Noel once said to me, he or she is indebted not to the giver as an individual but to the entire community. Community, in its broadest aboriginal definition, embraces everyone from ancestors to children as yet unborn, forming a matrix of responsibility and care that obliges a receiver of a gift and transforms possession *by* into possession *for*. These are also part of the forgotten truths at the base of the Christian gospel, though in reading the archbishop's notes I could see them living yet in the good faith and understanding of the one we call shepherd. Toward the bottom of one of his pages of notes there are some lines explaining how the sacred objects originally came into the hands of the oblates: "Gov't policy since 1880 to eradicate ceremonies, culture, etc. Some officials would confiscate items—others would offer money for them. Some, rather than die and leave these, would entrust them to missionaries." And then in a final line, "Gift—creates a reciprocal relationship of trust!"

Let the record show that the man who inherited an archdiocese wounded by its legacy of residential schools did not for a moment consider breaching that trust.

# 3. CONVERGE

*We must leave it to the humble and the ignorant*
*To invent the frame of faith that will form the future.*

—Robinson Jeffers, "Faith"

*In the nature of things everything that is faith must rise and every-*
*thing that rises must converge.*

—Pierre Teilhard de Chardin,
"Address to the World Congress of Faiths," March 8, 1947

There is more than you or I will ever comprehend or sense behind each ugly jab of rancor thrust from one bloodline to the other, man to man; and many hearts you'd think were fossilized until their story shows it beating yet with a stillborn bitterness, the loss of a fine love, mitigating, accommodating, holding us together in the awkward, wrestling embrace of the estranged.

Though I rarely take a cab in this city, I have twice had rides from an older man with a German accent who likes to play schmaltzy old Bavarian tunes on his tape deck. You open the cab door to enter and out come dulcet voices crooning of the motherland. On my second ride I glanced at his ID card hanging on the rear-view mirror to look for a German name, but it was covered with an oval medallion of Our Lady. Another German Catholic, and like many others I have met, a likeable, garrulous old fellow, free with his opinions and yarns.

As we headed south on a busy downtown street, three young Indian people dashed out in front of us. The cabbie, who never took his foot off the gas as we passed by them, said, "Hah! Just about had three points."

In this town you get accustomed to letting such comments go unchallenged but this time I didn't. "What did you say?"

"Wouldn't have to pay their way anymore."

"Is that what you really think?" I asked.

He laughed and shook his head ruefully, "You don't see what I see driving this cab. Drive enough drunk Indians around and you'll think different. On welfare check day I'll get forty fares and every one is a trip to the bingo hall. Bingo! While their kids go hungry and half-naked to school. I know—I drive them to school too. Nine-year-old kids stealing candy so's they can eat. Their mothers get eighteen hundred dollars a month in welfare—that's what they cost you and me—and it all goes on bingo, booze, and drugs! I drive them every day to houses where they pick up drugs or drop it off. I can tell you where twelve different drug houses are in this city. That's where your tax dollars are going."

He went on at length with details about bingo, hungry children, and drugs, but I interrupted.

"So, why is this happening? Don't you ever ask yourself how this came to be?"

"I'll tell you why," he said, pulling the cab over to drop me off. "The kids grow up seeing their moms get nothing but welfare and then spending it on this stuff. It's all they know. They grow up thinking it's the way life is."

We had parked and he turned in his seat to face me.

"Look, I was married to a woman, half-Cree, half-French. Thirty-three years we had together. Met her when she was fourteen, married her when she was nineteen. Do you think I loved her? By God, she was the finest woman ever lived—hard working, gentle, beautiful…She had no time for people who wouldn't help themselves. And now she's gone."

Then he flipped down the sun visor and showed me a school photo of a healthy mixed-blood girl, twelve years old or so.

"There's my granddaughter. I'm raising her by myself now. She moved in with us when she was two."

He pulled out a well-thumbed packet of photos. "Here we are camping together with her brother. There, that's the two of them. Such great kids."

I looked at the photographs, admired his grandchildren, thanked him for the ride, and paid the fare. As I walked away from the cab, he finished looking at the photographs, returned them carefully to their envelope.

There is something of that cabbie in all of us who have come late to this continent, to the degree that we regret all that we have lost in our relations with the aboriginal yet remain in ignorance and shame on our side of the river that runs between us.

"I do not know much about gods," T. S. Eliot wrote in his "Dry Salvages," "but I think that the river / Is a strong, brown god—sullen, untamed, and / Intractable."

Not knowing either, I think that the river may be matter—that matrix of spirit in rose and thorn and dust—in a kind of motion that allows us to honor its implacable currents and depths, and with it the bewildering truth that reconciles the irreconcilable. It does not permit an easy knowing, and the only way to move through it is with a respectful "I do not know" displacing every need and desire in the heart.

It's safer to stay on shore and admire the river, but there are brave ones and fools who do wade in, some led by their curiosity and a desire to possess that which lies on the other side, some by self-loathing and a rejection of their own heritage, one or two by the river's own constant allure. Few are able to say "I do not know" in the face of mystery, to respect aboriginal ways of being as a wildness that will always resist our appropriations.

In recent years, elders have opened some ceremonies, the sweat lodge in particular, to white people. There was a day not long ago when a well-timed remark about one's recent experience at a sweat might have carried a certain prestige in some conversations, but nowadays, as often as not, one or two others will chime in with stories of their own epiphanies in the lodge. Such disrespect and superficiality from spiritual tourists has been one of the costs of opening up the ceremonies. With white people now crowding into sweat lodges and sometimes outnumbering their indigenous hosts you'd expect resentment, or at least a scornful laugh or two. If it is there it is hidden or else dampened by their overriding certainty that the circle of indigenous wisdom doesn't open for the facile and acquisitive among us.

I cannot join in a sweat without thinking of the shameful efforts by clergy and government to suppress indigenous religious practice; nor without amazement for the way sacred ceremonies are now shared openly with the blessings of elders who say that they were given by the Creator and must therefore not be hoarded. The lodge is sometimes described as an accommodation between humanity and the Creator that helps people rise to a spiritual plane in this life. Used properly, it is also becoming a place of accommodation between the indigenous and nonindigenous peoples of the Great Plains.

Regrettably, the same cannot be said in general for our churches, though there are some exceptions. Inner-city aboriginal ministries, now focusing more on emotional and family needs than on evangelizing people when they are vulnerable, are beginning to adjust some of their spiritual language and to use smudging ceremonies and bannock (for the host) in their services. Aboriginal catechists are hired in a Catholic diocese to find ways of integrating indigenous traditions with Christian practice and belief. Workshops on "Sharing Faith within Aboriginal Culture" are held in church basements to get aboriginal and nonaboriginal people talking with one another. Much of this is helpful as far as it goes but, against the horizon of all our actions in establishing a faith alien to this soil, these measures seem minuscule and piecemeal, the begrudged offerings of a people who are uncertain of the survival of their own faith. Just as our governments in recent years have made transfers of resources to First Nations that seem generous (at least until you compare them to all that has been taken from this land's original peoples and harnessed to our engines of wealth), and then wonder why the anticipated social and economic transformations have yet to occur; likewise our churches make cautious, reluctant steps toward reconciliation, complete with apologies for past wrongs and promises to do better, and then wonder why their congregations in urban areas still include so few Indian and Métis families.

The great mass of churchgoing Christians on this continent are not likely to wake up to the gospel this week or the next. No less human than their counterparts at any other point of history or in any other religion or civilization, most will continue serving self, family, and tribe, ignoring the people digging in the garbage in their back lane, waiting for more virtuous and deserving poor to happen along, comforting themselves with illusions of a faith unchanged by time or context. In my own church and diocese it is typically not the leadership so much as the congregation that is reluctant to move. Last year the diocese tried to engage the laity in "Vision Quest," a grassroots discussion of the future direction of the church, globally and locally. The name, in a well-meaning but clumsy use of this aboriginal term, inadvertently begged the question of a more indigenous way of faith here, but the process that unfolded had nothing to offer aboriginal people. Participation was poor in general and the aboriginal voice was not well represented. As always, Christianity ossifies wherever most of the people in the pews sit in comfort, never having to worry about what they will do to feed and clothe their children.

Any real evolution and accommodation seems always to occur far from the cities and centers of first world power. In parts of

Africa, the local church is adapting to indigenous cultural traditions in an integrating movement that has the Vatican's blessing. In
Latin America, where 473 years ago the Great Mother Tonantzin
showed herself to Juan Diego on Tepeyac Hill in the form of
Tequantlaxopeuh (she who crushes the serpent's head), speaking
his native language, moving bishops with visions of Mary, and
unleashing a powerful vernacular Catholicism impregnated with
indianismo, there are lay communities, priests, brothers, and missionaries who are living a faith that blends the truth of Jesus and
Saint Paul with the earthy spirituality ancient in the rivers, hills,
and forests.

In South Dakota, at Blue Cloud Abbey, a Benedictine community named for a Lakota chief, the brothers run an aboriginal
cultural center and consider intercultural and coreligious awareness
to be part of their primary apostolate. In the Anglican diocese of the
Arctic, the new bishop is Inuk, Andrew Atagotaaluk, and he was
installed as such in a church where the pulpit looks like a dogsled
and the crucifix is made entirely of narwhal tusks. Here and across
Canada's north there are missionaries, mostly oblate, saying Mass
in Native languages, taking risks, joining people in the sweat lodge,
bringing Native ceremonies into their services. The confluence is
even more distinct at a pilgrimage site such as Manito Sakahigan
(Lac Sainte-Anne), where forty thousand aboriginal people converge every July to honor the mother spirit dwelling in sacred
waters and embodied in Our Lady. Coming to the site from hundreds of miles away by foot, bicycle, bus, and car, Cree, Déné,
Blackfoot, and Métis offer up songs that are sometimes Christian
hymns, sometimes Native chants, prayers to both Jesus and Manito,
immersing themselves in the healing powers of a lake that cares not
whose gods are invoked nor what materials or words are plied, for
a miracle is nothing if it is not a confluence of the divergent forces
in our lives.

It is sometimes hard to say how much of this is healthy coreligious energy and how much is imperialist Christianity devouring yet another indigenous religion. Noel Star Blanket, bearing the nativity of this encompassing religion in his own name, is encouraged by the new tolerance and wider ecumenical spirit but has his doubts. He talked to me once about the divide he has seen in some Cree communities between traditional and Christian Indians. There are Christianized bands in the north, he said, where the leadership is hostile to any efforts by their people to revive Cree religious traditions. In one case, the band council put a stop to a sweat lodge that had started up on their reserve.

"I spend a lot of time talking to my family, my community, and others about this whole mentality of Christian versus traditional Indians," Noel said. "My sister passed away in early September. I came out to the funeral and I saw the priest and the nun burning sweetgrass in recognition, in deference to the First Nations people. Some people in our communities, the more staunch or puritanical traditional people, will say that's a blasphemy, but I'm a little more open than that. I say that's good if the priests can recognize that. It's a real turnaround from the days when Chief Star Blanket was thrown back into his tipi.

"The Christian churches have called us pagans and heathens and every other thing under the sun from day one. I've harbored a prejudice about Christianity since those days—thinking of what they did to my grandfathers. And I've become politically aware, *acutely* aware of that, and I must admit I still harbor that today."

Out of his pride in all that is native within himself, his nation, and all the other nations that have emerged from the first peoples of the continent, Noel is saddened to see the blood of his race more diluted each generation within the deluge of newcomers. And sadder yet to see his own people so ready to adopt the colonizer's culture, the addictiveness and wealth mongering, filling a spiritual void with consumption and pleasure. He sees this acculturation everywhere but it is worst in the eastern half of the continent, he says. He talked about a recent trip to some reserves in the East where everyone is Christianized. "Those people have completely lost what they had. Sure, they have their romantic notions, put them on their rugs and up on their walls, but they don't speak their language and don't follow any traditional practices. I'm sorry to say it but they are brown white people who happen to live on reserves.

"It's different out here in the West. We have a genuine opportunity to identify, to cultivate, nurture our culture, to carry those traditions from a First Nations perspective, yet still do it within the context of a larger society."

Not surprisingly, there are traditionalists, people Noel calls "purists," who see the acculturation and respond by rejecting white values, even ones that may align with their own. "These people want absolutely nothing to do with white people, with Christianity, with mainstream. They take only trappings, will not take any teachings or morality or anything else from white people. So there are two worlds. Two islands. And I see those going down separate roads."

Noel spoke about his son, in university now and moving confidently with a strong group of friends of every racial and religious heritage. He is impressed at how open and respectful they are with one another, how comfortable they are with their own diversity. His son speaks very little Cree, but Noel brings him along sometimes when he attends ceremonies. He wants him to remember his origins no matter where he goes, what he does in life. "I tell him, 'Make sure you know where you come from. Make sure you understand where you are going, who you are.' But I let him make his own decisions about life. Each generation evolves, every generation creates their own."

Noel has seen too much to be any more than cautious in his hopes for that next generation. If there is any hope, he said, it is in people beginning to live from the best tenets of their own faiths.

"I've met many fine Christian people of all sects, fine Jewish people too. I see a lot of change coming in the churches, in their attitudes toward Native peoples, and I see a lot more of that happening, that reconciliation. If we all—native and non—lived according to our principles we'd have a good world here. But we're weak, we're human beings. As we say in our language, *kitimākisiw*, "we are pitiful.""

As I left the house the next morning I saw the aboriginal couple who live down our street. Unlike many other aboriginal families in the neighborhood, they appear to be living in much the same fashion as their white neighbors. Dressed in business suits and carrying briefcases, they hop into an SUV at 7:30 and drive to work. When I say hello they seem surprised, even more reticent than most aboriginal people I know, and I imagine what their lives might be like, if they feel estranged from everyone else in the city: from nonaboriginal people to whom they are still Indians, and therefore not the kind you invite over for dinner or out to the cabin for the weekend; and from their own who might say that they have sold out, become acculturated.

Acculturation, assimilation, integration. These are the terms we use when we talk about the way ahead in a land where the indigenous, though very much alive, is moving, transforming as the colonizers and the colonized begin to converge. Some of us catch ourselves wishing for ways to freeze the flow of things, keep cultures and bloodlines vital and distinct as they have been in the past, but then realize the futility and the apartheid inherent in such a desire. As disheartening as it is to see people abandon their native faith and traditional ways and surrender to the homogenous, televised superculture, there will always be those who quietly replant the heritage of their ancestors within the soil of the here and now.

Something new is rising from those roots, something fresh emerging from the old and good, something not dependent on the daily practice of the majority but nurtured by the few and the small.

But there is another way of looking at this coming together, particularly here, where the birthrate of aboriginal people doubles that among nonaboriginal.

Whenever we spend an afternoon at the beach up the valley from our cabin I notice people segregating themselves at the waterfront park. There are no signs—Aboriginal Bathers, Nonaboriginal Bathers—to show us the zones but it is remarkable how little we mingle. The aboriginal people—the Cree, Nakota, Dakota, and Saulteaux, who come from reserves, and the Métis, who come from towns nearby—keep apart from the white people. Many of the aboriginal families arrive later in the afternoon, as we often do, avoiding noonday heat and taking advantage of sun-warmed water. They set up for the day either at the far northern end of the beach or under the trees where they like to barbecue: grandparents and great-grandparents sitting in elm shade, parents grilling hamburgers, the kids in the lake. The adults seldom sit on the beach itself amongst the tanning cottagers who have walked or driven from their resort properties around the rim of the lake. The older aboriginal children, most in T-shirts and cutoffs, play in the water with complete abandon, while their younger siblings on the shoreline create worlds with sticks, pebbles, and piles of water weeds.

No one on the beach plays with as much gusto as some of the aboriginal children, who splash around like Labrador puppies, bounding over waves, dunking one another, throwing weed balls, jumping off each other's shoulders, diving for crayfish, yelling, crying, laughing. If you look carefully you will see their parents and grandparents keeping an eye out, watching from the shade seventy-five yards away.[9] They are not like the white moms and dads two or three paces away from their charges, instructing the children on how to play politely and safely: "That's deep enough."

"Don't splash that girl." "No, keep your hat on!"

Interaction between white and aboriginal kids is rare. White parents ignore the aboriginal kids, though occasional eye contact and a disapproving word or two will occur when a toddler from an aboriginal family begins using someone's inflatable dolphin or when a little brown-skinned boy climbs repeatedly up and down the slide while a line of little white girls wait their turn at the top. Heads swivel, *Is there no one watching this child?*

One Canada Day afternoon we brought two canoes down to the beach so our older kids could paddle around the rim of the swimming area. Hot day, calm lake, beach and lawn areas full of families and teenagers; parking lot filled with trucks hooked up to boat and Sea-Doo trailers. For a change we sat at the north end of the beach in the shade. There were one or two other white families there as well that day, perhaps because the prime real estate on the beach was already occupied. Two large aboriginal families were clustered around picnic tables and barbecues while their children swam away the afternoon. Some of their teenaged boys were launching Roman candles from the other side of the bush behind us, the heads of every white mother and father in the vicinity turning with each crack and whistle—*Don't these kids have parents? No wonder their children die young. Why can't they control their kids the way we do?*

Behind that racist desire for them to be more like us, and within the memories of my generation, lurks the dirty secret of an unwritten, unspoken assimilation policy, the descendant of a written one that our legislators reluctantly repealed in the middle of the last century. It was still there when we were children, and its legacy remains, not as policy but in the failure to understand the reasons for high aboriginal youth mortality rates, in the nostalgia for the noble savage, and in our assumptions and even wish that the indigenous will vanish into the general population, surrender to the inevitability of becoming us.

I stood in the shallows watching my two youngest girls. The

nine-year-old, Sage, was out alone in chin-deep water, diving repeatedly, so I glanced at her often to make sure she resurfaced after every plunge. After a few minutes I noticed a young Indian girl, about Sage's age, who seemed to be diving next to her, facing the same direction but off to one side by fifteen feet or so. Sage would dive or do a handstand and then the other girl would do the same. This continued for some time, the two of them playing parallel to one another but not talking, not even acknowledging one another. My youngest, Maia, took my attention for a spell and when I looked back to check again on Sage, she and the girl were an arm's length apart, diving and somersaulting, but now stopping to look at one another, smiling as they wiped water from their eyes.

A few minutes lapsed as I toweled Maia dry and got her onto a blanket on the sand. When I looked up again, Sage and her friend were playing a game with black stones from the lake bottom. They were taking turns tossing a stone into deeper water. Then the two of them would swim over to the ripples where it had disappeared and dive down to retrieve it.

As I watched Sage and the girl play, I allowed myself to imagine that, just as First Nations people are becoming more like us, we in turn are becoming more like them. The population of this piece of the plains has been stable now for nearly seventy years, but the ratio of aboriginal to nonaboriginal is changing rapidly. Faced with statistics that show the steady departure of nonaboriginal people for more prosperous and populated cities, and a sharp birthrate differential favoring the aboriginal population, government planners are in a dither. Community workers say that the trend is already bringing social inequities to a crisis point because our economy, social support, and education systems are not yet ready to engage all this aboriginal youth effectively. Unemployment, crime, teen pregnancy, drug and alcohol addiction, and suicide continue to curse the lives of many young aboriginal people. But out of those increasing numbers and out of that crucible of disadvantage there are also many more educated, healthy, and energetic indigenous men and women contributing to the energy and life of our towns and cities. With more Métis and First Nations people graduating from universities and colleges, working in offices, schools, construction sites, banks, stores and museums, the old barriers between the races are weakening, and our children are leaping across them in every possible way. Despite all that divides us yet, young white people and young aboriginal people are falling in love with one another, marrying, and having babies. If this is assimilation we are neither capable of stopping it nor of understanding exactly who is assimilating whom. Yet the overwhelming political power and numerical advantage of the colonizer is on the wane, while the power of the indigenous appears to be growing, winnowing the population down to those who haven't the resources to head for that better elsewhere and those who know who they are only in relation to this place they have chosen, forsaking all others.

The land is always on the side of those who commit themselves to it long-term, who are native or who are willing to become native to the place. A land with a short growing season, cold winters, and a terrain that commands wild-eyed poetry from its dwellers and dewy-eyed nostalgia from its expatriates is before too long going to shed its drift of gold miners and distill into a mestizo population where the question of who is native is seldom asked anymore. Human sexuality becomes a tool in the hands of creation, plundering that "sacred reserve of energy, the very bloodstream of spiritual evolution," which Teilhard so audaciously ascribed to love.[10] Though we may want to resist all that reduces cultural diversity, we are in the end helpless before the exertions of nature and happenstance that pull a man and a woman together. No nation can live in isolation, reproducing itself and its culture indefinitely. It, too, is an organic creature, bound not by our intentions and myths, but by wild forces that we cannot fully appropriate.

Language is the marker that traces our mingling across the boundaries where some would resist or enforce assimilation. If we have any cause for optimism here on the Great Plains, it is in the survival of plains Indian languages into the twenty-first century. I have perhaps thirty or forty years left to watch things change here. I am hoping that the Cree, the Saulteaux, the Déné, the Nakota, and the Dakota people will continue speaking, learning, and sharing their beautiful languages. Learn the words your grandfathers spoke; let us learn them too. Take back your names—Assiniwasis, Ahtahkakhoop, Nanaquewetung, Okemahwasin—even if they are hard for English speakers to pronounce. We will be better for the effort of our tongues. Someday my granddaughters will marry your grandsons, and when they do, I want them to carry the names that speak of these rivers, these creatures, this land, and all its progeny.

A few weeks after that Canada Day we were on the West Coast. It was the last day before we had to head back east from a family camping trip that had taken us up the long incline of prairie to the alpine meadows of Lake O'Hara, then across the British Columbia interior and the coastal ranges to the outfall of great rivers where the westering multitudes, having come to a boundary, now clog the deltas with their deluxe bivouacs and boulevards. On the final leg, we ferried across the strait, passing smaller islands, then drove up the hump of the largest one on salmon and log-bearing highways. And when we arrived we camped for several days behind beaches scoured by winds that rise from the rockbound capes of Japan, bringing across the ocean weather that is often anything but pacific. Yet on our last morning it was peaceful. A brooding mist had draped itself over our campsite in the pine and fir woods—the first trees on a shore that runs with flats of sand down scalloped miles of coastline punctuated by volcanic, barnacled points at the tips of each bight or bay.

As I packed the car I realized that my binoculars were gone. I'd left them between the front seats of our van, which I had neglected to lock for the night. When the children found a splash of beer on one of the seats, I gave up looking. Through those lenses in the past few weeks I'd watched a male hermit thrush, seen the saffron lining of his mouth as he sang out his soul from a rock perch in the avalanche runway above Lake O'Hara and, a few days after that, a gray whale mother and calf rising like islands in the kelp beds off Meares Island.

I spent the early part of the morning in a funk, annoyed at myself and at the thought of being without binoculars for the remainder of our vacation. Once we got down to our favorite stretch of beach, I sat on the packed sand and tried to forget that a pod of dolphins or a slaty-backed gull might be passing by just out of sight. Besides, the fog was so thick I couldn't see more than a couple hundred feet anyway. Our youngest children were racing chunks of driftwood on a small creek that tumbled out of the forest and onto the intertidal zone before mingling with the rising tide. I took Karen by hand so we could go for a last barefoot beach walk while Kate kept an eye on her brother and sisters. I wanted to show Karen something that our son, Jon, and I had discovered the day before. We'd been walking just out of reach of the waves across a wide and utterly empty expanse of hard sand. Jon said something about there being nothing to run into or trip upon, that you could walk blind and it wouldn't make any difference. So we closed our eyes and tried it, walking fifty, then one hundred, two hundred paces or more at a time, sightless, unconsciously orienting ourselves along the waterline by the hiss and sigh of wave fall.

Karen and I did the same, except we set out across the beach, walking slowly toward the ocean. It was somehow exciting and meditative at the same time, to hold hands and walk in that blind hush toward the sea we knew lay ahead. Having closed our eyes to an emptiness covered in mist, I felt as though we had quietly stepped into another realm, somewhere natal, ready to be born or give birth.

After a hundred paces or so we let go of one another's hands, separated a bit and kept walking sightless toward the rising sound of the waves. We'd gone a long stretch in silence when I heard Karen, somewhere on my left, say, "Stop. Open your eyes." When I did I saw at my feet a single eagle feather that had been tossed up by the surf. Bald eagles patrol those coastlines steadily; they are abundant here, I told myself, as I bent to pick it up. Everyone who looks will find an eagle feather on this beach. But it was a flawless primary from just inside the eagle's wingtip and it was here in my path when I was walking with my eyes shut through a mist...

I felt blessed, knowing the spiritual power an eagle's feather holds for Indian people, but over time I came to see the experience of losing my binoculars and finding a feather as a chastening taunt, reminding me that no amount of imagination or argument will make me anything more than a white, middle-class urban intellectual. It took me three months to get over the temptation to assume some kind of facile benediction from the events of that day and to convince myself that it was all right to replace the binoculars.

Even so, the time without a glass between wild things and me yielded its own blessings. On late August mornings at home, at the beginning of the songbird migration, I'd go out for walks along the creek that passes through the city, eyes unaided by binoculars. For several days it was strangely humid and the park smelled like northern woods, damp and a little fetid, with the tang of willow sap and ripening fruit. I would stand next to the creek among forty-foot willow trees watching bands of common birds forage: five robins, a yellow warbler, two warbling vireos, two redbreasted nuthatches, a trio of juvenile flickers. I tried to disappear while I smelled their world, heard the lisping notes, barely there, with which they stay in contact with one another as they rollick through the trees.

Once, I listened in on another conversation. Four people out walking their dogs, apparently strangers to one another, had converged on a pathway and were chatting amicably, introducing their dogs with obvious affection and pride. I've seen this happen before and have always found it oddly annoying. I harbor secret hostilities toward dog walkers, perhaps from the countless "Oh, don't worry, he's just being friendly" encounters between their surrogate children and my actual and terrified ones. It has always seemed incomprehensible to me that three or four people who have nothing in common other than a pet at the end of a leash will stop to talk with one another in tones that one ordinarily reserves for family reunions.

This time, though, as I listened I began to hear something else in their talk. These people, I realized, truly love their dogs and the animal elicits from them the kind of attention that we are capable of applying to the least in creation if we make the effort. Dog owners share as a bond this encounter with the personality of their pets. The rest of us who do not understand are inclined to ridicule them for treating an animal like a person, but that is the shame of our blindness. Someone who comes to know a creature, even a pet, gains a glimpse of what David Abram has called "the animate terrain,"[11] by sensing and becoming engaged with the "more-than-human" personality in that creature, which is, in Christian terms, the presence of God, an incarnation. Few pet owners would think of it this way, but most recognize an intelligence and personality in their pets. With dogs it is obvious, easy to know even for those of us who have become inured to the presence of God in creaturely life. But there are others, gifted with time and circumstance and sensitivity, people like the boy mystic in Wicklewood, who attend to the smallest creatures hour after hour, by stages coming to know the divine personhood within the smallest of the wild.

For a moment, watching and listening to the birds passing among the willow trees I thought I gained a shade of who they are and felt a longing, a leaning toward them that I could not entirely satisfy. I remembered Benedict's *Obsculta*—listen carefully, and incline the ear of your heart—and Father James telling me of the need to pay attention, come to know the personhood in Christ, the Christ in personhood. It is there, an enlivening, particular intelligence, "the image of the unseen God" (Colossians 1:15) waiting to be felt and heard and known in each organism and locality: skunkbrush and coulee, pocket gopher and grassland, damselfly and slough.

If our world seems godless, we have made it so in the generalizing summaries of both science and religion. Our language knows better, though, in the way we refer to the personal attributes of someone or something with the phrase "by nature." We could as easily say "by God" though that may be heresy in some circles. Saint Paul's doctrine of the preexisting Christ in creation has always been hard to grasp, even more so after Teilhard got hold of it and began to speak of the Christogenesis, but there *is* something there in those early letters of the old tent maker that bears our pondering. It was on the Jesuit paleontologist's mind in his final days. On the last page of Teilhard's diary, April 7, Holy Thursday, 1955—he died, three days later, on the morning of the resurrection—he wrote down some cryptic notations, under the heading of "What I believe." At the top of a list of two items is a line that reads "1) St Paul...the three verses:" It is thought to be a reference to 1 Corinthians 15: 26, 27, and 28, and indeed at the end of that line Teilhard included the Greek for the final phrase in verse 28, a favorite he would often cite: "*En pasi panta theos*" (God all in all).[12]

In another letter, this one to the Hebrews, Paul wrote that God "made everything there is" through Christ, who he says is "the radiant light of God's glory and perfect copy of his nature" (Hebrews 1:2–3). In Greek the actual phrase is *charakter*, meaning the very imprint of something's substance, like a seal made in clay or wax. There are mystic depths here sounded perhaps by Teilhard and a few others, while the rest of us are satisfied to remain somewhere nearer the surface, but it is within our human capabilities, as sensuous and spiritual beings, to know something of God's imprint upon all of the creation, to recognize the All in All, and render that divine seal its due in the way we acquit ourselves.

That imprint and radiant light was present the day we placed our seal—not with clay or wax but with smoke breathed by our forbears through sacred stone—upon the paper where other characters had been printed to make specific covenant between the people of the Pipe and the people of the Crown, the colonizers who mistook and still mistake that sovereign symbol for a representation of the temporal reign of kings and queens. The aboriginal people, whose genuine respect for the Crown has always puzzled whites, given their resistance to empires and empire builders, recognize something else behind that authority, something that exceeds symbolism and monarchy. Some elders refer to the Crown as an equal and sacred counterpart to the Pipe, invested with a similar power to unify once separate peoples, to bring together in peace. They hint at the One who is fit to wear that Crown, not actually naming Christ, but referring to the character of the divine person who is held in such esteem by the white civilizations and in whose sight the treaties were made.

And it is our children, and the children yet to come, each marked by that imprint, who hold us to the terms of our covenants. When Noel talks about his great-great-grandfather Chief White Calf signing Treaty Four, he says that they did not sign for themselves but for "the children yet unborn." This is easily dismissed as rhetoric, but it was a primary provision when the treaties were signed. When you read the documented remarks of each chief who signed the treaties, you can hear, even in the awkwardness of translation, their reluctance and fears, tempered always by a resignation to making sacrifices today to secure a future for their people. In assenting in Treaty Six to negotiate the sharing of lands to the northwest of the territories covered by Treaty Four, Chief Mistawasis said, "What we speak of and do now will last as long as the sun shines and the river runs; we are looking forward to our children's children, for we are old and have but a few days to live."[13]

Later in the fall, I spent a day with some of those future ones envisioned by the treaty signers. Sage's fifth grade class was heading out to the Treaty Four grounds to join in the annual celebrations now held each September on the reclaimed site on the edge of Fort Qu'Appelle. I was there, along with several other parents, to help supervise on the bus trip and at the site, which would be thronging with schoolchildren from the city. One of the other chaperones, a white man married to a status Indian woman, had the busload of children chanting, "Treaty Four! Treaty Four! Treaty Four! Treaty Four!" as we rolled down the highway toward the valley. Up and down the aisle he went, videotaping the children as they sang. It was a strange and inspired moment, one that would not have happened even ten years ago. Something is changing, and I imagined I could actually see it underway as we hurtled back toward the old treaty grounds, our children jostled shoulder to shoulder, as though we were moving together toward a better place, where indigenous values would become part of what it is to be a dweller on these plains. When we arrive it may look like a fifteen-tipi circus of plastic handicrafts, greasy food, and powwow dancing, but there will be larger forces at play, by stages showing us that this treaty is an invitation. Should we ever decide to accept it, honor it, even resanctify it in ceremonies where priests and elders exchange sacraments, our treaty could one day yet become the covenant it was meant to be: a sacred land trust binding us to one another and to our responsibilities toward 75,000 square miles of the Creator's imprint.

The meeting grounds where we will find possibilities for such a reconciliation is any place where we can share our religious traditions in mutual respect and openness. The Church of Our Lady Parish in Moose Jaw has bought a tipi with money they raised specifically for that purpose. For the past few years they have been hosting ceremonies and cross-cultural workshops led by an elder from Piapot First Nation and they decided it was time to create a better space in which to learn and celebrate together.

These kinds of gatherings are happening quietly here and there across the Northern Great Plains. People here learn of them through a friend of a friend or someone sends them an invitation and, after some hesitation, curiosity wins out and they decide to go. This last spring someone sent me an invitation and the timing could not have been better.

The day before we'd been out to the Land for our first trip of the year. The snow had melted weeks earlier but the ice had just come off the lake. As we coasted down our hill to park by the side of the cabin I could see right away that something was wrong. The tipi poles, which we had left standing naked for the winter, were down. There are few forces in nature that can knock down a well-anchored tipi frame, but a human being is one of them. There were tire tracks pressed into the long grass and running out across the meadow toward the site where the poles were all akimbo. I walked down there to discover that someone had cut the anchor rope, making it relatively easy to lift the frame and upend it. Four pole tips had snapped off. Three were now so short that they'd have to be replaced. Mike had left spares by the site and these were now mixed up with the rest of the poles in a pile of giant pick-up-sticks. Though I'd never raised the frame without help and instructions, I decided I had to give it a try.

After taking the poles apart and laying them side by side, I found the three that looked to be the original tripod poles that form the basis of the frame. It is all oriented by the pole that rests on the northern point of the circle so I dug around in the grass until I located the anchor hole that lined up with the landmark across the valley above which the North Star hangs on clear nights. Then I lashed the tripod poles together where the peak of the frame would be. I used piles of rocks to hold the butt ends of north and south poles steady and poised above their respective anchor holes as I tried and failed repeatedly to get the tripod upright. Eventually, after learning how to align the rocks and poles properly, I managed to hoist the threesome aloft, each pole slipping into its original hole in the turf. The rest of the poles, each tipped with their colored ribbons, went into place one after the other in a spiral that was not quite as lovely as the original but filled out the frame well enough. I picked the last pole up off the grass and thought of Grace's warning about tipis drawing children, and just then I heard my youngest daughter's voice ring out, "Dad! Wait! We've got something!" Maia was running full gallop down the path from the cabin, followed by her friend Zoë, who had come out to the Land for the weekend. Behind the two of them trailed a red satin ribbon from a short stick that looked to be the very end of a tipi pole. I glanced down at the pole in my hands. The tip had been snapped off.

"Here!" said Zoë, arriving breathless and handing the bit of wood to me. When it fit first try, we all laughed. Some carpenter's glue finished the job. It was a long, straight pole and when I put it in place it was by far the highest, its scarlet flag sailing two feet above the other colors. Sage helped march the sisal rope around the structure, lashing the poles together where they cross at its apex. As she carried it the fourth and final lap around the frame, staring up at the crossed poles and ribbons, she asked me, "Why would someone do such a thing—knock down a tipi? I don't get it."

There was no good answer for the question. I said that I didn't know, but when it happens all anyone can do is put it back up again.

I walked inside the tipi frame through the door space and, using a rock for a hammer and two cherrywood stakes, I drove an anchor into the ground on the one side of the fire pit. I wrapped the end of the sisal around it in a figure eight, yanking it down with all my weight and fastening it with a couple of half hitches.

The next day I received an invitation to a gathering to be held the first weekend in May at an acreage east of the city, the home of Harold and Audrey Zettl. The Zettls are rare Catholics who have chosen to take the gospel to heart and let it shape their family and livelihood. When I first met them twenty years ago they were the amazing couple who had started the Harvest Community, a small farm and workshop that continues to provide work and the experience of rural life for a few disabled people. Recently Audrey has been working all over Canada's north as a nurse in Cree, Déné, and Inuit communities.

I had not seen the Zettls for several years, and the creek valley by their home is always a good spot for a walk, so I decided to join the gathering for the Saturday morning, saving the rest of the weekend for some springtime chores long overdue at home. As things turned out, I didn't get home until a little after midnight, for it was a day that wouldn't let me go. As the sun warmed us and the wind dropped, strangers opened their hearts to one another, and the hills along the creek invited us to listen to each other's stories, prayers, and wishes.

The Zettls' acreage is the last lot in a string of properties that form the remnant of another German-Catholic colony, also named Saint Peter's and with its own early-twentieth-century shrine to Our Lady. This Saint Peter's, too, is held fast to a small prairie creek. Many Bones, the spring-fed tributary of Pile-of-Bones, is a narrow stream like the Wolverine so there are stretches where you can leap easily from bank to bank even in spring. Its valley, one hundred feet deep in places and a half-mile wide, forms a significant corridor of native prairie that snakes southeast toward its confluence with the larger Pile-of-Bones. It is in these smaller, shallower meltwater channels rather than the great glacial spillways that one senses most acutely the bodily absence and ghostly presence of the buffalo. Local farmers speak cautiously about kill sites, tipi rings, and buffalo pounds, later perhaps mentioning their box of artifacts stored in the cellar.

The artifact that interested me at the Zettls' acreage was an ancient-looking longbow mounted above the door just inside the log-walled rec center where we gathered for our meals. I asked Audrey about its origins.

"Oh, that's old Father Metzger's bow."

Metzger, I learned, is the legendary patriarch of the colony, famous for building the shrine and fieldstone grotto across the road from the Zettls' place. Born Heinrich Metzger in Alsace, France, in the 1870s, this frontier cleric was an artist early on in life, having studied at the École des Beaux Arts in Paris. He went on sketching trips to Italy as a young man and then somewhere along the line decided that he was called to be a priest. A few years after his ordination he emigrated to the New World, eventually finding his way to Many Bones Creek, where he built his chapel in the wilderness. The romantic ethos of Christ in the wilderness—evinced in Caspar David Friedrich's paintings of decrepit cathedrals surrounded by moody skies and crucifixes upon mountain crags—had captured the European imagination during the years Metzger was studying to be an artist and priest. At the same time the mythology of the American West presented in novels and travelogues had set the hearts of young European men astir with longings for wild frontiers.

Arriving at Saint Peter's to serve the new German colonists, the young Metzger resumed his painting whenever he could take time away from pastoral duties. His subject matter switched from landscapes to the people he found most interesting in his new home: the aging warriors and chieftains of the plains, now treated as refugees in their own land. At the old schoolhouse in the colony, long out of use, I saw a photograph of Metzger, dressed in his black cassock, his face as white as sanctuary linen, and flanked by several sun-baked Indian men in full ceremonial garb. Perhaps the bow had been a gift from one of his Cree or Lakota friends. No, Audrey said, it was his own bow; he liked to hunt.

Reading about Metzger later I would find out that he also painted the interior of another church in the nearby colony of Saint Joseph's. But it was his portraits of Indians that drew me to his story and I managed to find photographs of three. One is a head-and-shoulders painting of Chief Matore Tchanka, who fought alongside Sitting Bull at Little Bighorn. Another, more a tableau than a portrait of an actual person, shows an elder sitting on a rock next to a stream, head lowered, his expression far away and melancholic. Metzger titled this piece *Dreams of the Past*, a suitably romantic name for an image that looks like an illustration in *Boys' Life* or a Fenimore Cooper novel. The third painting shows Grey Owl nursing one of his pet beavers. It was years after Metzger's death before it was revealed that Grey Owl was Archie Belaney, an Englishman in whom the myth of the noble savage had produced a desire so strong he manufactured his own indigenous identity, which he parlayed into a series of popular books and a speaking tour back in Britain.

It is hard to fault Metzger for falling prey to the dominant mythologies of his era. The romance of the vanquished and virtuous savage is a kind of tonic to soothe the remorse that follows conquest—one that both the conquered and the conquerors still are too often happy to imbibe. In Metzger's time Indian people appeared to be in an irreversible decline and had behind them a history that was in every way more appealing than the reality of the vagabonds who straggled into town now and then. To his credit, though, this priest seems to have made a real effort to befriend the Indian people of his area, not simply as subjects who would sit for his portraiture but as frequent guests camping next to his rectory.

That rectory is now the home of the Zettl family and it was part of the day's charm to think that the tipi we sat in was by no means the first to be pitched on that stretch of grass. As the leader spoke to us that morning, both in English and Cree, my thoughts went to old Metzger walking through the willow flats at the bottom of Many Bones valley, his bow strung, arrows in their quiver, hoping to touch something pagan in his own bones. Was his faith, even in the subtlest of ways, influenced by the hours he spent with hunting peoples, for whom the idea of a pastor would have held little meaning? If we have become in this past century less willing to be herded, more inclined to look for God and spirit beyond the domestic fold of church and doctrine, we can trace the shift I think to indigenous spirituality, the ways of Esau that have influenced us more than we will ever realize or admit.

Later in the day we listened to a talk by a Saulteaux elder who leads the rain dance ceremonies for many of the Treaty Four nations. He spoke of old prophecies and new and a coming convergence of all races and religions. In the midst of all this I was startled to hear him mention Mount Carmel, the original one in the Holy Land, which he said was a gathering place for spiritual seekers regardless of their ethnic or religious heritage. Then he told us that he has for many years been a member of the Baha'i faith, because it is a religion that not only welcomes him as an aboriginal person, but even insists that he retain and foster his own religious traditions as a Saulteaux. He referred to Messianic prophecies in the Old Testament that Baha'i people believe are being fulfilled today on Mount Carmel. The religion's founder, Baha'u'llah, during his imprisonment in Turkey, envisioned the day when he would pitch his tent on the Holy Mountain. When he was released in 1891 he walked overland to Mount Carmel and set up camp near the Carmelite Monastery just above the cave of Elijah. There he made the pronouncement that the faithful know as *Lawh-i-Karmil* (the "Tablet of Carmel"), an inspired dialogue between the prophet, Baha'u'llah, and the mountain itself. The Baha'i consider this revelation to be Baha'u'llah's charter for believers to build a center for the faith. Today the Baha'i World Centre, with its grand buildings, terraced gardens, shrines, and monuments, dominates one side of

Carmel overlooking the city of Haifa.

The man who presides over the rain dance ceremonies finished his presentation with a description of his duties and the four days without food or water he must undergo in preparing for the annual ceremonies. His bearing throughout the talk, whether he was describing the prophecies of Baha'u'llah or his own role as a Saulteaux elder, was deferential and modest, claiming nothing for himself other than his gratitude for the tasks he has been given.

Later, the Zettls gathered us into the upper room of their rec center for the evening meal. After we were seated, Audrey stood by the doorway beneath Metzger's bow to offer a blessing. Her words were thoughtful, well chosen, reflecting the spirit of openness and hope that had enlivened the day. She took care to avoid the traditional Christian prayer format that comes automatically to a cradle Catholic, and when she went silent at the end, with all of us waiting for some kind of closer, well aware that the customary one might not be appropriate, the room was taken momentarily by an awkward quiet. Then someone, one of the aboriginal participants I think, shouted a hearty "Amen!" and the room broke into laughter.

After supper I went off by myself into the quiet of Many Bones valley, and on my return I walked past Metzger's church and back behind the Zettls' house to sit down at the fire pit among the others. One of them, a man my age from Sweetgrass, began talking with pride about the old ways of getting a meal on the table: snaring grouse on their dancing grounds, building a fish-basket trap out of nothing but rocks and willow, sending your horse around the poplar bluff to distract deer hunkered down in the thicket.

At dark we entered the tipi for another ceremony. Two of the leaders took turns singing songs to the beat of a skin drum, their voices lifting Cree and Saulteaux prayers up through the smoke hole to the stars. The inside of the lodge was hung with fourteen willow offerings we'd prepared earlier in the day—short sticks of peeled willow lashed together with strands of rawhide and painted with dabs of the sacred colors: blue, white, yellow, red, and black. As we made them we were to think of prayers for our families, our communities, and ourselves, aware that the next morning the offerings would be blessed and set adrift on the waters of Many Bones at a particular spot where the people have always come to address the spirit of water.

When the ceremony was over, I put my shoes back on and walked out of the lodge and into the dark of the maple grove where the old trees were breathing in the exhalations of another day. Through the far side of the trees I came out to an expanse of grass stretching away from the old rectory. Light from the house cast yellow rectangles onto the lawn behind the trees and when I looked up I saw within the window the Zettl family, gathered around an old upright piano, singing while Harold played. Seeing but unseen in the shadows of their yard, I paused, watching their faces, the silent song and laughter of a family drawn back together. It was midnight; time to go home to mine.

&#8270;

The following morning at Mass as the priest was preparing the gifts, he lifted bread above the altar and said,

> Blessed are you, Lord, God of all creation.
> Through your goodness we have this bread to offer,
> which earth has given and human hands have made.
> It will become for us the bread of life.

The altar server standing beside him was a young aboriginal girl, perhaps twelve years old. As she turned to hold something for the priest, the long braid running down the center of her back faced the congregation. It was tapered at the same angles as a braid of sweetgrass I'd received at the ceremony the day before. It was a gift of openness and community, for sweetgrass is a symbol of the coming together of many hearts into one. Then the priest,

> Blessed are you, Lord, God of all creation,
> Through your goodness we have this wine to offer,
> Fruit of the vine and work of human hands.
> It will become our spiritual drink.

What if I were to pass the braid of sweetgrass on to her? Would she remember other ceremonies she'd attended, or would she think of those who've told her that such things are superstitious, unholy?

> Lord, we ask you to receive us and be pleased with
> The sacrifice we offer you with humble and contrite hearts.

I thought of the others down at Many Bones Creek standing in the willows beside that creek no wider than this altar.

> Lord, wash away my iniquity; cleanse me from my sin.

The Christians there at creekside all have mothers and fathers, siblings, who would disapprove, call this placing of the lattice of willow upon the waters voodoo or the work of pagans. As the leader lifts his heart and voice to the sky in the blessing song, he gives no thought to them or to those among his own who say the traditions must not be squandered on the newcomers.

> We sing in antiphon,
>> The Lord be with you.
>>> And also with you.
>> Lift up your hearts.

We lift them up to the Lord.
Let us give thanks to the Lord our God.
It is right to give him thanks and praise.

Prayers over bread and wine, willow branch and rawhide, placed into a consecrating flow we honor but do not command. Each recalling the prayers of ancestors:

Take this, all of you, and eat it:
This is my body which will be given up for you.

A sparrow sings, a bell rings, and we dream we are one body, braided together in the drift of willow sticks on this creek, in the breaking of bread in this chapel. Something of them in us, something of us in them; we who are pitiful and broken alone, become healed and worthy together.

Lord, I am not worthy to receive you,
But only say the word and I shall be healed.

That consecrating word spoken by the Creator into the land and into our hearts is not English or Latin or Aramaic, not even Cree or Saulteaux. It is the Creation itself and its long desire to redeem the irredeemable.

In such ways as this we hold up our lives and the lives of all who share this world in sin and sanctity, so that God might bless the whole of it and wash away all that keeps us distant from one another. Then, once in a while, when our hearts are so inclined, we might be privileged to brush up against the promise of that unity, feel the pull of the river, even hear something of its one true song, the one the mystic must hear more fully, the single strain that contains all others, forming music from the incomplete, the yet to be consummated.

Faith, in opening upon that infinite horizon and a multitude of mysteries, explains very little, other than the wisdom that to be deepened, truly pressed up against the bosom of the All in All we must lose something—a life or some piece of it—mourn its passing, and then, clinging only to its blessings, give it away freely to the wind that has already breathed life into the new spirit waiting for a Pentecost that is never really about conversion, and always about convergence. And then it matters not if we are the Jews and they the proselytes, or the other way round, for these tongues of flame gloss our saying and our hearing into wild translations we can never wholly circumscribe.

# AN EVENING PRAYER

*In the beginning there were not coldness and darkness; there was
the Fire.*

—Pierre Teilhard de Chardin, "Hymn of the Universe"

The sun hangs now just above the wrinkled verge of the earth,
looking as distant as the other stars it outshines by day. For
several minutes we wait and watch in silence on our seat, a limestone boulder, as the orange disk falls beneath the horizon. An owl
utters the eventide offering from the woods that flank the hill—a
pagan sound, unmoved by death and other revolutions. A violet
curtain is filtering the afterglow and just above it Venus has risen,
lighting a candle to the old goddess right where the sun stood
twenty minutes ago.

Small anvil-topped thunderheads are gathering in the north-
west. A storm could pass over this hill in the next hour. We will be
gone by then. The statue of Our Lady will stand unattended in the
dark, but protected by rods that ground the fire of prairie storms
into the hillside whenever a charged cloud reaches for her. To be
with her at such a moment and watch a thunderbolt strike, see the
twenty or fifty thousand amperes crackle in a luminous web around
her form, a fiery ligature tracing our religious yearnings from earth
to heaven and back again—that would be a wild ascension. In the
protective shadow of a Holy Mother wrought from older matriarchs, we'd muster the courage to speak.

Here we are, the people who traded many gods for one, and the spells of nature and narrative for the magic of text. In the name of Our Lady who is the very spirit of acceptance and release in the face of tragedy, we acknowledge and proclaim all of the death and bitterness and sorrow that we have poured into the chalice of our history: the long descent from our hunter origins, leaving behind the multiple spirits enlivening the world to take up the plow, the word, and inevitably the sword; the centuries of invasion, empire, and war that bracketed the arrival of new and encompassing faiths, making the voices of the land ever harder to hear as we hung new worlds and their people on timbers crossed by our greed and their suffering. And there were redemptions too, for even in the building up of new civilizations dedicated to the Incarnation and its rooted-ness in the cycles of creation, in the attempt to follow that good news, and in its ultimate corruption to serve the appetites of princes and bishops, we have time and again been saved from utter decay and degeneration by the exertions of a few holy people; and even after exhausting the wild leaven of the Old World and coming to places new only to the children of Jacob, bringing with us upheaval and destruction, taking Esau's birthright whenever the hunt failed, we have come face to face with our ancestors here, found beauty again, forged something new from the vernacular and indigenous encountering the alien and imperial.

This, our humanity, we offer up to the heavens, though we would retain its blessings, its lessons and its chastening. Opening up our hands, we release our grieving and our blaming, make peace with our origins, and let all of it rise to the domain of angels and eagles.

One year after I said good-bye to my aunt, the family storyteller, I went back again to the landscapes of my ancestors to assess the damage from another loss.

A news clipping came in the mail—"VALLEY BURNS AGAIN." The paper said the fire started as a windrow burn lit by the man who owned the land once farmed by my grandfather. It tore through the old farmyard and consumed the house where he had spent his last years, the house where I took up residence for part of one summer to write histories of the valley. When the wind came up, the fire lifted into the scrub oaks and breached the valley rim. Tearing down the long hogback slopes to the bottomland, it took another abandoned farmstead. Volunteers came from town and farm with pumper trucks, but the fire was too big by then, headed all directions at once: across the top land and down into the mouth of the creek valley, down the main valley walls to the east and west.

Out of control for thirty-six hours, they said. At one point the wind turned up the creek valley to the north and people feared for the village, Hazelcliffe. The farmers lit a backfire across the oak and ash and maple hills, a firebreak across that smaller valley, and there the inferno ended in ashes. Two homesteads, landmarks of first settlers, and hundreds of acres of oak were gone. Two potash mines lost power for their mills on the surface and their miners underground when the fire burnt up the poles carrying 230,000 volts of electricity up the valley side.

There are stories of my grandfather starting fires himself now and then at the mouth of the creek and into the main valley—fires that sometimes scorched a pole or two along the rail line—but he picked his moment, appraised the wind and the moisture in the woods so that the flames would stay on the grassy hilltops, not reach the store of fuel in all those gnarled oaks. The last fire he saw in those hills, though, was an accidental one of unknown origins in the fall of 1966. He was living in the house on the valley rim with a widowed daughter-in-law, the wife of his favored first son, dead since 1949. That time, too, the house was in the path of the fire but his oldest daughter, the one who kept the stories, was on the switchboard at the time and put out a general ring. The volunteers, more numerous in those days, came out to the hills to help, but the one who saved the day was his first grandson, favored son of that favored son. He was on a tractor in the valley bottom when he saw the fire drawing up the hill toward his mother's home. Turning the tractor and cultivator around he dropped the blades into the grass at the base of the hill. He plowed a fireguard straight up the hill across the path of the fire, up slopes too steep for the tractor, knowing others had died on safer slopes with machines turning over on top of them. Though he stayed on the tractor and kept the farmstead from burning that day, two years later he was killed when his truck rolled off the highway and burst into flames.

Loss and renewal, whether in the myths of a civilization or the legends of a family, seem to lead us always from fire to fire. This time there was no grandson there to plow the guard, no daughter to send out the general ring. The farmstead burned to its footings in the first hours of the fire. The day I went out to face the ruins a friend came along. Rob is a forest ecologist used to seeing the results of pine, poplar, and spruce fires. He wanted to see what the outcome of an oak fire was like, and I was more than happy to have him with me, for I was hoping, but not quite believing, that there would be some solace in the long truths of nature.

The farmhouse was completely gone, nothing left but charcoal scattered with steel and glass remnants that made it through the blaze. "Must've been a hot fire," Rob said, looking at the strangely bubbled shards of window glass, the spirals of steel wire where an old tire had burned down to its radial mesh. It was odd to find all the metal still there: bed frames, pieces of the oil stove, and nails everywhere. During the fire, nails would have been raining down through the flames from rafter, roof, and wall; hundreds of them, each one held by my grandfather as he hammered the place together half a century ago.

I saw for the first time just how small and shallow my aunt's root cellar had been. The once cool and dark burrow so cavernous and mysterious with its odors of potato sacking and roots was now utterly exposed to the sun: a little hole strewn with the detritus of human striving. One day it will be just another prairie depression, a sunken grave as smooth and evocative as a buffalo wallow, pronouncing, "Something died here, yes, but something lived too."

In the cellar bottom I found a warped whiskey bottle. It had collapsed and rippled from stem to bottom, as though someone had squeezed the stale air from its belly. Somehow, most of the stout-posted picket fence my aunt once used to protect her garden had survived the fire. Within its enclosure next to the ruins, small patches of yellow iris and orange lilies bloomed—the remains of perennial beds that were the glory of that hillside farm.

As Rob and I walked over the rim of the valley, there was a mild sweetness in the air, like caramelized sugar, and that is what it was: the sugars in the burnt forest turned to carbon. We moved quietly through a forest of blackened, skeletal oaks, the sun shining on places that had not seen full sun in many years. The scorched trunks and branches cross-hatched the hills with flat black streaks. In patches where the fire had burned most intensely the trunks downed by the blaze had apparently disappeared, leaving nothing but a spectral image of themselves, a streak of pale gray ash across the blackened ground where they had fallen. A tree of any size can be reduced to a smear of ash in a hot enough fire, but these shadows seemed only the faintest of traces, barely there to mark the passing of lives that had served beetle and jay, fungi and squirrel, for eighty years or more. It was as though someone had spirited their bodies away, leaving the merest marks to show where they had died.

Though death was all over the hillside in standing charcoal and ashen shadows on the grass, it was the birth and life that was bewildering. Green things sprang forward underfoot, demanding to be recognized as the foreground, middle ground, and background of everything that was gone. I found an orchid, a yellow lady slipper or moccasin flower, fully formed and unmarred. There were patches of oaks, sometimes only one or two, that had survived here and there in places where the fire had missed or passed low through the understory. Bur oaks have a corky bark, Rob said, that helps them to survive low-level blazes. Those that are not weakened by the burn will be the veterans of the fire, the old matriarchs that will live to see the next one, thriving on increased nutrients in the soil and reduced competition from neighbors. At the base of every dead oak, every scorched maple, every skeleton of buffaloberry, choke-cherry, and saskatoon-berry bush, there were exuberant sprouts of new growth already jumping toward the sunlight. Thirty days since the flames rolled through in their paschal revolution—it happened the week of Pentecost—and already fierce green shoots were rising three feet above ground.

Downslope on the open patches of mixed-grass prairie the green was bright enough to make you think the fire had not gone out altogether, had merely shifted along the light spectrum. From a distance the grass looked like a green Persian carpet, uniformly verdant, unblemished, as though Khidr had run through the hills with a torch dripping green fire. No dead grass thatching beneath the growth of the year, no shrubs or woody vegetation, just the bare black ground providing the contrast that sent each new blade and stem into sharp relief. It was a new-made landscape, the lives of other years atomized into the rich black earth placed at the feet of the resurrected. On my hands and knees I could make out the charred tufts of sedges and grasses hidden amidst their perfectly formed successors.

Everything had, in van der Post's words again, "a glow upon and within them as if they had just come fresh and warm from the magnetic fringes of whoever made them." Plants seemed to be spaced one beside the other in a spontaneous exactitude: no large gaps but no crowding either; every leaf of breadroot, every periwinkle bloom of pentstemon, every blade of wheatgrass, every blanketflower etched in flawless clarity.

After a fire, Rob said, the individual plants all die back and then quickly reemerge from their crowns. He called them geophytes, ground lovers, lovers of earth. Other plants regenerate from seed after a burn. Pincherry seeds, for example, can survive eighty years in the soil waiting for a fire to bring them to the sun.

We talked about the likely ebb and flow of the blaze during the thirty-six hours it burned. At night, when the humidity rose and the atmospheric pressure fell, the fire would have come down from the tops of the trees to smolder on the ground until daybreak, when the sun would have called it up again, the fire in stored solar energy rising to the fresh solar energy of the new day.

A priest in the Ordo Desert or a half-mad prophet at El Marahka evokes a similar energy in a movement of desire from God to man and back again. It flares from the pith of matter, arises in our longings, placing us on heights of land where we dance to the rhythms twinned within the womb of civilization.

The sun is down from this Carmel where, instead of Baalites, a girl, virginal and native to the land, gave up her life. Somewhere in our bones we bear the truths of ascension and Pentecost, but no one can say the burning that will make us fit to climb once more to places where the spirit has descended.

The sun will rise again tomorrow, and when it does the two brothers will still be wrestling, locked in their proprietary struggle.

"Let me go for the day is breaking," the elder will cry.

"Give me your blessing," the younger will reply, "and then I will let you go."

In the heat of every sunrise, every conflagration and holocaust, there is the possibility of reconciliation, the healing of Jacob's wound, and the promise that one day the Green One will leave his cave again and throw his cloak over the wrestling brothers. What a shining that will be, green gilt with the fire that is the very face of God.

POSTSCRIPT

---

# WIND

# BIRDS

On that morning after Pentecost when we walked the beaches of the reservoir listening for plover call notes above the roar of the wind, there were times when the walking felt like prayer. Mindfulness comes more easily when you have to make your way across acres of small speckled stones that could in this step or the next one resolve into the pattern of a nest. Focusing on the patch of beach ahead, choosing the location of my next footfall, I walked my section parallel to the other counters. We covered miles in this way, together but alone.

When the morning of counting nests and pairs was over, we drove several miles to another stretch of beach where Paul hoped to show us the first hatchlings of the year. There we walked as a group, observing pairs of plovers as we advanced along the waterfront. From Paul and one of his crew, an American PhD candidate named Katherine, I learned to identify some of the behaviors biologists categorize as either courtship or territorial. When some species, ours included, assert territorial interests it can be ugly business. When piping plovers get territorial it can easily be mistaken for a dance. I sat on the beach next to Katherine and we watched two male plovers scurry and stop, scurry and stop in perfect unison a few inches apart from one another. They never turned to face the other, but ran in parallel lines and loops stopping and starting on unseen cues. They looked like they were celebrating what it is to be a young male plover on a fine stretch of sand covered with just the right kind of pebbles. Katherine said it was a territorial defense display called parallel running. She sees it often on the Gulf Coast wintering grounds where she did her master's thesis on the piping plover. There she watches the same behaviors being played out not on northern lakes and sloughs but on broad algal flats on the Texas coast where it bends down toward the mouth of the Rio Grande.

Earlier we had witnessed what Paul and Katherine called the "tattoo step," whereby a male plover, his chest puffed out and his head held high—looking something like an animated bowling pin doing an elaborate goose step—walks slowly and deliberately. It's all very grand and martial, with the object of his desire standing by and doing her level best not to let out a nervous titter, which can't be at all easy because this is the prenuptial promenade. We did not stay to see things advance that far, though I expect it was the brief and inelegant wing-flapping, neck-biting affair most waterbirds go in for.

Higher up, away from the waves and amid the patches of beach grass, there was a nest of plovers that by Paul's calculations would be fledged by now. We watched from a distance, listening for plovers, while Paul approached the nest site. Finding the spot he called us over and showed us a few flakes of stone concentrated in a pattern barely distinguishable from the pebbly background. The eggs were gone but Paul said he could tell it had been a good hatch. The young would be in the grass nearby, escorted by the parents. Piping plovers produce precocial fledglings, which means they hatch out feathered and ready to run in a few hours.

We heard an adult plover call as we kneeled by the nest. Paul had everyone back away to stand along a ridge above a patch of sweet clover on the beach where we could watch for movement. In a few minutes we spotted one and then the other adult, running, looking agitated, and calling in sharp peeps. These, Paul said, were alarm notes intended to keep the young still during danger. If we waited, the adults would eventually give the two-note *peep-lo* call, which is the all-clear signal, and the fledglings would likely emerge.

After a short spell, the *peep-lo* call came and we strained our eyes for a glimpse of the young. At first we saw nothing and even lost sight of the adults, whose calls seemed to be getting more distant. We shifted our position to watch from another vantage. I began hearing the signal call again and then saw one of the parents briefly slipping back into cover. I walked toward the clover for a closer look. Finding one of the parents in a clearing in the clover, I kept it in my binoculars. Something small moved at its feet and before I realized what I was seeing a fledgling had zipped across the clearing and out of sight with amazing speed.

"I think I just spotted one," I called to the others, as I continued to watch. Just then another sand-colored ball of fluff scurried up to the parent and into cover. Soon we saw all four of the young. Paul tries to band as many plovers as he can so he got out his banding gear as the rest of us moved in to round up the fledglings. After a bit of a chase we caught the first three easily in our hands and placed them in a margarine tub. The fourth, however, seemed to be missing. I kept an eye out for it as Paul and Katherine banded the other three. After scouring the grass edges where we'd seen the others, my eyes settled on the foreground, bare and mottled with the colors of water-washed stones. I don't know if the wind moved its feathers or if I just happened to look in the right spot, but I found it there, sitting in the open looking like any other pebble on the beach. Unlike its siblings it made no effort to escape when I went out to retrieve it. An infant plover in the hand is all fluff and sticks, a cotton ball on toothpicks. It seemed smaller than the others, and it didn't squirm in my hands as I carried it back to the banders.

"Not sure this one is healthy, Paul."

He banded the runt and made note of its weight, six grams—a little less than the weight of a dollar coin. Then I carried the plover chicks toward the parents, who were fluttering as they paced and called out to their young. I put the tub on the beach and gently turned it on its side. Three plovers ran out and across the stones to their mother and father. The runt slid out and just sat there blinking, pathetic and utterly helpless. I backed away to watch. Several minutes passed as Paul finished up his notes. The little plover never budged.

We get so used to wild things running away from us that when they don't we know something is afoot. Maybe that is why the old iconographers chose to show the infusion of the Holy Spirit as a bird coming toward the faithful. I told Paul that the plover had not moved from where I had placed it.

"Better bring it in," he said, "see what we can do."

Again the bird made no attempt to flee at my approach and allowed me to pluck him from among the stones. I held him in the palm of my hand close to my chest, the way one always holds something vulnerable, mysterious, and precious, and walked back to where Paul and the others were kneeling in a circle on the sand. As I handed Paul the fledgling, something in the gesture, the kneeling, and our circle of care burned into me a recognition of sacrament, the here and now ceasing to matter, love nearly itself, the stillness and intensity of moving toward communion.

Paul took the bird and touched it gently with a forefinger. Nothing. It seemed all but dead. The rest of us waited for Paul to pronounce it so. Instead he lifted it up near his face and breathed some encouraging words into the ball of down. He set it onto the beach gingerly while the rest of us waited for any encouraging signs. It didn't move.

"C'mon," Paul said and he prodded it one more time; this time a little harder. On a ridge of sand twenty yards away the parents called out again.

At once the little bird drew itself erect, wobbling on its preposterous legs a moment before scurrying off across the stones toward its parent, the mother I think, who was waiting at the edge of a stand of beach grass. After her straggling child made it up the slope, the adult plover faded into the wall of green. The little one followed and was gone like a figure more believed than felt and seen, gone to the grass and the stones and wind that knows them all.

# NOTES

---

**Shelter 2**

1. Thomas Hardy, *Return of the Native* (Hertfordshire, UK: Wordsworth Editions Ltd., 1995), p. 55.

2. Ibid., p. 16.

3. Ibid., p. 22.

**El Marahka III**

1. Don McKay, "Baler Twine: Thoughts on Ravens, Home, and Nature Poetry," in *Vis à Vis: Field Notes on Poetry & Wilderness* (Wolfville, Nova Scotia: Gaspereau Press, 2001).

**El Marahka IV**

1. International Committee on English in the Liturgy, Inc., *The Liturgical Psalter: A Text for Study and Comment* (1994). A translation of Psalm 24:3, from Hebrew into English poetry, from the English translation.

**El Marahka V**

1. David Abram, *The Spell of the Sensuous* (New York: Vintage Books, 1996).

2. The Egyptians and Zoroastrians were monotheists first, but they never matched the Yahwist tradition, with its elaborate scriptures mediating man's relationship with a single God.

**El Marahka VI**

1. Talmudic tradition has it that he injured a sinew in his thigh. In deference to this event, the sciatic nerve is removed from kosher meat.

2. Laurens van der Post, "Witness to a Last Will of Man," in *Testament to the Bushmen* (London: Viking Penguin, 1984), p. 161–162.

**Shelter 7**

1. T. S. Eliot, from "East Coker," in *Four Quartets* (London: Faber and Faber, 1963).

**El Marahka VII**

1. Abram, *The Spell of the Sensuous*, p. 254.

**Shelter 8**

1. Ron Rolheiser, *The Holy Longing: The Search for a Christian Spirituality* (New York: Doubleday, 1999).

**El Marahka X**

1. Pierre Teilhard de Chardin, *Hymn of the Universe* (New York: Harper & Row, 1965).

2. The following story is pieced together from his handwritten and unpublished memoir. The family, preferring to remain anonymous, has asked me not to use any names.

**Wild Grace**

1. There is some confusion regarding Round Hill and Mount Carmel. Local historian Norman Duerr tells me that Round Hill is another hilltop nearby and that Hattie was likely buried at the base of that hill, near a large boulder. As recently as 2002, says Duerr, crow feathers have been placed by someone in a careful wreath around the rock, as well as on top. He believes the feathers may have been offerings made by some of the Duck Lake Cree who attend the annual Catholic pilgrimage at Mount Carmel. Regardless of where Hattie died, her story remains a point of convergence for aboriginal and nonaboriginal pilgrims who come to Mount Carmel to pray.

2. William Butler, *The Wild North Land* (London: Simpson, 1873).

**Songs**

1. See Andrew Britz, OSB, "Enriching the Rosary," *The Prairie Messenger*, October 23, 2002.

2. Samuel Noah Kramer, *The Sacred Marriage Rite: Aspects of Faith, Myth, and Ritual in Ancient Sumer* (Bloomington: Indiana Univ. Press, 1969), p. 90.

**Scapular II**

1. Rolheiser, *The Holy Longing*, p. 6 ff.

2. Pierre Teilhard de Chardin, "The Spirit of the Earth," in *Building the Earth* (New York: Avon Books, 1969), p. 64.

3. Ibid., p. 70–71 ff.

4. Reverend Alban Butler, *The Lives of the Fathers, Martyrs and Other Principal Saints*, vol. V (D. & J. Sadlier & Company, 1864).

5. Jacobus de Vitriaco, *Libri Duo: Quorum Prior Orientalis, siue Hierosolomitanae: Alter Occidentalis* (Douai, 1597), p. 86.

6. Alfred Guillaume, *Islam* (London: Penguin Books, 1954).

7. Maria Rosa Menocal, *The Ornament of the World* (Boston: Little, Brown, 2002).

8. There were times of religious persecution in Andalusia, such as the pogrom in Granada in 1066.

9. From A. Yusuf Ali's translation of the Q'uran.

10. Annemarie Schimmel, *Mystical Dimensions of Islam* (North Carolina: Univ. of North Carolina Press, 1975), p. 429.

11. The Sufi mystic Hallaj was crucified for claiming to be a *hulûl*, an incarnation. After his execution in 922, the ecstatic experiences of Sufis became secrets of the order.

12. *The Kulliyat of Shams-i Tabriz*, p. 292.

13. *Diwan of Muin-ud-Din Chishti*, ode no. 70, p. 102.

14. Andrew Harvey and Eryk Hanut, *Mary's Vineyard: Daily Meditations, Readings, and Revelations* (Wheaton, IL: Quest Books, 1996).

15. Peter Lamborn Wilson, *Sacred Drift: Essays on the Margins of Islam* (San Francisco: City Light Books, 1993), p. 140.

16. Guillaume, *Islam*, p. 149.

17. Elias Friedman, OCD, *The Latin Hermits of Mount Carmel* (Rome: Institutum Historicum Teresianum, 1979), p. 197–99.

**Leaven II**

1. The complete text of the letter was originally published on the order's website, www.eriebenedictines.org.

**Leaven III**

1. Richard Rohr, *Hope Against Darkness* (Cincinnati: St. Anthony Messenger Press, 2001), p. 34, says that the cross, often mistaken as merely a symbol of self-inflicted suffering, is in fact a paradox of opposites. "There is a cruciform pattern to reality."

**A New Small-Rented Lease**

1. Garma C. C. Chang, trans., "Maharatnakuta Sutra," in *Dharma Rain: Sources of Buddhist Environmentalism*, ed. Stephanie Kaza and Kenneth Kraft, p. 14–15 (Boston: Shambhala, 2000).

2. Wendell Berry, *The Unsettling of America* (San Francisco: Sierra Club Books, 1977), p. 130.

3. Ibid.

4. Sally Fitzgerald, ed., *The Habit of Being* (New York: Farrar, Straus and Giroux, 1979), p. 229.

5. Raymond E. Brown, Joseph A. Fitzmyer, and Roland E. Murphy, *The Jerome Biblical Commentary*, vol. II (Englewood Cliffs, NJ: Prentice Hall, 1968), p. 82.

**Into the Presence of God**

1. Bruno Doerfler, OSB, *Across the Boundary* (Muenster, Saskatchewan: St. Peter's Press, 1988).

2. Ibid., p. 93.

3. Ibid., p. 64.

4. The Lebret Residential School, run by the Oblate Brothers of Mary Immaculate, had little of the physical and sexual abuse that has been providing newspapers with headlines. Many graduates have said that they enjoyed their time at the school and appreciated the education they received. Such testimony, however, says more about the poverty and hunger they had left behind on the reserves and about the culture of the oppressed than it does about the realities of residential school life. Not all children in the schools were beaten and molested, and not all schools were run by abusive people, but all

children were taken from their parents and forced to give up their language, religion, and traditions. Over time, this encompassing violence to the spirit has been more devastating to the indigenous peoples of this region than any assault on the flesh. It is the true crime described so heartbreakingly in John Milloy's *A National Crime: The Canadian Government and the Residential School System* (Winnipeg: Univ. of Manitoba Press, 1999).

5. Regina poet Judith Krause recalls seeing the Assumption Day canoe trips from her family cottage on Katepwa Lake.

6. E. Brian Titley, *A New Vision* (Vancouver: Univ. of British Columbia, 1986), p. 169.

7. Heard at a lecture by Reichers in February 2002. Reichers, a brilliant mind and entertaining speaker, is one of several theologians who, rather than write their thoughts down in books, seem to thrive on an oral level, following traditions of talk and argument that run back through Jesus to the rabbinical lore of Judaism.

8. In 1999, John Munro successfully sued for malicious prosecution and received a settlement of $1.4 million. The First Nations leaders, including Noel Star Blanket, have sued as well. Their case, twelve years later, remains tied up in the courts. They have yet to receive any compensation.

9. I've been told that this aboriginal style of parenting, which often is mistaken for neglect, is deliberate. Native children are given the freedom to explore their environment and learn from their mistakes.

10. Teilhard de Chardin, "The Spirit of the Earth," p. 64.

11. Abram, *The Spell of the Sensuous*, p. 254.

12. Reproduced in Pierre Teilhard de Chardin's *The Heart of Matter* (London: Collins, 1978), p. 104.

13. Alexander Morris, *The Treaties of Canada with the Indians of Manitoba and the North-West Territories Including the Negotiations on Which They Were Based* (Saskatoon, Saskatchewan: Fifth House Publishers, 1991), p. 213.

# BIBLIOGRAPHY

Abram, David. *The Spell of the Sensuous*. New York: Vintage Books, 1996.

Ali, A. Yusuf, trans. *The Holy Q'uran*. Beirut, 1934.

Berry, Wendell. *The Unsettling of America*. San Francisco: Sierra Club Books, 1977.

Britz, Andrew. "Enriching the Rosary." *The Prairie Messenger*, October 23, 2002.

Brown, Raymond E., Joseph A. Fitzmyer, and Roland E. Murphy. *The Jerome Biblical Commentary*, vol. II. Englewood Cliffs, NJ: Prentice Hall, 1968.

Butler, Reverend Alban. *The Lives of the Fathers, Martyrs and Other Principal Saints*, vol. 5. New York: D. & J. Sadlier & Company, 1864.

Butler, William. *The Wild North Land: Being the Story of a Winter Journey, with Dogs, Across Northern North America*. London: Simpson, 1873.

Chang, Garma C. C., trans. "Maharatnakuta Sutra."In *Dharma Rain: Sources of Buddhist Environmentalism*, edited by Stephanie Kaza and Kenneth Kraft, 14–15. Boston: Shambhala, 2000.

de Vitriaco, Jacobus. *Libri Duo: Quorum Prior Orientalis, siue Hierosolomitanae: Alter Occidentalis*. Douai, 15976.

*Diwan of Muin-ud-Din Chishti.*

Doerfler, Bruno. *Across the Boundary*. Muenster, Saskatchewan: St. Peter's Press, 1988.

Eliot, T. S. "East Coker." In *Four Quartets*. London: Faber and Faber, 1963.

Friedman, Elias. *The Latin Hermits of Mount Carmel*. Rome: Institutum Historicum Teresianum, 1979.

Fitzgerald, Sally, ed. *The Habit of Being*. New York: Farrar, Straus and Giroux, 1979.

Guillaume, Alfred. *Islam*. London: Penguin Books, 1954.

Hardy, Thomas. *Return of the Native*. Hertfordshire, UK: Wordsworth Editions Ltd., 1995.

Harvey, Andrew, and Eryk Hanut. *Mary's Vineyard: Daily Meditations, Readings, and Revelations.* Wheaton, IL: Quest Books, 1996.

International Committee on English in the Liturgy, Inc. *The Liturgical Psalter: A Text for Study and Comment,* 1994.

Kramer, Samuel Noah. *The Sacred Marriage Rite: Aspects of Faith, Myth, and Ritual in Ancient Sumer.* Bloomington: Indiana Univ. Press, 1969.

*The Kulliyat of Shams-i Tabriz.*

McKay, Don. "Baler Twine: Thoughts on Ravens, Home, and Nature Poetry." In *Vis à Vis: Field Notes on Poetry & Wilderness.* Wolfville, Nova Scotia: Gaspereau Press, 2001.

Menocal, Maria Rosa. *The Ornament of the World.* Boston: Little, Brown, 2002.

Milloy, John. *A National Crime: The Canadian Government and the Residential School System.* Winnipeg: Univ. of Manitoba Press, 1999.

Morris, Alexander. *The Treaties of Canada with the Indians of Manitoba and the North-West Territories Including the Negotiations on Which They Were Based.* Saskatoon, Saskatchewan: Fifth House Publisher, 1991.

Rohr, Richard. *Hope Against Darkness.* Cincinnati: St. Anthony Messenger Press, 2001.

Rolheiser, Ron. *The Holy Longing: The Search for a Christian Spirituality.* New York: Doubleday, 1999.

Schimmel, Annemarie. *Mystical Dimensions of Islam.* Chapel Hill: Univ. of North Carolina Press, 1975.

Teilhard de Chardin, Pierre. *The Heart of Matter.* London: Collins, 1978.

———. *Hymn of the Universe.* New York: Harper & Row, 1965.

———. "The Spirit of the Earth." In *Building the Earth.* New York: Avon Books, 1969.

Titley, E. Brian. *A New Vision.* Vancouver: Univ. of British Columbia Press, 1986.

van der Post, Laurens. "Witness to a Last Will of Man." In *Testament to the Bushmen.* London: Viking Penguin, 1984.

Wilson, Peter Lamborn. *Sacred Drift: Essays on the Margins of Islam.* San Francisco: City Light Books, 1993.